Reviews of *Systematic Trading* by Robert Carver

"A remarkable look inside systematic trading never seen before, spanning the range from small to institutional traders. Reading this will benefit all traders."

Perry Kaufman, author of *Trading Systems and Methods*

"Rob goes into a level of depth which most trading book authors either deliberately avoid or simply lack knowledge of. Rob's background in the industry is beyond reproach and the informational contents of his book shows his experience and depth of knowledge. If you want to enter the professional systematic trading field, Rob's book is a must."

Andreas Clenow, CIO Acies Asset Management
and author of *Following The Trend*

"Being a hedge fund manager myself and having personally read almost all major investment and trading books, this is by far one of the best books I have read in over 15 years on a tough subject for most."

Josh Hawes, Hedge fund manager

"Robert has had very valuable experience working for many years in a large quant hedge fund, which makes the book doubly worth reading.... Well worth a read for anyone who trades, in particular for systematic traders (whether you're a novice or more experienced)!"

Saeed Amen, FX trader and author of *Trading Thalesians*

Reviews of *Smart Portfolios* by Robert Carver

"I've been a fan of Robert Carver's work for quite a while now, and this book definitely adds to the knowledge and experiences he willingly shares with others. Carver skillfully mixes theory and practicality, making this a great reference guide for intermediate and very experienced traders alike. Highly recommended!"

Kevin Davey, Champion full-time trader, author of
Building Winning Algorithmic Trading Systems

"In Finance (like many other subjects) there is a large amount of research that is smart but impractical and an equally large amount of popular literature that is practical but dumb. This book is in that rare category of smart and practical – it is also an entertaining read in its own right."

Francis Breedon, Professor of Finance, Queen Mary, University of London
and former global head of currency research at Lehman Brothers

"The book is a solid piece of work so check it out... It's about the process and there are some really practical ways, mathematical ways, to put a good process in motion for your life."

Michael Covel, author of *Trend Following*

LEVERAGED TRADING

LEVERAGED TRADING

A professional approach to trading FX,
stocks on margin, CFDs, spread bets
and futures for all traders

Robert Carver

Hh

HARRIMAN HOUSE LTD

18 College Street

Petersfield

Hampshire

GU31 4AD

GREAT BRITAIN

Tel: +44 (0)1730 233870

Email: enquiries@harriman-house.com

Website: www.harriman-house.com

First published in Great Britain in 2019

Copyright © Robert Carver

The right of Robert Carver to be identified as the Author has been asserted in accordance with the Copyright, Design and Patents Act 1988.

Hardback ISBN: 978-0-85719-721-4

eBook ISBN: 978-0-85719-722-1

British Library Cataloguing in Publication Data

A CIP catalogue record for this book can be obtained from the British Library.

"When you combine ignorance and leverage, you get some pretty interesting results."

Warren Buffett, legendary investor

"… the best minds were destroyed by the oldest and most famously addictive drug in finance, leverage."

Carol Loomis, *Fortune* magazine 1998

"Spread bets and CFDs are complex instruments and come with a high risk of losing money rapidly due to leverage. 81% of retail investor accounts lose money when trading spread bets and CFDs with this provider. You should consider whether you understand how these products work and whether you can afford to take the high risk of losing your money."

Risk warning from a brokerage web page

Contents

About the Author   xiii

Preface   xv
   Who should read this book?   xvii
   How does this book differ from my first book, *Systematic Trading*?   xvii
   What's coming   xix

Introduction   1
   The mistakes that losing traders make   2
   Why leverage is dangerous   4
   Why you should use a system when you start trading   4
   How is this book different from other trading books?   5

Part One: Fundamentals   7

Chapter One – Types of Leveraged Trading Product   9
   Introduction to leveraged trading   9
   Three key characteristics of leveraged products   15
   What products are there for leveraged trading, and how do they work?   17
   Products and underlying instrument are different   35

Chapter Two – Getting Ready to Start Trading   38
   Choosing your trading software, hardware and data feed   38
   Choosing which product to trade   40
   Choosing your broker   42
   How much money do you need?   45

Chapter Three – Introduction to Trading Systems   46
   Why you should use a trading system   47
   Common arguments against using trading systems   49
   What makes a good trading system?   50
   Why you should avoid third party trading systems   52

Part Two: Starting to Trade   53

Chapter Four – Concepts   55
Some definitions   55
Risk and return concepts   56
Minimum trades and minimum capital   66
Costs   67

Chapter Five – Introducing the Starter System   72
An overview of the system   73
Which instrument and product to trade?   73
When should we open positions?   86
How large should positions be?   92
When should positions be closed?   106

Chapter Six – Trading the Starter System   119
Before you start trading   119
Tasks on day one   123
Tasks on subsequent days   140
Trading diary   145
Summary   161

Part Three: Diversifying   163

Chapter Seven – Adding New Markets   165
Advantages and disadvantages of diversification   165
The theory of diversification   172
Trading the Starter System adapted for multiple instruments   188

Chapter Eight – Adding New Trading Rules   192
The case for diversification of trading rules   193
My suite of trading rules   196
How do we use multiple trading rules?   209
Using multiple trading rules in practice   220

Part Four: Advanced Trading   221

Chapter Nine – From Discrete to Continuous Trading   223
Why it can be safe to trade without a stop loss   223
Continuous trading   225
Practical trading without a stop loss   228

Chapter Ten – Position Adjustment   239
   Adjusting position size for confidence: non–binary trading   240
   Adjusting position size for risk   253
   Adjusting position size without incurring heavy trading costs 254
   Practical non-binary trading   259

Chapter Eleven – What Next?   267
   Improvements to the Starter System   267
   Back-testing and designing your own system   268
   Semi-Automatic Trading   269

Epilogue   279

Glossary   281

Appendices   **289**

Appendix A: Useful Information   291
   Further reading   291
   Useful websites   292

Appendix B: Costs   293
   Transaction costs   293
   Holding costs   297
   Total costs   299
   Minimum capital and costs   300
   Smarter execution to avoid the spread   301

Appendix C: Calculations   307
   Back-adjusting prices   307
   Instrument risk calculation   313
   Moving average calculations   314
   Breakout calculations   314
   Performance ratio   315

Acknowledgements   317

Index   319

About the Author

Robert Carver is an independent trader, investor and writer. He spent over a decade working in the City of London before retiring from the industry in 2013. Robert initially traded exotic derivative products for Barclays Investment Bank and then worked as a portfolio manager for AHL – one of the world's largest hedge funds – before, during and after the global financial meltdown of 2008. He was responsible for the creation of AHL's fundamental global macro strategy, and subsequently managed the fund's multi-billion dollar fixed income portfolio.

Robert has Bachelors and Masters degrees in Economics, and is currently a visiting lecturer at Queen Mary, University of London. His first book *Systematic Trading: A unique new method for designing trading and investing systems* was published by Harriman House in 2015, and his second *Smart Portfolios: A practical guide to building and maintaining intelligent investment portfolios* came out in 2017. Robert trades his own portfolio using the methods you can find in his books.

Preface

Leverage (verb): use borrowed capital for an investment, expecting the profits made to be greater than the interest payable

Oxford Dictionary of English

Not so many years ago the use of leverage for trading was the exclusive domain of highly-trained investment professionals. Sharply dressed denizens of Wall Street or the City of London would happily borrow, and then gamble, hundreds of millions of dollars or pounds. But such risky behavior was not for the average Joe (or Jane).

Things have changed. With the right broker, and just a few hundred dollars or pounds, anyone can become a leveraged trader. In the US it is easy to buy stocks, or bet on them falling, with a *margin account*. UK traders can make *spread bets* or take out *contracts for difference (CFDs)* on their favorite shares, as easily as betting at the local racecourse. In both countries, and in many others, you can trade *foreign exchange (FX)* and *futures*.[1]

Leverage has levelled the playing field for smaller investors, but it has also made trading riskier. Leverage is inherently dangerous. With too much leverage a modest trading loss can be magnified into a wealth-destroying explosion. Leverage also increases the costs of trading: doubling your leverage will double your trading costs. Traders who manage to avoid a quick death from blowing up will instead die slowly, with high costs gradually emptying their accounts.

Because leverage is so dangerous, it is absolutely vital to use a safe level of leverage when trading. Deciding on how much leverage to use is the single most important decision that any trader will have to make.

To protect yourself from the dangers of leverage it is my belief that you should use a *system* when you start trading. This comes from my own experience: I have traded

---

[1] If you aren't familiar with some or all of these products, don't panic. I explain them later in the book.

leveraged financial products for an investment bank without a system, and for a multi-billion-dollar hedge fund[2] that traded exclusively with systems. Now I trade my own money using purely systematic methods.

Trading systems have a poor reputation, but a simple system is much less likely to lose money than an inexperienced trader. If you use a system when you start trading, it will significantly improve your odds of becoming a profitable trader. A good system will calculate the right amount of leverage, protecting you from the dangers of serious losses and high costs.

But finding a well-designed trading system is a daunting task. There are thousands of books and websites offering potential systems, many of which are badly designed and even potentially dangerous. Many system designers give scant attention to the importance of managing risk by controlling leverage.

Instead they rely on incorrectly calculated *stop losses*[3] to limit losses (and indeed, as I explain later in the book, a stop loss is unnecessary in a properly-designed trading system). They are obsessed with finding the elusive perfectly accurate trading rule, when it is far more important to control risk and trading costs. They try and predict the price changes in a single market, but a good system designer knows that diversifying across many different markets is likely to be far more rewarding.

In this book, I introduce a properly-designed, but also simple, trading system. I then explain how to improve its expected performance: by trading additional markets, and also through adding new features. Not everyone will want to continue trading with a system. As you gain skill and knowledge you may wish to start using your own intuition to make decisions about buying and selling. I will explain how to combine human judgement with a trading system, so that you remain protected from the dangers of excessive leverage. This method, which I call *Semi-Automatic Trading*, is described in the final chapter.

---

[2]   A hedge fund is a type of investment fund where leverage is usually used.
[3]   A stop loss closes your trade when the price reaches a predetermined point. I explain stop losses in more detail later in the book.

Who should read this book?

This book is for traders who want to learn how to trade safely using leverage. It covers:[4]

- foreign exchange trading (FX[5] or Forex)
- futures contracts
- contracts for difference (CFDs) trading
- spread betting
- trading stocks with a margin account

No prior experience or knowledge is required, so this book is suitable for newcomers to trading. But even experienced traders should find the book useful, since I will be challenging many of the preconceptions that most people have about trading.

You do not need much money to start trading leveraged financial products – just a few hundred dollars or pounds. However, you should only trade with cash you can afford to sacrifice, as with any kind of leveraged trading there is always a possibility that you could lose everything.

The examples in this book are aimed primarily at readers from the US and UK. However, traders from other countries can also use the system I explain. Be aware that local regulations may ban or limit the use of certain leveraged products. Tax laws will also be different from country to country.

How does this book differ from my first book, *Systematic Trading*?

If you read the 'About the author' page, you will see that I wrote another trading book a few years ago: *Systematic Trading* (*ST*). Perhaps you are browsing online or in your local bookshop and trying to decide which of these two books you should buy. Maybe you already own *ST*, and are considering adding this book, *Leveraged Trading* (*LT*), to your collection.

To help you decide, the main differences between the two books are:

- As the title suggests, *ST* is mostly aimed at traders who are enthusiastic about systems trading. *LT* helps new traders learn how to trade by using a system, but

---

[4] I don't cover options or binary options. These are fundamentally different products, and I would need to write at least one more book to explain them properly. I would advise beginner traders to avoid options. I would advise absolutely everyone to avoid binary options, which are incredibly expensive and dangerous.

[5] You will probably have heard the term 'Forex' used to describe foreign exchange trading, often pronounced 'Four-Ex' (which makes it sound like an Australian beer). I prefer the acronym 'FX', pronounced 'Eff-Ex', which is used by professional traders. It's also quicker to type.

then explains how to combine the system with their own human intuition; the method I've named 'Semi-Automatic Trading'.[6]

- The trading systems in *ST* require large amounts of capital (at least £100,000; around $130,000). The Starter System in *LT* needs just £1,100 or $1,500.

- *ST* is written for relatively advanced traders with some prior knowledge of certain financial concepts. *LT* is suitable for novices.

- *ST* is a generic book which doesn't go into much detail about individual markets. *LT* explains how to trade specific leveraged products.

- *ST* explains the various components of a complex trading system one by one; it isn't until the book is finished that you can see the entire picture. In *LT*, I introduce a simple system in its entirety which you can start using right away. I then go on to explain how, and why, you could make it more complicated.

- *ST* explains how to design trading systems from scratch, which requires using software to simulate historical system performance (a process called *back-testing*). In *LT*, I present a system I have already back-tested. I then explain how you can modify the system for different types of trading, and to cover different markets, without needing any further testing.

Because I have designed the trading systems in this book with the same principles in mind there are some ideas that readers of *ST* will find familiar, although there is no duplicated content in this book. I would recommend that you read *Leveraged Trading (LT)* if:

- You tried to read *ST* and didn't get it.

- You read and understood *ST*, but are struggling to build a simple system from scratch.

- You have not read *ST* and are an inexperienced trader who is unfamiliar with financial theory and back-testing software.

- You are specifically interested in trading leveraged products: FX, CFD, margin accounts, spread bets and futures.

- You do not have enough cash to trade the systems in *ST*.

- You are interested in combining your own trading intuition with a trading system: Semi-Automatic Trading.

Of course, if you find this book useful, are interested in purely systematic trading, and want to develop your own trading system further, then I'd definitely recommend making *Systematic Trading* your next purchase.

---

[6] I also discussed the idea of Semi-Automatic Trading in *Systematic Trading*, but there is much more detail in this book.

What's coming

This is a four-part book. **Part one** introduces each of the leveraged products we are going to use and explains how to make decisions about your trading setup.

Then in **part two** I introduce the Starter System. The Starter System is a very simple trading system which trades a single instrument, using just one kind of trading rule to decide when to open new positions.

Part three then explains how to extend the Starter System by *diversifying* into multiple instruments, and by adding new trading rules.

In **part four** I introduce some more advanced improvements that you can make to the Starter System. The final chapter of part four explains how you can continue your trading journey, either by progressing into designing your own trading systems, or becoming a *discretionary* trader who makes subjective forecasts about market movements whilst still using a system to manage risk: Semi-Automatic Trading.

At the end of the book there is a **glossary** and three **appendices**. Appendix A lists some useful books and websites; appendix B discusses the calculation of *trading costs*, and some techniques for reducing them. Finally, appendix C explains how to perform various other calculations required to run a trading system.

There are also many useful resources on the website for this book:

systematicmoney.org/leveraged-trading

These include spreadsheets that you can use to help implement all the trading systems in this book.

Introduction

Anyone who is contemplating risking some, or all, of their bank balance in trading needs to be aware of one important fact:

The majority of traders lose money.

There is plenty of evidence to support this depressing statistic.[7] For example, a US study in 1999 found that only 12% of traders were consistently profitable, whilst another in 2003 found that around two-thirds of day traders lost money. Before 2010, US brokerage firms did not have to report on customer profitability. You can see why they wanted to keep these figures under wraps; an analysis of this data in 2011 showed that only 25% of their customers were in profit.

Traders in other countries are just as unsuccessful as those in the US. French financial regulators found that 89% of customers trading foreign exchange and CFDs lost money. Meanwhile the Polish regulatory body estimated that 80% of traders were losers. In Taiwan, researchers calculated that only 13% of accounts were profitable in any given year, and only 2% were able to outperform the market consistently.

What about the UK? One of the quotes at the start of this book is from a UK broker: "81% of retail investor accounts lose money...". This figure is typical in the UK FX, spread betting and CFD industry.

---

[7] Sources: 'Report of the Day Trading Project Group', North American Securities Administrators Association (1999), www.nasaa.org/wp-content/uploads/2011/08/NASAA_Day_Trading_Report. pdf; Douglas J. Jordan and J. David Diltz, 'The profitability of day traders', *Financial Analysts Journal* (2003); www.financemagnates.com; 'Study of investment performance of individuals trading in CFDs and forex in France' Autorité des marchés financiers 2014; KNF report on trading in the over-the-counter markets, quoted in www.financemagnates.com/forex/brokers/knf-survey-polish-forex-market-shows-roulette-table-concept-80-lose-money; Brad Barber, Yi-Tsung Lee, Yu-Jane Lian, Terrance Odean, 'The cross-section of speculator skill: Evidence from day trading', *Journal of Financial Markets* (2014).

The mistakes that losing traders make

Perhaps the stark statistics above don't faze you. You firmly believe that you will be in the minority of successful traders, due to your superior skill, high IQ or work ethic. I'm afraid I have to debunk your illusion. You will mostly be competing with traders with equal or superior levels of ability, intelligence and commitment. And, in any case, there is no guarantee that being a better, smarter or harder working trader will automatically lead to profitability.

So how can you avoid joining the ranks of money-losing traders?

Importantly, all the research I've quoted above is based on studies of *amateur* traders, not professionals. Nowadays I only trade my own money, but in the past I have worked as a trader for an investment bank, and as a portfolio manager for a hedge fund managing billions of dollars. In my experience, professional traders don't make the same mistakes as amateur traders.[8] Amateur traders should learn from the professionals and avoid three key errors:

1. Overconfidence: overestimating how successful you will be at trading.

2. Over-betting: taking on too much risk.

3. Overtrading: trading too frequently.

Let's look at these in turn.

1. Overconfidence

It is very easy to become a trader. You just need a computer or smartphone, and some money (and with leveraged trading you hardly need any money at all). If it is very easy to become a trader, then surely it is very easy to become a *successful* trader? It is not. The markets are very hard to predict and even the best traders can't predict them perfectly (or even well).

Do not listen to the trading gurus who tell you that returns of 50%, 100%, 200% or more each year are possible if you buy their exclusive system or sign up to their virtual private trading room. Some professional trading funds, usually labelled with the moniker 'top hedge fund', will have the occasional stellar year: that's just the way

---

[8]   Maybe that should be: *most* professional traders don't make the same mistakes as amateurs. Hubris can affect even highly intelligent professionals and the very smartest traders are most at risk of believing themselves to be invincible. Take the hedge fund Long Term Capital Management (LTCM). LTCM employed star traders who'd worked at Salomon Brothers and several brilliant professors, including two Nobel Prize winners. They ran strategies with vast amounts of leverage and for a few years were incredibly profitable. Then, in September 1998, it all went horribly wrong, and the fund lost 90% of its capital within a matter of weeks. Nearly $5bn evaporated into thin air. There are plenty of other famous examples of professionals blowing up, but the vast majority of professional traders behave in a far more sensible way than the average amateur.

luck works. But over longer time periods, where their performance is more likely to be skill than luck, even the best hedge funds make relatively modest average returns of about 15% a year.

Small retail traders do have some advantages over large funds, but these are massively outweighed by other factors. These funds trade dozens or hundreds of financial instruments, employ many highly-qualified experts, and invest millions of dollars in technology. Do you really think you can do significantly better?

Whether you're new to trading in the financial markets, or you consider yourself an expert, it's important that you have realistic expectations of what is possible.

Overconfidence is problematic enough, but it also encourages traders to make two other types of error: over-betting and overtrading.

2. Over-betting

It is more fun to trade with the hope of making big bucks from a small stake, than to earn pedestrian returns barely better than you could get from a bank account.

For this reason, people are drawn to the very riskiest kinds of trading – like penny stocks or obscure cryptocurrencies that can go up 100% or more in a few days. Massive risk means you have a chance of a massive reward, but it also introduces the possibility of massive losses. The trader who loses 20% in a bad year has to make 25% before they are even. But a trader who loses 90% of their capital faces the near impossible task of increasing their account ten-fold to get back to square one.

Most amateur traders take too much risk and this is why most of them lose money.

3. Overtrading

Brokers constantly encourage their customers to trade more often. They provide fancy trading apps and pretty websites with nice charts. Many brokers have relationships with celebrity trading gurus who claim to be offering an educational service. Their real business is encouraging novices to trade more, so they can collect a cut of the brokerage commission which is generated.

Whilst writing this chapter I examined the accounts of a large UK CFD and spread betting provider. They made an average of $1,379 in revenue per customer. Revenue for a brokerage company is a cost for their customers. The customers had an average of $500 on deposit with the brokers at the end of the year. Running a brokerage firm is clearly more lucrative than being a client. According to an old story, a naive client visiting New York and admiring the boats of bankers and brokers asked:

"Where are the customers' yachts?"

Every time you trade you remove some money from your account and hand it to your broker.

Limit your trading to the absolute minimum. Do not assume you will make sufficient profits to cover costs which are inflated by overtrading.

Those are the mistakes that traders often make. Leverage will just make things worse. Let's see why.

Why leverage is dangerous

Leverage magnifies the three mistakes that retail traders typically make:

1. **Overconfidence**: If you overestimate your ability to predict the markets, you're likely to use more leverage. If you can easily make 10% a year, then why not use ten times more leverage and make 100% a year? But leverage magnifies your mistakes as well as your profits. If you're not as good as you thought, or if you get unlucky, then you'll lose a lot of money very quickly.

2. **Over-betting**: It's risky to trade Bitcoin, the cryptocurrency whose value collapsed by half in a little over two weeks at the beginning of 2018. But trading Bitcoin with added leverage is terrifyingly dangerous. Even relatively pedestrian assets like US government bonds can become risky if you use the maximum leverage allowed by many brokers.

3. **Overtrading**: Leverage also increases your trading costs, so if you are overtrading your account you will be more severely punished. Suppose you have $1,000 and decide to buy gold. You pay $10 in costs for a $1,000 trade. Using leverage from a particularly generous broker you could buy 50 times more gold: $50,000. This will incur 50 times more in costs: $500. Your trading costs as a proportion of your account value have gone up fiftyfold: from 1% ($10 ÷ $1000) to 50% ($500 ÷ $1,000). You have burned up half your account just paying costs.

Easy access for amateur investors to huge amounts of leverage is superficially attractive, but incredibly dangerous if used recklessly.

Why you should use a system when you start trading

A trading system can help you avoid the fundamental errors made by most amateur traders: overconfidence, over-betting and overtrading. The systems I show you in this book are all carefully calibrated to use the correct amount of leverage, and with a trading frequency that's crafted to suit the products you're likely to be trading. They are based on realistic expectations of typical future performance, rather than wildly optimistic predictions.[9]

---

[9] Having realistic expectations about performance also means that you shouldn't expect to make a consistent profit every year, never mind the 'guaranteed' daily or weekly returns promised by certain online trading gurus.

When you are an experienced trader you will want to start making changes to these systems, or even start making your own calls on the market. I explain in the final chapter how you can do this, whilst still ensuring you're safe from repeating the typical mistakes of amateur traders.

How is this book different from other trading books?

There are thousands of books on trading listed on amazon.com. Most of them will make promises about the untold wealth you can have if you'll just follow the author's advice. The writers appear to know what they are talking about: you can find many of them posing on Instagram or other social media in their palatial homes or private jets, surrounded by attractive people, and waving large wads of dollar bills.

Sadly, most of these images are a facade. Most celebrity 'traders' don't make huge fortunes from trading, although some make a good living from selling trading courses and books, and from kickbacks paid by brokers when they introduce new customers. The houses, jets and attractive people are usually rented for the day. You can buy a briefcase worth of fake money on eBay for a fraction of its face value. Truly successful traders usually keep very low profiles.

I take a different approach. Here is what someone wrote when reviewing my first book:

> "It's not often you come across a trading book that promises you nothing in terms of riches, trading from a hammock on a beach with your laptop or becoming a billionaire hedge fund yet delivers you most of the successful components to give you a trading edge over many other market participants."

> Review of *Systematic Trading*, on amazon.com

Just as in *Systematic Trading*, there is no secret recipe in this book that will allow you to make easy money in the market. I offer no guarantee of profits and you should not expect to make huge returns. Instead I offer a more realistic promise: if you follow my advice you will avoid making the errors that nearly every amateur trader makes.

Not everyone agrees with this approach. Here is a less complimentary book review:

> "I agree that the general principles set forth here are valid and useful. This work is marred, however, by an exceedingly pessimistic view of the kind of Sharpe ratios a skillful system developer can achieve..."

> Review of *Systematic Trading*, on amazon.com

(The Sharpe ratio, as you will discover later, is a measure of the profitability of a trading system.)

I respectfully disagree. Some people can indeed make very good money from trading. However, much of that is down to luck rather than skill, and few people will trade for long enough to know the difference. It is safer to be pessimistic: assume you don't possess special trading skills and that you may well be unlucky.

Consider a trader who is overly optimistic and trades accordingly, using too much leverage and trading too frequently. If they have been overconfident about their abilities, or if they are just unlucky, they'll end up with huge losses.

In contrast, a trader who is pessimistic about their likely performance will limit their trading and won't use too much leverage. If things turn out even worse than expected, then at least they will have limited their likely losses. However, if things go well they will be pleasantly surprised. They should bank the unexpected gain with cool detachment. The trader will not dwell on the missed opportunity of additional profits if they'd only taken more risk or traded more often.

So, this is not a book for fantasists. It's for realists who think that avoiding mistakes is paramount: controlling your risks and trading costs.

PART ONE
Fundamentals

CHAPTER ONE

Types of Leveraged Trading Product

IN THIS BOOK, I COVER several different kinds of leveraged products: FX, margin trading of stocks, CFDs, spread bets and futures. In this chapter, I explain how they work and the important differences between them. There is some technical detail, but this is necessary if you're going to trade safely with leverage.

Introduction to leveraged trading

Before I discuss specific products, I am going to explain the concept of leverage in some detail and introduce certain key features of leveraged trading. Once you understand the general ideas, you will able to grasp the finer details of each product more easily.

What is leverage?

Leverage, or *gearing* as it sometimes called, is the use of borrowed money to make a bet on the price of an asset. The simplest kind of leveraged trade is where we borrow money to buy an asset, hoping that the price will go up (trading jargon for betting on a price rise is *going long*).

House mortgages

This is like buying a house with a mortgage. If I buy a house that costs $500,000 and it goes up by 10% in price over the next year, then I will make $50,000. If I am renting the house out, then I'll also make a rental return. If you can earn $20,000 in rent after paying agent's fees and maintenance, then the total profit will be a handsome $70,000. In percentage terms, that works out to 14%: 10% from the property going up in price, and a 4% rental yield.

But most people don't buy houses outright, as only the very wealthy have that kind of spare cash. Instead, I would probably raise a deposit of $100,000 and get a mortgage for $400,000. Sadly, the bank is unlikely to give me the loan for free, I will have to pay some interest. With a 4% interest rate it will cost me $16,000 to service the loan for a year.[10]

The figures involved are summarised in the following table.

	I begin with **$100,000** in cash.
I borrow $400,000	This gives a total of $500,000 in buying power.
I buy a $500,000 house	My starting housing equity is the value of the house, less the outstanding loan: $500,000 – $400,000 = $100,000. For this simple example we ignore any costs such as agent's commissions or taxes.
After a year I have earned rent and paid interest	I earn $20,000 in rent and pay $16,000 in interest. This is a net return of $4,000.
The value of the house has gone up by 10%	My equity after one year is the value of the house, less the outstanding loan: $550,000 – $400,000 = $150,000. I have made $50,000 profit from the price gain.
	Total profit is **$54,000**.

Notice that I have earned money from two sources: (i) **the difference between rent and interest payments**, and (ii) a **leveraged gain in price**.

Even if prices are unchanged, I make profits because my rent ($20,000) is greater than the mortgage payment ($16,000). This difference between what I earn from owning an asset (for a house, rent) and what I pay to fund the purchase (mortgage interest) is known as *carry*.

This example is a **positive carry trade**. If the rent was lower than the mortgage, then it would be a **negative carry trade**.[11] Similarly, certain assets will earn a return when we buy them. Shares in companies pay dividends – a share of the firm's profits. Bonds pay a regular interest coupon. This return may be more than the interest we pay when borrowing (positive carry), or less than the interest (negative carry).

I have also profited from a leveraged increase in price. In the original example (with no mortgage) I earned $50,000 on a $500,000 investment from the price increase: 10%.

---

[10] I am ignoring any repayment element of the mortgage. It is common to buy investment properties with an interest-only mortgage. This also makes the example more relevant for leveraged traders, who do not have to repay their loan until the end of the trade.

[11] You will sometimes hear traders talking about the 'cost of carry' for a negative carry position.

With a mortgage, after the house increases in value by 10% I still make $50,000, but this is now a 50% return on my $100,000 deposit. That is a five-fold improvement.

Leveraged trading works in a similar way, but the deposit is known as *margin* (hence, *margin trading* is another term used for leveraged trading).

Leverage ratios, leverage factors and margin percentage

Leverage can be measured in several different ways. The first is the **leverage ratio**. Suppose you have $100 and want to invest $300; you will have to borrow another $200. The leverage ratio is the ratio of the borrowed amount, $200, to the cash you have, $100. So the ratio is $200:$100, which simplifies to 2:1.

I prefer to use **leverage factors**. The leverage factor is your total investment, $300, divided by the cash you started with, $100. Here the leverage factor is $300 ÷ $100 = 3. The total investment is equal to your original cash plus the borrowing. For a leverage ratio of X:1 the corresponding leverage factor will be (X + 1).

A leverage factor of 1 means no borrowing and trading purely with your own cash. A leverage factor below 1 equates to using only part of your money, for example a factor of 0.5 implies that only half your cash is invested.

Many brokers quote leverage using **margin percentages**. This is equal to the margin as a percentage of the value of the trade. If you want to invest $300, and this requires $100 in margin, then the margin percentage is $100 ÷ $300 = 33.33%. For a margin percentage of X the leverage factor will be 1 ÷ X.

In our house example, the **leverage ratio** is $400,000:$100,000, or 4:1. The **leverage factor** is $500,000:$100,000 which equals 5. The **margin percentage** is $100,000 ÷ $500,000, or 20%.

Notice that the improvement in returns earned through price increase from using a mortgage (five-fold: 10% return without a mortgage, to 50% return with a mortgage) is equal to the leverage factor (5).

Who decides how much leverage you can use when you buy a house?

The bank will set a maximum level, but you as the buyer can use less leverage if you wish. For example, if the bank allowed a leverage ratio of 4:1 you are not forced to use all of it: you can use less, but you cannot use more. If you want to buy a bigger house, you will have to stump up a larger deposit.

Similarly, when trading with leveraged money, the broker will set a maximum leverage ratio, or an equivalent minimum margin percentage. Depending on the product, this limit will be decided by the broker, by the regulatory authorities, or by the rules of the market you are trading in. You can use less leverage if you want, but not more.

What is the point of using less leverage?

House prices generally go up in value, and we would all prefer to live in nice big expensive houses, so why not use the maximum leverage allowed? Unfortunately, leverage is a two-way street. If I buy a $500,000 house with a $100,000 mortgage, and the price goes down by 10%, then I will lose $50,000; half my deposit.

With houses this isn't such a big deal. Unless I need to sell up and move in the next couple of years, or switch my mortgage provider, then I can just wait for prices to go back up again. But when we are trading with leverage in the financial world, brokers use a method called *mark to market*.

Mark to market

Mark to market works as follows: each day the broker calculates the market value of everything you have in your trading account, and they compare this value to the equity in the account. They then recalculate your leverage. If the leverage ratio is too low, so that you have insufficient margin, then they will demand a margin payment to top up the account until the ratio is acceptable. This is known as a *margin call*. If you don't meet a margin call, your broker will start to close out the trades in your account, a process known as *auto-liquidation*.

We don't have mark to market in the housing market, but if we did then it would work like this: suppose you buy a $500,000 house with a maximum allowable leverage factor of 5. Your opening 'housing account' will look like this:

- House value: $500,000

- Loan: $400,000

- Equity = House value – Loan = $100,000

- Leverage factor = House value ÷ Equity = 5

Then, say, the day after you buy your house it falls in price by 1%. Now your account appears less attractive:

- House value: $495,000

- Loan: $400,000

- Equity = House value – Loan = $95,000

- Leverage factor = House value ÷ Equity = 5.21

To return the leverage factor to a value of 5, you would need to add $5,000 to the account. Your 'housing broker' would send you a margin call for this amount. If you met the margin call, your leverage ratio would now be acceptable:

- House value: $495,000

- Cash value: $5,000

- Total value = House Value + Cash value = $500,000

- Loan: $400,000

- Equity = Total value – Loan = $100,000

- Leverage factor = Total value ÷ Equity = 5.0

However, if you didn't pay the margin call then the broker would have to auto-liquidate: sell assets in your account, and use these to pay off the loan. It isn't normally possible to sell part of a house, but let us assume that it is, and the broker sells $20,000 worth of the house (perhaps a small bathroom, or a section of the front lawn) and uses this to pay off part of the loan.

- House value: $495,000 – $20,000 = $475,000

- Loan: $400,000 – $20,000 = $380,000

- Equity = House value – Loan = $95,000

- Leverage factor = House value ÷ Equity = 5.0

One of the dangers of auto-liquidation is that your broker isn't concerned with getting a good price, just reducing their risk as quickly as possible. You might end up with even larger losses because your broker has just dumped your assets on the market.

What if house prices moved very quickly, by 20% or more, and you lost more than the initial $100,000 investment before the broker had collected more margin, or auto-liquidated the position? Although house prices are unlikely to move that quickly, this is a very real possibility in the financial markets. The 'housing account' will have a negative value, and in theory the broker could demand further cash to bring it back to zero.

In reality, what actually happens depends on the exact rules of the brokerage account and current regulatory framework. Some brokers also offer *guaranteed stop losses*, which mean you will never lose more than a certain amount on a given trade. However, these come with additional fees. Since July 2018, under new European Union rules, retail traders in certain products are protected from negative account balances. If you empty your account and still owe the broker money, then they have to write off the debt.

However, under current US regulations you may be on the hook to pay up further money to offset the extra losses incurred. This isn't just a theoretical problem: whilst I was writing this book in November 2018, a US trading advisor (optionsellers.com) managed to lose all their customers' money and left them liable for additional losses.

Mark to market makes it vital that you get your leverage ratio correct. Too high, and you will have to pay margin calls or face auto-liquidation. Too low, and you will be giving up potential profits.

Short-selling

So far, we have expected house prices to go up. What if we thought house prices were going to fall, rather than rise? We can use a type of trade called *short selling* (also known as *going short*, the opposite of going long).

Short selling is selling something that you don't own, in the hope that it will fall in price and you can buy it back cheaper.

You can't short sell houses, but if you could this is how it would work. First, you need to borrow a house from someone else, paying them a small fee for the privilege. You then sell that house to a willing buyer, and wait for house prices to fall. Assuming that prices do fall, you can then buy the house back more cheaply. You then return the house to its original owner, keeping the profits for yourself.

With a mortgage purchase you borrow money to buy a house, but when short selling you borrow a house and sell it in exchange for money. You also have to worry about the cost of carry. For a mortgaged purchase this is the difference between the rental income, and the cost of financing your purchase. However, for short selling the payments are different. Instead of paying interest to borrow money, you will pay a borrowing fee to borrow the house. In theory, you will also earn interest on the money you generate by short selling. Instead of being paid rent, you will have to pay rent to the original owner of the house.

If buying an asset is a positive carry trade, then selling short will be a negative carry trade. If you earn \$4,000 a year from going long a house (the net of rent and mortgage payments), then logically you will have to pay \$4,000 to go short. However, you won't normally pay exactly the same carry that you would earn from being long. Banks pay lower interest rates on deposits than they charge for mortgages. Instead of earning interest at the mortgage rate of 4%, you will probably be earning much less, perhaps only 2%. The difference is a *financing spread* and is a source of revenue for the bank. Similarly brokers also earn a financing spread on the different rates they charge for long and short margin trades.

Here is a detailed example of a (theoretical) short sale in housing:

EXAMPLE: THEORETICAL HOUSE SHORT SALE ON MARGIN

	I begin with **$100,000** in cash. Just like with a mortgage the cash is needed to cover any potential losses that the trade will make.
I borrow a $500,000 house and sell it	The leverage of this trade is calculated in the usual way: **Leverage factor = Position value ÷ Equity** **= $500,000 ÷ $100,000 = 5.** As with margin buying there are leverage limits for short selling.
	I now have $600,000 in cash and am exposed to house prices falling.
Over the year I earn or pay: rent, interest and borrowing fees	I will earn 2% interest on my deposit of $600,000 = $12,000. I have to pay a borrowing fee on the $500,000 house, at a rate of 1% that is $5,000. I have to pay $20,000 to the original owner of the house to compensate for lost rental income. Net payment (negative carry): **$13,000**.
After a year the value of the house has fallen by 10%	I buy back the house I have sold for $450,000. I have made **$50,000** in leveraged capital gains.
I return the borrowed house	Again, we ignore any other costs such as agent's commissions or taxes.
	Net profit is **$37,000**.

This is difficult to do with houses as people don't like lending them out for other people to temporarily sell, and you will struggle to find someone willing to sell their house at a loss a year after buying it from you. But it is common practice in financial markets.

Three key characteristics of leveraged products

Leveraged products differ from each other in the following ways:

1. They are either physical products or derivatives.

2. Derivative products can be dated or undated.

3. Products can be traded on exchange or over the counter (OTC).

1. Physical vs derivative

It could be possible to bet on the price of housing going up or down without actually buying or short selling, if you could find someone to take the other side of the bet. If you went long, and prices went up, then you would make a profit. However, if prices fell then you would lose. Either way, the loser of the bet would then pay the winner.

Similarly, financial traders can use *derivatives* to bet on market prices. A derivative is a type of financial product that you can use to benefit from price changes without actually owning the asset. It will pay you what you *would* have earned from buying on margin (if going long the derivative), or selling short (if going short).

The returns on a derivative bet have to be equivalent to those of the physical asset, or it would be possible to buy an asset whilst placing a short bet against it, and be guaranteed to make a fixed profit or loss irrespective of price movements (which would be called an *arbitrage* trade). Hence, you will also earn any positive carry or pay negative carry that you would have earned or paid on the underlying asset.

Incidentally, non-derivative products are often called 'cash', 'spot' or 'physical' to distinguish them from derivatives.

2. Dated vs undated

Derivatives come in two variations: *dated* and *undated*. An undated derivative works like a normal margin trade. You put the trade on and can hold it for as long as you like. There is no specific date that you have to close the trade before. But a dated derivative is for a specific date, known as the expiry date.

A dated derivative for houses would work like this: you could go long and bet that the price of your $500,000 house will be higher in one year. If it was currently January 2020, then the expiry date of the trade would be January 2021.

You also receive any positive carry or pay negative carry when you make a dated bet. Unlike undated bets the carry isn't paid to you over the life of the trade, but it is embedded within the price of the derivative.

So, for example, if buying a house is going to earn $4,000 in carry over the next year, then the dated bet price would include a $4,000 discount on the $500,000 spot price: $496,000. If nothing happens to house prices, and the underlying house still costs $500,000, then a long bet would make $4,000 in profits by the end of the year. Conversely if you had gone short, then you would have lost $4,000 as the dated price rose from $496,000 to $500,000; equivalent to the negative carry of a short position.

Notice that there is no financing spread for dated derivatives: the negative carry when short is identical to the positive carry when long. Because the carry is embedded in the price it has to be the same for both long and short traders.

You do not have to hold a dated derivative until the expiry date. The position can be closed at any time before the expiry. But if you want to keep a position open when expiry is looming, you can close your trade in the expiry date you are holding, and simultaneously open the same trade in the next expiry date. This is known as *rolling* your trades.

3. Exchange vs OTC

Brokers act as intermediaries between you and the market. But what is 'the market'? There are two types of financial market, exchanges and over-the-counter trading.

An exchange is a formal venue for trading, where you can't trade on an exchange without being a member. Brokers are either members of the exchange or will send your orders to member firms. Exchanges used to be based in physical locations, where people in colorful jackets made weird hand signals at each other, but now the vast majority of trading is done electronically. Futures and shares are traded on exchanges.

Over the counter (OTC) trading is done outside of exchanges, over electronic links between large banks and brokers, and between brokers and their customers. When trading spread bets, FX and CFDs, your contractual relationship is with the broker and your order is not sent onwards[12] to an exchange. These are all types of OTC trading. I will discuss the pros and cons of exchange and OTC trading more in chapter two.

What products are there for leveraged trading, and how do they work?

In this section we will be looking at specific examples of leveraged products:

1. Buying stocks on margin

2. Short selling stocks

3. Exchange traded funds (ETFs)

4. Foreign exchange (FX)

5. Contracts for difference (CFDs)

6. Spread bets

7. Futures

8. Dated CFD and spread bets

---

[12] However, the broker will usually hedge their risk by doing a similar trade of their own in the wider OTC market, or on a formal exchange. I will discuss this more in chapter two.

1. Buying stocks on margin

The first type of leveraged product we'll consider is *buying stock on margin*. This is equivalent to buying a house with a mortgage. This is straightforward to do with stocks if your broker lets you have a *margin account*.

Imagine that we want to invest $6,000 in Citigroup shares, but only have $3,000. We can borrow the other $3,000 for a leverage factor[13] of $6,000 ÷ $3000 = 2.

Sadly, the broker is not lending $3,000 as a charitable gesture. They will charge a premium interest rate for the privilege. Interest rates are set relative to a *reference rate* like the London Interbank Offered Rate (LIBOR), with an additional *funding spread*. Brokers charge a higher interest rate on any borrowing by adding a spread and pay a lower interest rate on deposits after deducting a spread.[14]

When buying stock, my broker currently charges an interest rate which is equal to USD LIBOR, *plus* a funding spread, for a total of 3.2% a year. Brokers also make money by charging *commission* (a fee for each trade that you do), or a *trading spread* (you pay a higher price when buying, and receive less for a sale), and sometimes both.

As an example of how trading spreads work, suppose that a broker will charge $71.25 if we want to sell Citigroup and $71.30 if we want to buy. The rate the broker will buy at (and we sell: $71.25) is the *bid*, and the rate they will sell at (and we buy: $71.30) is the *offer*. The spread is $71.30 – $71.25 = $0.05 per share.

An example of a stock margin purchase is shown on the page opposite.

As when buying a house, our profits are magnified by leverage. The share price went up by around 5% but we made 10% in profits. Profits have doubled as expected from our leverage ratio of 2 (the negative carry of $8.10 is negligible in this case). Of course, if we had made a loss that would also be magnified.

We usually receive *dividends* on stocks, which are analogous to the rent received by a housing investor. Dividends are a regular payment made by most companies to their shareholders and are usually paid quarterly or every six months. In the one-month period in the example we didn't get a dividend payment.

---

[13] Typical leverage ratios are lower for stock margin trades than for other types of leveraged product. Under current US law leverage ratios are limited to 1:1 under 'Regulation T', equivalent to a leverage factor of 2. Another type of account, 'portfolio margin' is available to certain investors, and may allow higher leverage.

[14] Some of this funding spread is because brokers can't borrow or lend at LIBOR themselves, and is a true reflection of their cost of doing business. But most of it is a source of profit for the brokers. Indeed, brokers in OTC products will not need to borrow or lend at all if they can find two customers with offsetting trades. In this case, they can keep the entire funding spread.

EXAMPLE: BUYING STOCK ON MARGIN

We start with $3,000	
We borrow $3,000, giving us a total of $6,000	Leverage factor is $6,000 ÷ $3,000 = 2. Interest rate charged by my broker for USD margin purchases is currently 3.2% per year.
We buy 84 shares of Citigroup, leaving us with $9.80 in cash	The broker currently has a bid-offer spread of $71.25 to $71.30 with a $1 commission on each trade. We pay $71.30 per share, which means we can buy 84 shares[15] at a cost of 71.30 × 84 = $5,989.20 leaving us with $6,000 – $1 – $5,989.20 = $9.80 left in our account.
We wait one month	Interest paid is 3.2% a year on $3000, which over a month is around 0.27%: $8.10.
We sell our Citigroup shares	The broker makes a spread of $75.00 to $75.05 with $1 commission. We sell our shares at $75.00 which gives us 75 × 84 = $6,300. After deducting $1 commission this is $6,299.
We have $303.89 in profit	We have the $9.80 left over from our initial trade, plus $6,299 from selling our shares, minus $8.10 in interest: $6,300.70. After repaying our $3,000 loan we have $3,300.70. This is a profit of $300.70, or around 10% of our initial investment of $3,000.

Buying stock on margin also differs from buying a mortgaged house in one crucial respect. If house prices fall substantially, I will have a loan that is larger than my house is worth. But as long as I keep paying my mortgage the bank won't care until I come to sell or remortgage.

But this isn't true when you buy stock on margin: we have to worry about mark to market. If the price of Citigroup stock started to fall, then our broker would be on the phone screaming for more cash to cover the losses.[16] If I didn't co-operate with my broker's demands then my Citigroup stock would get auto-liquidated. Remember: auto-liquidation is bad and to be avoided at all costs.

---

[15] We actually have enough money to buy 84.15 shares, but you can't buy fractional shares, so we round down.

[16] In reality, only large institutions that owe their brokers millions get called on the phone. Ordinary folks like us will get a sternly-worded email.

Incidentally, you may be wondering why we bother working out small amounts of money like the $2 in commissions and $8.10 in negative carry in the above example. The total of these costs works out to about 0.34% of our initial $3,000 cash investment. Even if I include the effect of paying the trading spread, the cost of the trade is still less than 0.5%. This pales in insignificance to our 10% profit.

However, as we shall see in later chapters, trading costs are actually extremely important because, unlike our profits, they are guaranteed. We pay them on every trade regardless of its profitability. If we don't have an accurate idea of what our costs are, then we can't know how many trades we can afford to do without paying too much to our brokers. All successful traders have an excellent grasp of what their trading costs are, and you should emulate them by not ignoring the odd few quid or dollars in costs.

Margin accounts are relatively common in the US, but harder to find in the UK.

- Margin buying is a physical trade where we buy the underlying asset with the help of leverage.

- Stocks are listed on exchanges like the New York Stock Exchange (NYSE) and the London Stock Exchange (LSE).

- With no set end date for the trade, margin buying is undated.

2. Short selling stocks

Short selling is selling stock that you don't own, in the hope that it will fall in price and you can buy it back cheaper.

Short selling is not universally admired. Many people believe it is immoral to bet on a company's share price going down. Over 200 years ago, Napoleon Bonaparte claimed that short selling was unpatriotic, and numerous politicians have subsequently agreed with him. Historically, short selling has frequently been banned or heavily regulated. During the 2007–2008 financial crisis, it was illegal to short the shares of banks and other firms in the financial industry. This seriously affected the hedge fund I was working for at the time, since we had to keep checking if a given trade was permitted.

Nevertheless, most economists believe that short selling allows the market to become more efficient. Without it share prices would climb too high, resulting in more spectacular crashes.

Short selling, and buying stock on margin, are two sides of the same coin: both use leverage to make bets on the price of the same underlying asset.

Buying on margin	Short selling
We want shares to go up in price.	We want shares to fall in price.
At the start of the trade we borrow money, and then use it to buy stock.	At the start of the trade we borrow stock, and then sell it, receiving money.
We pay interest on borrowed money.	We pay the owner of the shares a borrowing fee. This depends on the stock and how many people currently want to borrow it. We get interest on the cash proceeds from short selling (at least in theory – many brokers don't pay this).
We receive dividends on the stock.	We reimburse the owner of the stock for any dividends they would have received.
If stock prices fall, we pay margin calls.	If stock prices rise, we pay margin calls.
At the end of the trade we sell the stock we bought and repay the borrowed money.	At the end of the trade we buy back the stock we shorted and return the borrowed stock.

As they use leverage, buying on margin and short selling both require the use of a *margin account*; in this book I'll use the term *margin trading* to cover both types of trading.

Two things that make short selling weird

The slightly weird thing about short selling is the concept of **borrowing stock** and having to pay a fee for the privilege. But this is no different from buying on margin, where we 'rent' money and pay a fee – the interest payment. When selling short you are renting stock for a borrowing fee.

The even weirder thing about short selling is that you have to **reimburse dividend payments**. To understand why, here is a simple example. Suppose Mr A is the original owner of the stock. Miss B wants to sell the stock short, so she borrows it from Mr A. Miss B then sells the stock to Mrs C.

When a dividend is paid it will go to the current owner of the stock, Mrs C. However, Mr A is also expecting to get his dividend payment: the loan contract doesn't affect his rights to a dividend (in fact Mr A may not even realize his stock has been lent out by his broker). So, Miss B has to pay Mr A the dividend they would otherwise have earned.

Here is a tangible example of a short sale. We want to bet on Citigroup stock falling in price, and we want to short up to $6,000 in stock. With a maximum leverage factor of 2 we must have at least $3,000 in our trading account. The stock borrowing cost is 4.8% per year, and no dividends are expected to arrive during the next month.

EXAMPLE: SHORT STOCK SALE

We start with $3,000	
We borrow and sell 84 shares of Citigroup, leaving us with $8,984 in cash	The market currently has a trading spread of $71.25 to $71.30 with a $1 commission. We sell 84 shares at $71.25 per share realising 71.25 × 84 = $5,985 leaving us with $3,000 + $5,985 – $1 = $8,984 in cash.
We wait one month	The borrowing cost is 4.8% a year on $6,000, which over a month is 0.4%: $24. We have to reimburse the owner of the stock for any dividends, but none are due. We may also earn interest on the $8,984 we have in our account. In this example I assume the broker will not pay interest.
We buy back the Citigroup shares	The broker makes a spread of $69.95 to $70.00 with $1 commission. We buy back our shares at $70.00 which costs 70 × 84 = $5,880 plus the $1 commission: $5,881.
We have made in $91.50 profit	We had $8,984 less borrowing costs of $24; once we've paid for the stock buy-back ($5,881) we have $3,079. That is a $79 profit on our original investment of $3,000; around 2.6%.

- Short selling is a physical trade where we borrow the underlying asset.
- Stocks are listed on exchanges.
- With no set end date for the trade, short selling is undated.

3. Exchange traded funds (ETFs)

Exchange traded funds (ETFs) are a special type of share which allows you to get exposure to indices, such as the S&P 500. ETFs are also available that track many other kinds of assets, such as bond indices and commodities. You can buy them with leverage, or sell them short. This opens up trading in many different kinds of assets to owners of margin trading accounts. This is a real boon for US traders, who are not currently permitted to use certain other kinds of leveraged product.

There are also ETFs that come with their own leverage included. These are potentially very dangerous. You cannot control the amount of leverage they use, and they have very high fees. Avoid these products.

Margin trading of ETFs has the same characteristics as margin trading of stocks: they are **physical** products, which are **exchange traded**, and **undated**.

4. Foreign Exchange (FX)

FX, forex, foreign exchange; whatever you call it, is one of the most popular products for leveraged trading. Trading FX is just betting on the exchange rate of one currency against another.

Almost anyone who has been on vacation to another country understands foreign exchange. If I want to visit New York, I'll exchange some of my British pounds for US dollars. Right now, I can buy $1,000 for £750 (an exchange rate of £1 to $1.3333). In the jargon, betting that the pound will get weaker relative to the dollar means I have 'gone short' pounds versus dollars' or *sold* GBPUSD.[17] Alternatively, if I thought the pound would strengthen, I could have gone long or *bought* GBPUSD.[18] As yet this is not a leveraged trade, because I haven't borrowed any money.

Suppose the exchange rate moves in my favour and falls to $1.25 per £1. My $1,000, which I bought for £750, is now worth $1,000 ÷ 1.25 = £800. I have made a £50 profit.

FX trading in real life works in exactly the same way, with two important exceptions. The bad news is that nobody gets to visit the Big Apple. The good news is that we don't need to come up with £375. The FX broker will lend us most of it.

As with margin trading, the amount a broker will lend depends on their maximum *leverage ratio*. Many FX brokers offer a ratio of 30:1 or higher.[19] But let's use a more modest leverage limit of 9:1. That means with a £75 deposit we can borrow 9 times that amount, £675. That gives us a total of £750 to trade with.

---

[17] When we write currency pairs the first currency (here GBP) is the one that will appreciate in value versus the second (here USD) if the exchange rate goes up. The first currency will depreciate relative to the second if the rate falls.

[18] Somewhat confusingly with FX there are two possible ways to describe any trade. Going short GBPUSD at a rate of 1.3333 is equivalent to going long USDGBP at a rate of 0.75 since 1 ÷ 1.3333 = 0.75. In both cases we want dollars to get stronger relative to pounds, but with a short GBPUSD trade we want the quoted rate to fall, whilst for a long USDGBP trade the rate needs to rise. Fortunately, there is a convention that dictates how the rate is quoted for a given pair of currencies. In this case GBPUSD is the market tradition.

[19] I'll explain how to calculate the optimal leverage ratio later in the book.

My broker currently charges an interest rate to borrow British pounds which is equal to GBP LIBOR (currently 0.3%) *plus* a funding spread of 1.5%, for a total of 1.8% per year. The broker will also pay interest on any dollars I deposit with them. This is equal to the reference rate, 1.7% for USD LIBOR, *minus* a funding spread of 1.5%, equal to 0.2% a year.

The traded spread is 1.3334 – 1.3332 = 0.0002. FX spreads are often expressed in *pips*. A pip is 1 ÷ 10,000 or 0.0001. The spread here is 2 pips wide.

Here is an example of an FX trade:

EXAMPLE: WINNING FX TRADE

We start with £75	
We borrow £675, giving us a total of £750	Leverage factor is £750 ÷ £75 = 10. Interest rate charged is 1.8% per year.
We exchange £750 into $999.90	The broker makes a trading spread of 1.3332 to 1.3334 with zero commission. We go short GBPUSD: buy $ and sell £ at an FX rate of 1.3332, which gives us £750 × 1.3332 = $999.90. We now have a *short open position* in GBPUSD: we want the GBPUSD rate to fall (GBP to weaken, USD to strengthen).
We wait a month	Interest paid is 1.8% a year on £675, which over a month is around 1.8% ÷ 12 = 0.15%: 675 × 0.15% = £1.01. Interest received is 0.2% a year on $990.90, or 0.0167% a month, which is: $0.17.
We now have $1,000.07	This is the initial amount we converted, $999.90, plus the deposit interest ($0.17).
We convert $1,000.07 into £799.99	The broker makes a trading spread of 1.2499 to 1.2501 with zero commission. We sell $1,000.07 and buy £ at an FX rate of 1.2501, which gives us $1,000.07 ÷ 1.2501 = £799.99. Our position in GBPUSD is now closed.
We repay our loan and we are left with £61.98	£799.99 after deducting the interest paid of £1.01 is £798.98; after repaying our loan of £675 we have £123.98. This is a profit of £48.98 on our original deposit of £75, which gives us a return of 65.3%.

Notice the effect of leverage: the currency moved by around 6% (from 1.3332 to 1.2501) but we made around ten times that (65.3%). Of course, if the FX rate had gone the other way, we'd have lost money.

- FX trading is a physical trade where we use leverage to borrow currency.

- FX trading is done over the counter (OTC), not via an exchange.

- With no set end date, FX trading is undated.

5. Contracts for difference (CFDs)

At this point you might think that leveraged financial trading is very complicated. You have to borrow something (money, shares or foreign currency), pay various kinds of fees, and keep track of interest and possibly dividend payments.

But what if someone was prepared to do all that work for you?

Then you could just say "I want to bet on the pound going down against the dollar (short GBPUSD)" or "I want to bet on Citigroup shares going down in price (short Citigroup)", and they would take care of the finer details.

That someone is your friendly neighborhood CFD broker. CFD stands for contract for difference. You enter into a *contract* with your broker where they will pay you the *difference:* the movement of the relevant price during the life of the contract. A CFD is a *derivative* product, as we don't ever own the underlying asset.

Let's implement a short GBPUSD trade using CFDs. We'll first consider an undated CFD trade with no set expiry date, and then look at dated CFDs later in the chapter. Unlike the trades we've seen so far, CFDs are offered only in standard units. A single contract with my broker for GBPUSD is for £10,000 worth of currency. My broker has a minimum margin requirement of 3.33%, equating to a leverage factor of 30. As I will discuss later in the book, this is too high. To use a more sensible leverage factor of 10 we'd need to deposit £1,000.

We start with £1,000	
We bet £10,000 on GBPUSD falling	The CFD provider is making a spread of 1.3332 to 1.3334 with zero commission. We'd get 1.3332 as our price for a short position. The value of our contract is 10,000 × 1.3332 = $13,332.0 We've effectively borrowed 10,000 – 1,000 = £9,000. Our leverage factor is 10,000 ÷ 1,000 = 10; the same as in the earlier FX example.
We wait one month	Unless you open and close an undated CFD trade on the same day you have to pay a daily *financing cost*. Financing costs are usually charged on the entire position value, not just on the £9,000 that we've effectively borrowed. Let's assume this cost is identical to the earlier example, where we paid interest on our GBP at 1.8% a year and received it on our USD at 0.2%. For CFDs these two rates are netted off to calculate the financing cost: 1.8 – 0.2 = 1.6%. 1.6% a year over a month is around 1.6% ÷ 12 = 0.13%, and 10,000 × 0.13% = £13.33
We close the trade and make a profit of £651.41	The broker makes a spread of 1.2499 to 1.2501 with zero commission. We receive 1.2501 as we are buying (to close our short position). The value of our $13,332 contract is now $13,332 ÷ 1.2501 = £10,664.75 Our profit is £664.75. After paying the financing charge (£13.33) we have made £651.41. As with the earlier FX example. this is around 65% of the £1,000 in cash margin we had to post.

You can also use CFDs to bet on share prices. Going long in a particular share through a CFD is similar to buying stock on margin. When you buy shares through a CFD you normally receive the same dividend as if you'd bought the shares on margin, although many brokers only pay 80% or 90% of the dividend, keeping the difference for a little extra profit.

Similarly, betting on share prices falling with a CFD is just like selling short. When you go short a stock via a CFD you will be charged 100% of the value of any dividend payments that are due.

Dividend dates

There are three important dividend dates:

- The date when the size of the dividend payment is announced.

- The ex-dividend date. If you buy the stock on or after this date you won't be entitled to the dividend.

- The payment date: when the dividend is actually paid.

Suppose a stock is trading at $100 the day before the ex-dividend date and is due to pay a $10 dividend. All other things being equal, the stock will drop $10 in price when the market opens on the ex-dividend date, as anyone buying the stock that day will not receive the relevant dividend. To smooth out this price drop, CFD providers normally credit holders of long positions with the dividend on the ex-dividend date, rather than waiting until the payment date. If you are short, they will debit your account on the ex-dividend date.

As with all leveraged trading, CFDs are subject to margin calls if the market moves against your position, and auto-liquidation if things go really wrong. Finally, an important feature of CFDs is that they can be used to trade many different kinds of financial products, not just FX or shares, including ETFs, commodities and cryptocurrencies.

At the time of writing it is difficult for most non-professional traders in the US and certain other countries to access CFDs. You should check the local regulatory situation before you trade.

- CFDs are derivatives.

- They trade over the counter (OTC).

- With no set end date, they are undated. Some special types of CFDs are dated, and I will discuss these later.

6. Spread bets

I have casually used the term 'bet' quite a few times because, in my opinion, trading and gambling are essentially identical activities on which only the underlying asset is different.

Trading and gambling

Surely gambling is the refuge of sad addicted losers, whilst trading is a respectable profession? This is a massive oversimplification.

There are a whole series of activities which involve taking risk: betting on horses or football games, trading, and investing (the boundary between trading and investing is also a matter of some debate). Even putting your money in the bank, or under your bed, is a risk-taking activity: you risk the bank going bust, or inflation depreciating the value of your wealth.

In fact, it's irrelevant **what** the risk-taking activity is, but **how** you do the activity signifies whether you are a loser or a respectable risk taker.

Sad, addicted losers take dangerously large risks in situations where the odds are against them: betting on long-shot horses, sticking dimes or 50p pieces into slot machines, investing in dodgy unregulated products, trading binary options, or day trading (and I explain why that is dangerous later in the book).

Smart gamblers take modest risks when the odds are favorable: betting on horses where they have a proven edge, card counting in casinos, long-term investing in diversified portfolios, or trading with a system.

However, there is a big *legal* difference between trading and gambling.

Spread betting in the US is currently illegal. US readers should hastily skip to the next section, lest they be tempted to break the law.

In the UK gambling profits are tax free (the government gets its cut by taxing bookmaker profits). But taxes on share trading are potentially taxable. This creates a gaping loophole. If you try and predict share prices by buying shares (possibly on margin) or going long a CFD, you have to pay tax on any profits. But if you place a spread bet on the share price then your profits are usually tax free.[20]

---

[20] It's not all good news, since you can usually offset trading losses against profits. You can't do this with gambling losses.

Tax

Most traders have to worry about tax, unless they are living in an exotic offshore location. It is impossible for me to cover this subject comprehensively here as tax rules are complex, always changing, and different for each country. This is a very brief overview of how taxes affect most traders, but you will need to find out what the local rules are and you should consult a professional tax advisor.

It's unusual for individual traders to have to worry about **income tax**, since it will be unlikely that their trading will be classified as a proper business. Tax authorities are reluctant to allow this, since you would be able to offset your trading losses against other income and reclaim the tax on the costs of running your trading business (such as data feeds).

The main tax that affects traders is **capital gains tax**. Essentially, if you buy something cheaply and sell it for a higher price, then you have to hand over some of your profits to the government. In the UK, spread bets are free from capital gains tax, but otherwise this tax is hard to avoid.

Dividend income from physical positions in shares and ETFs are also subject to tax. Traders who own derivatives do not receive dividends, but the treatment of carry and financing costs for spot FX and undated derivatives is very complicated, and you will definitely need to check this with a professional.

In certain countries you have to pay a transaction tax when you buy shares. This is known as stamp duty in the UK and is currently 0.5% of the trade value. You can avoid paying stamp duty by using derivatives like CFDs or spread bets. Usually ETFs are also free from stamp duty.

You can also avoid tax by trading inside a tax-free wrapper: 401K and Roth IRAs in the US, ISAs and SIPPs in the UK. Unfortunately, not all products are available inside these wrappers. Finally, it is possible to adjust your trading strategy to reduce the tax that is payable. This is a complex area that I will not cover in this book.

Betting on share prices in this way is known as *spread betting*. The name comes from the trading spread quoted by brokers. Like CFDs, spread bets are a **derivative** product where we don't actually own the underlying asset. We'll first consider **undated** spread bets, and then look at dated spread bets later in the chapter.

A spread bet works in a very similar way to a CFD, if we ignore the different tax and regulatory treatment. With a spread bet we bet a certain amount 'per point'. A point is a given movement in the price. For GBPUSD a point is usually equal to a *pip*, a 0.0001 move in the currency. For simplicity the price is often quoted in points. The GBPUSD rate would be quoted at 13333 rather than 1.3333.

The minimum bet per point with my broker is £1 per point. A single point of GBPUSD at a price of 13,333 has a notional value of 13,333 × £1 = £13,333 worth of currency. To keep our leverage factor[21] at 10 we'd need to deposit £1,333.30.

As with spot CFDs, because there is no fixed expiry date, we have to pay a daily financing charge. For this reason, these undated spread bets are often called *daily funded bets*.

Here's how it works in detail:

We start with £1,333.20	
We bet on GBPUSD falling at £1 per point	Just like other products spread bets are traded with a spread (and sometimes commission). The broker's current spread is 13,332 to 13,334 with zero commission. We receive 13,332 as our price for a short position in GBPUSD.
	Our exposure is £13,332. The leverage factor is £13,332 ÷ £13,33.20 = 10.0, the same leverage as in earlier examples.
We wait one month	Unless you open and close a daily funded spread bet on the same day you have to pay a financing charge.
	We assume it is identical to the earlier CFD example, 1.6% a year or 0.13% for one month. On £13,332 this is £17.33.
We close the trade and make a profit of £488	The broker makes a spread of 12,499 to 12,501 with zero commission. We'd get 12,501 as we are closing our short position and buying back GBPUSD.
	The price has moved by 13,332 – 12,501 = 831 points. We bet £1 per point, so our profit is £831. After paying the financing charges we have made £813.67, or around 61% on our original investment.

We can also spread bet on share prices. As with CFDs, if you place a long spread bet on shares then you receive a dividend credit to your account on the ex-dividend date. Your account will be debited if you have a short position on shares. Also, just like CFDs, spread bets can be placed on a variety of financial instruments as well as FX and stocks.

Naturally, spread bets are subject to margin calls, and auto-liquidation.

---

[21] Most brokers will allow much higher leverage than this.

- Spread bets are derivatives.

- They trade over the counter (OTC).

- With no set end date, they are undated. Some special types of spread bets are dated, and I will discuss these later.

7. Futures

The final leveraged financial product we consider are *futures*. These are a bet on where the price will be at a *specific future date*. So, futures are a **dated product**, and also a **derivative**, since we don't actually own the underlying asset. Unlike the other derivatives we have seen so far (spread bets and CFDs) they trade on exchanges. The terms of the trading contract are standardized and set by the exchanges.

The specific date of a future is known as the **expiry**, or **settlement**, date. There are normally a variety of settlement dates on which we can bet. The dates that are available depend on the underlying asset you are trading. A future that expires on a specific date is known as a **contract**.

For FX, the relevant futures have contracts which expire every month.[22] Other futures, such as the US S&P 500 equity index, have *quarterly* contracts: every three months there is a new futures contract you can bet on. You can bet on what the price of the S&P 500 will be in March, June, September and December. Most futures have quarterly or monthly expiries, but there are some oddities. The gold future on the Chicago Mercantile Exchange has expiries every two months: in February, April, June, and so on.

Some futures, like crude oil, have actively traded expiries stretching years into the future. Others, like the future on the S&P 500, only have active trading in the *nearest* contract (the next contract to expire). We can hold a futures position to expiry, close it earlier, or roll it to the next futures contract. However, every time you roll you will have to pay transaction costs on the roll trade (trading spread, and commission), and possibly capital gains tax.

There is no explicit financing cost for futures, and if you buy a future based on an equity, you wouldn't actually receive any dividends (nor will you have to reimburse dividends if you sold). The price of futures already reflects the financing cost, plus any dividends if relevant. If the underlying price doesn't change then the movement in the futures price will reflect the positive or negative carry that would be due in the underlying asset.

---

[22] These are the 'IMM FX' futures which trade on the Chicago Mercantile Exchange. To be pedantic, they actually have monthly expiries for the next year, and quarterly in subsequent years. In practice, the most popular contract tends to be the next quarterly contract; i.e., March, June, September or December, whichever is next.

As an example, consider the GBPUSD spot FX trade example from earlier in the chapter. The interest rate to borrow GBP was 0.3%, and the rate you could earn on USD was 1.7%. In the original example the broker added and deducted financing spreads from these rates, but these will not apply to futures. The positive carry from shorting GBPUSD is equal to 1.7% − 0.3% = 1.4%. With a current FX rate of 1.3333 the futures price for GBPUSD in one year's time must be: 1.3333 × (1−0.014) = 1.3522

If you go short the future at 1.3522, and nothing happens to the FX rate, then in one year's time when the future expires it will be worth exactly the same as the current FX rate: 1.3333. Going short the future at 1.3522, which ends up being worth 1.3333, will earn you (1.3522 − 1.3333) ÷ 1.3520 = 1.4% in profits: exactly the same as the positive carry.

What if the future wasn't priced at 1.3522? If it was priced differently, then you would be able to do a spot FX trade and perfectly hedge it with a futures trade, leaving you with a guaranteed *arbitrage* profit.[23] Notice that the difference between future and spot price only reflects the cost of carry: it doesn't mean the market expects the price of GBPUSD to be higher in one year's time than it is now.

The futures price is the same for both buyers and sellers (at least in principal, ignoring the trading spread which would make the price slightly higher for buyers), so both will earn or pay the same amount of carry. Neither buyer or seller has to worry about the financing spread which would reduce the positive carry earned on a short spot FX position, and increase the negative carry on a long position.

Like CFDs futures have specific contract sizes. The contract size for the GBPUSD future on the CME (Chicago Mercantile Exchange) is £62,500. Because of the large contract size many futures can only be used by larger traders. AHL, the multi-billion dollar hedge fund I used to work for, are big players in the futures market, and I still trade them myself.

The margin required on a GBPUSD futures contract is currently $1,800. With an exchange rate of 1.3333, the margin corresponds to 1,800 ÷ 1.3333 = £1,350.03, so the maximum leverage factor we are allowed is currently 6,2500 ÷ 1,350.03 = 46.3. This is lower than is theoretically possible with spread betting or CFDs, but still much higher than the leverage factor of 10 we opted to use in earlier examples.

---

[23] This ignores the financing spread and other costs. In practice, arbitrage trading is only possible for large institutions which do not have to worry about financing spreads.

We start with £6,250	
We go short one GBPUSD futures contract	Futures typically have narrower spreads than CFDs or spread bets, but on the down-side you usually have to pay a commission on each trade.
	The spread is 1.3333 to 1.3334 with £1 commission per contract. We'd get 1.3333 as our price for a short position.
	We effectively borrow 62,500 – 6,250 = £56,250. Our leverage factor is £62,500 ÷ £6,250 = 10, the same level of leverage as in earlier examples.
We wait one month	There is no financing charge with futures, and so no ongoing costs (unless we traded just before the contract expiry date, in which case we'll need to pay the costs of rolling the position).
We close the trade and make a profit of £4,158	The spread is 1.2500 to 1.2501. We'd get 1.2501 as we are buying to close our short position.
	In futures there is a set value to each fractional movement in price. For GBPUSD futures we earn $6.25 for each 0.0001 move in price (one pip).
	We make 10,000 × (1.3333 – 1.2501) = 832 pips.
	This is a profit of 832 × $6.25 =$5,200 or $5,198 after paying two chunks of $1 commission; i.e., 5198 ÷ 1.25 = £4,158.40; that is a 66.5% profit on our initial investment of £6,250.

We can also face margin calls with futures. If we deposited £6,250, we would have no problems until we lose more than £4,900. At this point, we have less than £1,350, and since £1,350 per contract is required for margin, we need to cough up some more dough or face the dreaded prospect of auto-liquidation. When trading futures the extra cash needed after losses is called *maintenance margin,* or *variation margin,* to distinguish it from the *initial margin* required in our account before we trade.

- Futures are derivatives.
- They trade on futures exchanges, like the Chicago Mercantile Exchange (CME).
- They have set expiry dates, so they are dated.

8. Dated CFDs and spread bets

The final category of product we need consider are the **dated** variations of the OTC derivative products: CFDs and spread bets:

- Spread bets based on futures.

- CFDs based on futures.

- Quarterly spread bets and CFDs, not based on futures.

It is easier to create a dated OTC derivative if there is an exchange dated derivative that you can base it on. This makes it easier for brokers to calculate prices, and to hedge their risk, and for customers to check that the pricing is fair. Futures are readily available for many different markets, so dated spread bets and CFDs are usually created with reference to a futures price. However, futures are unavailable for many FX rates, individual shares and ETFs. In these cases, the broker has to create their own derivative product from scratch.

Each of the products listed is traded with a set expiry date. So, when shorting GBPUSD with one of these products, you need to specify that you are 'shorting GBPUSD expiring in June 2019'. You can close the position at any time before the expiry, or, if you want to keep it alive when expiry is imminent, you can close your trade and open the same trade in the next expiry date. As with futures, this is known as *rolling* your position.

Where relevant, expiry dates usually match the underlying future, although not all possible future expiries will be available as spread bets and CFDs. Where there is no underlying future, expiries are normally quarterly.

As with futures, there are no financing costs or dividends paid or received: the positive or negative carry of a dated product is built into the price.[24] In theory, there should be no funding spread for these products, although some cheeky brokers may still charge one.

Trading spreads on dated OTC products tend to be wider than on undated products, but if you trade infrequently, they will work out cheaper, as you do not pay a hefty interest rate spread. However, dated products are not entirely free of holding costs, since when you roll a dated product you have to close one position and then open another, which will mean paying a trading spread and possibly some commission. Determining which is the most cost-effective product depends on your trading style, and I return to this question later in the book.

- These products are all derivatives.

- Although they may be based on exchange traded futures or share prices, they all trade OTC.

- They have set expiry dates, so they are dated.

---

[24] Dividend payments if we are betting on share prices, and interest payments for bonds, are also included in the price. For many dated products the price is based on the relevant future and, as we've already seen, futures prices have financing costs embedded within them.

SUMMARY OF PRODUCT CHARACTERISTICS

Stock margin trading*	Physical	Undated	Exchange
ETF margin trading*	Physical	Undated	Exchange
Spot FX	Physical	Undated	OTC
Spot CFD	Derivative	Undated	OTC
Daily funded spread bet	Derivative	Undated	OTC
Future	Derivative	Dated	Exchange
Quarterly spread bet and CFD	Derivative	Dated	OTC
Futures based spread bet	Derivative	Dated	OTC
Futures based CFD	Derivative	Dated	OTC

Includes short selling and buying on margin

Products and underlying instrument are different

There is an important distinction between the type of leveraged *product* (CFD, future, FX, spread bet…), and the underlying *instrument* the product is derived from. Sometimes these are the same: we trade FX with spot FX and trade stocks with stock margin buying (or short selling). But we can trade a CFD, spread bet, or future on almost anything: FX, shares, cryptocurrencies and so on. These different groups of instruments are called *asset classes*.

Table 1 shows which leveraged products can commonly be used to trade underlying instruments in various asset classes. Not all brokers will offer the options shown, and some products are illegal in certain countries.

TABLE 1: LEVERAGED PRODUCTS AND UNDERLYING INSTRUMENTS

	FX	Shares	Share indices	Bonds and indices	Interest rates	Volatility	Commodities	Crypto
Undated products								
Spot FX	✓							
Cash CFD	✓	✓	✓	✓			✓	✓
DFB spread-bets	✓	✓	✓	✓	✓	✓	✓	✓
Shares on margin		✓						
ETF on margin	✓		✓	✓		✓	✓	
Dated products								
CFD on future	✓		✓	✓	✓	✓	✓	
Quarterly spread-bet / CFD	✓	✓						
Spread-bet on future	✓		✓	✓	✓	✓	✓	
Futures	✓		✓	✓	✓	✓	✓	✓

Some of these underlying instruments we have seen before, whilst others are new:

FX	Buying one currency, like USD, whilst selling another, such as GBP.
Shares	A share in the ownership of an individual company like Citigroup. Shareholders are entitled to a share in the profits, paid via dividends.
Share indices	A group of shares which form an index, like the US S&P 500 or UK FTSE 100.
Bonds and bond indices	Bonds are issued by both governments and companies and entitle their owners to interest payments. Like shares they can form part of an index. Futures on government bonds are based on a specific bond, though the precise bond used changes over time.
Interest rates	Common interest rates that traders bet on include LIBOR and EURIBOR. These are the London and European interbank offered rates respectively, the interest rates which banks lend to each other at in the London and European markets. The US equivalent is the 'Eurodollar' rate.
Volatility	Volatility is a technical term for how much prices move up and down. It is possible to bet that share prices will get riskier, or less risky. The flagship volatility product is the VIX index, which measures the riskiness of the S&P 500 US equity index.
Commodities	Commodities are real and tangible, unlike the purely financial assets we've seen so far. They include energies (such as crude oil), agricultural products (e.g., corn), and metals (like gold).
Cryptocurrency	A relative newcomer to the investment space, cryptocurrencies are a form of electronic money. They are based on a new fangled technology called the blockchain. The oldest and most infamous cryptocurrency is Bitcoin, but there are now thousands of them.

CHAPTER TWO
Getting Ready to Start Trading

My FIRST JOB IN THE financial world was rather mundane. I worked part time answering the phones in a broker's call-center, whilst studying for an undergraduate degree in economics. This was in early 2000, and although the firm offered online dealing, most older customers still preferred to do their trades whilst speaking to a real person. They had grown up in a world where computers were an expensive luxury, and the only source of share prices for amateur traders was the business pages of a daily newspaper. A friendly and helpful voice on the telephone was an important factor when deciding which broker to trade with.

The world has moved on rapidly since then, there is more to choosing a broker than finding one with a polite telephone manner, and it is essential to acquire certain electronic tools before you can begin trading in today's markets.

In this chapter I will explain three choices you need to make before starting trading. So, this involves selecting:

1. your trading software, hardware and data feed

2. which product to trade

3. your broker.

I end the chapter with a discussion of how much money you will need to begin trading.

1. Choosing your trading software, hardware and data feed

If I asked you to describe a successful trader in their native working environment, you would probably picture someone sitting at a desk with four or more computer monitors. Dazzling arrays of coloured lines festoon the monitors – all produced by an expensive trading software package – analysing streams of data costing thousands of dollars per month. A top-of-the-range laptop is perched on the desk, whilst underneath it a sleek computer workstation sits, gently humming with latent power.

Both machines are plugged into a superfast internet connection which leads straight to the exchange, ensuring their orders are at the head of the queue.

This picture is very misleading. I blame all the YouTube videos put out by trading 'gurus'. My favorite video consists of a two-minute tracking shot, showing all 41 monitors that someone allegedly uses to trade. It's true that when I was working as an investment bank trader, I did indeed have six monitors and two computers, but a set up like that is complete overkill for an amateur trader.

I recently watched a documentary where an inexperienced trader, who had just completed an introductory course, invested thousands of pounds on a fancy dual monitor trading setup. That hardware cost somewhere between 10% and 50% of the money they had set aside for trading. This is analogous to buying a top of the range power saw to cut two pieces of wood in half. There is no guarantee of higher trading profits if you buy more data, monitors or computers, and for most people these are completely unnecessary.

I manage my own portfolio of shares and funds on the single screen of a battered old laptop, bought second hand for $300. A separate machine, with zero monitors, sits in the corner of my study automatically trading futures: cost $500. My portfolio is relatively large and complicated for an amateur trader, and yet the cost of this budget one-screen setup comes in at significantly less than 0.1% of my portfolio value.

For my data feeds, I pay an annual charge of less than 0.003% of my account balance. I do not pay big bucks for a fast internet connection: I will never be faster getting my orders to market than deep-pocketed institutions, so there is no point playing the speed game against them. That is a competition with no second prize.

The most basic system in this book requires access to financial data which is available for free on numerous websites, and a few calculations which can be worked out on a pocket calculator. Even the more complex systems in the book can be deployed with free data plus any spreadsheet package.[25]

It's possible that you may end up automating your trading, which will require further investment, or that with some experience you might need a more powerful machine, but to begin with, almost any computer or internet connected device is sufficient. Do not spend money on fancy hardware or software: save it for trading.

---

[25] The spreadsheets can be accessed from the website for this book, systematicmoney.org/leveraged-trading

2. Choosing which product to trade

The leveraged products discussed in chapter one are all superficially similar. Usually we buy something which we finance with some of our own cash, plus a chunk of borrowed money. When short selling we borrow the stock rather than the money. Using leverage magnifies our potential profits, but also increases any losses.

In the case of futures, spread bets and CFDs, the loan doesn't really exist, but we still have to pay a financing charge. Dated products do not have explicit financing charges, but there is an implicit charge built into their price. Finally, with all products, we can face margin calls if prices move against us, and if things go badly wrong, our position will be automatically liquidated.

However, despite their many similarities, there are still some important differences between the various products.

Position sizing and leverage

Re-read the examples above for trading GBPUSD with different products and you may notice something interesting. All four examples had a leverage factor of ten, but the amounts of money involved were quite different. To trade the future, we used £6,250 in margin; the spread bet and the CFD came in at £1,333 and £1,000 respectively, and we traded FX with less than £100. As a rule, futures are only accessible to relatively large traders. In contrast, spread bets and CFDs offer smaller, minimum size positions, making them more suitable for the average trader, whilst position sizes in FX can be very small indeed.

The allowable maximum leverage also varies from product to product, but, as you will discover later in the book, a prudent trader would rarely use the maximum allowable leverage.

Costs

Futures are often used by CFD and spread bet brokers to hedge their exposures, futures that their own clients can't trade because of their large margin requirements. These brokers perform the same service as a wealthy kid buying sweets for their poorer friends. Most of the children can't afford to buy an entire bag, so the richest buys sweets in bulk, and then sells a few to each of their customers. The whole bags of sweets are like the futures that less wealthy traders can't afford and the individual sweets are spread bets or CFDs.

Naturally the well-heeled child is going to make a profit on this. They might sell a $1 bag of 20 sweets for 10 cent each, totalling $2 for a $1 profit. Similarly, brokers aren't charities – they have to cover their operating costs, any losses from feckless clients who go bust, and still make profits for their owners.

As a result, CFD and spread bets are usually more expensive than futures. CFD and spread bet brokers will usually quote wider traded spreads than on futures. But, if you don't have the capital to trade futures, you will have to stick with CFDs or spread bets; just like the poorer kids have to buy their sweets at a mark-up.

Calculating the cost of trading different products and instruments is a relatively complex task. I will return to this subject in chapter four.

Trading with a broker versus on exchange

You trade on an *exchange* when you trade futures, or use a margin account to trade shares, although your trades are always routed via a broker. With spread bets, CFDs and FX, you are trading directly with the *broker*. Trading with a broker is relatively risky, whilst trading on an exchange is safer. When you trade on an exchange the settlement of your trades is guaranteed by a *clearing house*. These are highly regulated organisations with significant capital backing from many different sources, and an implicit or explicit government guarantee. They are much, much safer than any broker.

The pool of capital within a clearing house guarantees that your broker can collect any profits you have made from traders who have lost money. It is very unlikely that you will lose money because a clearing house has gone bust, as no clearing house has failed in over thirty years.[26] But, in the seven years I spent working in hedge funds, three large brokers effectively went bust (Lehman Brothers, Bear Stearns and MF Global).

However, the presence of clearing houses does not mean that exchange trading is completely safe. Brokers still hold your cash in their own accounts. In reputable jurisdictions, like the US and the UK, these accounts are supposed to be segregated to prevent brokers stealing or 'borrowing' your cash. Should your broker go down the tubes, government insurance and bankruptcy courts might repay your money, but it could take a long time. I have friends who are still owed money by MF Global as I write this chapter, seven years after its bankruptcy.

Nevertheless, brokers trading on the OTC market have a much higher failure rate than those which pass customer orders on to exchanges. As well as the safety net offered by the clearing house, brokers who are exchange members are governed by stricter rules, which help protect traders. Generally, it is safer to use a broker that sends your trader to an exchange, than to use a broker that doesn't.

---

[26] The last clearing house to fail was the Hong Kong Futures Exchange in the aftermath of the 1987 stock market crash. It was rescued by the government, so traders didn't actually lose any money.

3. Choosing your broker

No dealing and direct market access

Irrespective of where your trades eventually end up, brokers will deal with your orders in a number of different ways. I've listed these in order of preference; the first type of broker is the best, and the final type is the least desirable.

HOW YOUR ORDERS ARE DEALT

Straight through (also known as 'pass through')	If you are using an exchange traded product (like a share, ETF or future) then your broker will usually pass your order straight through to the exchange. In this case you have a legal contract directly with the exchange, not with the broker. This reduces your risk, since exchanges and the clearing houses that sit behind them are safer than brokers.
	If a broker uses pass through orders they will usually offer *Direct Market Access*, which allows you to put orders on the exchange at a given price level. This can reduce your trading costs considerably. I explain how in appendix B, from page 293 onwards.
Full hedging	If you are trading OTC and not dealing with an exchange, then your legal relationship is with the broker, *not* the exchange. Remember FX, spread bets and CFDs are all OTC products.
	With OTC products some brokers will deal with you directly, then immediately *hedge* the risk by doing exactly the same trade on an exchange (if you're familiar with how bookmakers work this is like 'laying off' bets). This approach is sometimes described as *no dealing desk*. Spread bets and CFDs are often hedged with futures, whilst FX trades are usually hedged in the interbank market.
	This type of broker may also offer Direct Market Access.
Partial hedging	Other OTC brokers will not hedge your risk immediately, but gradually build up a backlog of un-hedged trades. Some of these will partly offset your order, so when the broker finally comes to hedge they will have a smaller net exposure. This is more profitable for the broker, but also riskier.
No hedging	Finally, there are OTC brokers[27] that never hedge their risk. Their exposure is always the opposite of yours. You should be extremely wary of these people, since they will always make bigger profits if you lose money. They might be tempted to manipulate the price against you.

---

[27] Technically they aren't even brokers, since a broker is an intermediary between you and the market, and your orders never reach the market. The US term 'bucket shop' is more appropriate.

When you are trading with a broker who does not pass through your orders to an exchange, **they control the price they are quoting you, not the market**. This can lead to some serious problems.

PROBLEMS WITH BROKER-QUOTED PRICES

Indicative prices	The broker quotes you a price, but you can't actually trade at that level.
Re-quotes	The broker quotes you a price, but when you come to trade the price has changed.
No quotes in chaotic markets	When the market is moving too quickly, brokers stop quoting entirely so you can't trade at all.
Missed stop loss	A *stop loss* is an instruction to close a losing trade if the price reaches a particular level. When the market is fast moving, the quoted price may 'gap' beyond your stop, so you will receive a fill that is worse than your stop. This will also happen when you are trading directly with the market, but some brokers create artificial gaps by deliberately or 'accidentally' delaying their prices. To avoid this, many brokers offer *guaranteed stop losses*, but using these will increase your trading costs.
Stop loss triggered by spread widening	You enter a stop loss order, but when the market gets close to it the broker widens the spread so that your stop is triggered. Your trade is prematurely closed even though the mid-market price never reached your stop level.
Fake stop loss triggers	You enter a stop loss order, and the broker's quoted price moves down to that level, resulting in your trade being prematurely closed, even though the real market never actually reached that level.

Apart from the last problem, which is downright cheating, these are all justified by brokers as they protect their dealing desks from excessive risk. Clearly brokers want to maximize profits, whilst letting their customers take all the risks.

There is one superficial advantage of trading with a broker that doesn't pass orders through to the market: **you can sometimes trade when the exchange is closed**. But you should never do this. Because brokers can't hedge their risk when the market is not open, they will quote much wider spreads, making after hours trading much more expensive.

You might have to do some digging to find out exactly how your broker trades. If you cannot find the information on their website, then contact them and ask them for their execution policy. A reputable broker will reply, if you don't hear back then they're probably best avoided.

Access to the instruments and products you want to trade

I have not explained how to choose which instrument and product to trade. That is coming in chapter six. But, if it turns out you want to spread bet the UK FTSE 100 equity index, then you obviously need a broker who offers this product. If you want to trade inside a tax-free wrapper (UK ISA or SIPP, US IRA or 401K), then again you should check your broker offers this.

You can have more than one broker if a single provider doesn't satisfy all your needs. I use five brokers! One is cheapest for futures and margin trading, but they don't offer spread betting, so I do that elsewhere. Another broker is particularly competitive with the fees on their ISA accounts, whilst yet another is best for SIPPs. If you have a large portfolio, **it is safer to split it between brokers**; if one fails at least you won't be destitute.

Minimum account size

Some brokers require you to deposit a certain minimum amount of money before you start trading. This is particularly common for brokers offering margin accounts or futures trading. As I write this you need at least $2,000 to open a margin account in the US, and many brokers require more. The broker I currently use for futures and margin trading has a minimum of $10,000.

Currently in the US there is a 'Pattern Day Trader' rule, which requires a minimum account value of $25,000 at all times for traders who frequently day trade (opening and closing positions in a single day). However, as you will discover later in this book, I don't recommend day trading. Hence, this particular minimum is not an issue.

Financial stability and regulation

You need to be able to trust your broker. After all, you are going to be handing over your money to them. Choose a broker that is regulated by a competent authority: the SEC in the US, and the FCA in the UK. Stay away from businesses that are based in shady offshore jurisdictions. For example, Israel and Cyprus are delightful places to go on holiday, but they also have a history of hosting dubious brokerage firms.

Strict regulation does not guarantee your broker won't go bust. Giant US bank Lehman Brothers employed hundreds of compliance officials, but they still ended up in bankruptcy in 2008. Do some research to check how financially stable your brokerage is. When brokerage MF Global went bankrupt in 2011, the hedge fund I was working for at the time had seen it coming and we had already withdrawn the vast majority of our cash.

This research is a lot easier if your brokerage is a publicly listed company, or part of one. Do not be tempted to cut corners by giving your money to a small firm with opaque accounts, even if they seem amazingly cheap.

Costs

The final, important factor when choosing a broker is how much they will charge you to trade. I always pick the cheapest broker, as long as they don't play games with my orders, are financially stable, and offer the products I want.

Be wary of brokers advertising superficially cheap headline deals. "Trade for free with zero commission" usually means their trading spreads are wider than the competition. I will explain later in the book how you can calculate the true cost of different products and brokers.

Irrelevant factors when choosing a broker

Brokers compete to have the flashiest websites and mobile trading applications. But these are not important. Indeed, an overly complicated interface can make trading harder. Brokers also highlight their generous leverage policy. But you can mostly disregard maximum leverage limits, since **sensible traders never use as much leverage as brokers would let them**.

Ignore brokers who claim to have some special insight into the market – they don't. The last thing you need is a broker who wants to give you advice on when, and what, to trade. These brokers usually charge higher fees, or will find some other way of extracting money from you to pay for their 'valuable' advice.

Something that might become important later in your trading career is the ability to trade automatically through an API,[28] which is the system I use for trading futures. Right now, this is a feature you don't need to worry about.

How much money do you need?

To run the Starter System – the most basic trading system in this book – you need a minimum of \$1,500 or £1,100 (unless your broker requires a larger deposit). This is money you can afford to lose. You should not have borrowed it or be relying on it as a deposit for a house purchase. Trading is a dangerous business, and even if you follow the rules in this book to the letter there is still a risk you will see some, or all, of your cash disappear.

---

[28] Application Programme Interface: the method by which your computer communicates with the broker's computer.

CHAPTER THREE
Introduction to Trading Systems

IN 2012, I WAS WORKING at AHL, a large systematic hedge fund. My job was to manage the fixed income portfolio. This involved a vast number of trades in different kinds of leveraged instruments, all betting on interest rates across many countries. One of our larger positions was in debt issued by a particular European government, which we were exposed to via bond futures.

One day, I was in the staff restaurant deciding which of the delicious menu options I should sample, when a *Very Senior Person* from the parent company of AHL tapped me on the shoulder. He was originally from a non-systematic trading background, where decisions were made based entirely on human judgment.

"Get rid of those bond futures," he said, "I have a contact in the finance ministry who tells me they are going to release some very bad economic news."[29]

"Unfortunately, we can't do that," I replied nervously, "We're running a purely systematic fund, and we cannot override the strategy which the computer is running."

He hissed and stalked off. Difficult as it was to ignore the demands of such a senior manager, I had to let the trading system run unimpeded.

Systematic trading is trading 'by the book'. It's following the rules. It's not ignoring some of the rules because you think you know better. It's not following the rules most of the time, then putting them aside when they don't suit you. In this chapter, I'll explain which rules you can safely ignore when you have more trading experience, and which rules should **never** be broken.

---

[29] Had I acted upon the information then it probably would not have been 'insider trading' – a criminal activity. Insider trading rules don't normally apply to the government bond market. Naturally, I would have checked with a lawyer first.

Why you should use a trading system

Trading systems have two jobs:

1. Deciding when to open a new position, and whether to go long or short.

2. Deciding the size of position you should have, and how long to hold it for.

I believe that everyone should use a system for the latter, and almost everyone should use a system for the former.

Why you should (usually) use a trading system to decide whether to buy or sell

Humans are really smart. They can analyse complex information, detect clear patterns in murky data, and their capacity to understand other people is vital when playing games like poker.

But humans are also really dumb. They are emotional. They frequently ignore rational analysis and make decisions purely on gut feel. Their decision-making is hampered by behavioral biases and they do the same stupid things over, and over, again. They overestimate their ability to predict the future. This is not just my opinion. There has been plenty of research by Nobel prize winning economists and psychologists,[30] showing how and why humans make key errors.

Take one specific example of human incompetence: most people sell out quickly when they make profits, but hang on to positions where they are suffering losses. This makes no rational sense. The market doesn't know or care where you entered the trade and is utterly indifferent to your profits or losses, so it is irrational to get rid of winning trades and hold onto losing ones.

Psychologically, however, it makes perfect sense. Humans enjoy the feeling of being right when they have made money and want to quickly bank their profits in case they evaporate. When losing, they do not want to sell, thus admitting they have made a mistake.[31] As a result, where there has been a slew of good news stocks can experience some weakness, as they have been sold by humans taking a quick profit.[32]

---

[30] Nobel laureates in the field of behavioural economics, the study of human failings in financial decision-making, so far include: Richard Thaler (2017), Robert Shiller (2013), and Daniel Kahneman (2002).

[31] Technical note: This theory of changing risk aversion was developed by Daniel Kahneman and Amos Tversky, "Prospect Theory: An analysis of decision under risk" *Econometrica* 1979. Investors may also be suffering from other cognitive biases such as anchoring and framing.

[32] Sometimes it can make sense to sell after good news. There is an old saying "Buy the rumour, sell the fact". If you have bought in anticipation of good news, it is logical to sell once all the news is factored into the price. But it is hard to judge the point at which the price fully reflects the news, so most traders will sell too early, and would be better off waiting.

Simple trading systems have a number of advantages over human beings.

Firstly, they won't succumb to human biases.

Secondly, they can *exploit* those biases. If human traders continue to do the wrong thing, then doing the opposite thing can be a profitable strategy. The Starter System I introduce in chapter five does exactly that; it reverses the human predilection to cut winners and let losses run. It identifies trends in the market and then follows them: it's a *trend-following* or *momentum* system.

Thirdly, running a trading system is a *repeatable* process. Traders who rely on gut feeling can have bad days when they are not emotionally or physically 'in the zone'. If you are following a system, then you can still trade just as effectively, even if your team lost a big game yesterday or you are suffering from a heavy cold.

Repeatability also means your system can be simulated using historical data: a process called *back-testing*. Back-testing will tell you if something worked in the past. This is no guarantee it will work in the future, but it's a good start nonetheless. More importantly, back-testing indicates how you should expect your system to *behave*. How likely is it you will lose 10% of your account in a week? How many trades should you expect to do every year? Back-testing can answer these questions, and many more.

I will not cover the mechanics of back-testing in this book.[33] You do not need to do any back-testing, since I have already back-tested all the systems in this book.

Repeatability also means your system can be *automated*, but again that is not covered here.[34]

If a system is repeatable then you can easily apply the same rules to many different instruments, giving you *diversification*. Diversification is the holy grail of finance, as it results in a significant improvement to your expected trading returns. I discuss diversification further in part three of this book.

In summary, **simple systems make better trading forecasts than the vast majority of human traders**. Some very experienced people can predict the market with better accuracy than any system, but traders who are just starting out should instead delegate their decisions to systematic trading rules.

---

[33] Instead see my first book: *Systematic Trading.*
[34] I discuss the mechanics of automated trading systems at length in multiple articles on my blog, at qoppac.blogspot.com

Why you should always use a trading system to decide the size and duration of your trades

I frequently get asked: is trading an art or a science? My answer: the decision to go long or short is perhaps an art for a few gifted traders, but **choosing position size and trading frequency are definitely a science where you should follow set rules**.

Certain highly skilled and experienced traders can do better than simple trading systems when it comes to making buy or sell decisions. This is the part of a trading system whose rules you can consider breaking: once you have gained enough experience and can be confident of your ability. I discuss how you can know if you are ready for this in the final chapter. But I firmly believe that you should *always* stick to a system when it comes to deciding (i) how large your positions should be, and (ii) how long you should hold them for.[35]

Why? Well, human traders are usually overconfident. They overestimate how good they are relative to other people, and they make predictions about the future whilst underestimating uncertainty. Most traders conclude that it is possible to make consistently high trading profits.

This leads to two serious problems. Firstly, people assume that it's safe to make huge bets, boosting their returns further using massive leverage. Secondly, they want to trade more often, with each extra trade 'guaranteed' to make further profits. These are both huge mistakes.

By contrast a properly tested trading system will give you a realistic idea of what your likely profitability is. It is possible to calibrate the system to ensure that you have the right amount of leverage. You can also calculate your likely trading costs and adapt the system to keep costs down to a sensible level.

Naturally, I've already calibrated all the systems in this book, so they don't bet the farm and pay reasonable costs. Once you have a good system, then following it rigorously will ensure you avoid the usual human failings of taking too much risk and trading too frequently.

Common arguments against using trading systems

I often encounter disbelief that a simple system can do a better job of trading than a skilled human. Here are some of the arguments I've heard, and my responses:

---

[35] This advice doesn't just apply to amateur traders. Professional investors are also pretty lousy at deciding when they should sell. "While investors display clear skill in buying, their selling decisions underperform substantially – even relative to strategies involving no skill such as randomly selling existing positions." From: Akepanidtaworn, K. et al, 'Selling Fast and Buying Slow: Heuristics and Trading Performance of Institutional Investors', https://ssrn.com/abstract=3301277 (December 2018).

People are smarter than computers	True. But does being smarter automatically make you a better trader? Is the smartest person on the planet also the best trader? No: the best trader on the planet is pretty smart, but there are thousands, if not millions, of people smarter than them.
	Also, as I have already pointed out, even smart people behave irrationally.
The system doesn't know about this particular event, but I do	So what? Can you predict the outcome of the event, better than other traders can? Can you predict how the market will react to the event, better than the rest of the market can? No? Then knowing about the event isn't helpful.
Systems can't adapt when the market changes	This is a valid point, and there are two possible solutions:
	(i) keep updating the system as the market evolves, so it adapts to new conditions. This approach is suitable for sophisticated traders using systems which trade very frequently, generating large amounts of data which can be used to recalibrate the system.
	(ii) use systems whose source of return has persisted for a long period of time. This is my preferred option. The Starter System I introduce in chapter five exploits an effect called *momentum*, which has been around for decades if not centuries.[36]
All trading systems are over-fitted or curve-fitted garbage	*Over-fitting* and *curve-fitting* both mean the same thing: creating a trading system which assumes the future will be almost exactly like the past. Such a system will perform unrealistically well when tested on historic data but will fail when traded with actual money in the future.
	Whilst over-fitting is a very real problem in trading system development there are techniques you can use to alleviate its effects. Naturally I used these methods myself when developing all the systems in this book.
The market is very complex so how can it be predicted with a simple system?	Good trading systems don't try and perfectly predict every microscopic price movement. Instead they forecast broad market movements, knowing that they won't get every prediction correct.
Trading should be fun. All these rules are so boring.	If your motivation for trading is purely to have fun, then be my guest. Give this boring book to a friend and trade the way you want. Just make sure you only put 'play money' in your account, money you can lose, money you would otherwise spend on another form of entertainment, like visiting the casinos of Las Vegas. Because you are probably going to lose.
	But if you are trading to make money, then you are better off sticking to the rules.

---

[36] There have been several tests of momentum with large historical data sets. One study which goes back 200 years is by Christopher Geczy and Mikhail Samonov, 'Two Centuries of Price-Return Momentum', *Financial Analysts Journal* (2016).

What makes a good trading system?

There are three characteristics of a good trading system:

1. No excessive risks.

2. Doesn't trade too often.

3. Doesn't assume the past will repeat exactly in the future.

Let's look at each of these in turn.

1. No excessive risks

Overconfident traders take too much risk. They get greedy. They use too much leverage. If you can earn $500 on a trade by risking $100 of the $1,000 in your account, then surely you can earn $5,000 by risking the entire $1,000?

As I will explain in chapter five, ramping up your leverage beyond sensible levels can turn a winning strategy into a sure-fire loser. Keeping your leverage at the right level will improve the chances that you end up profitable, even though it means sacrificing a tiny chance of a really big payoff.

2. Doesn't trade too often

Many people assume trading is a simple numbers game. Trade more, and you will make more. If you can make $100 trading once a week surely it makes sense to trade every day and make $500 a week? Or trade hourly and make $4,000 a week?

But trading faster means you are handing over more money to your broker, via the trading spread, commissions, or both. Your trading profits are going to need to overcome the headwind of all those extra costs. Unlike costs, those extra profits are uncertain. There is a remote chance you could end up making sufficient additional profits to cover your costs, but it is more likely you will end up worse off.

Good systems keep their costs low and trade relatively slowly.

3. Doesn't assume the past will repeat exactly in the future

This is the sin of *curve-fitting* or *over-fitting*. It is analogous to the common human trader error of *overconfidence*. An over-fitted trading system will have a complex set of rules and dozens of parameters – the numbers that control how the rules behave. It will work fantastically well when run over historic data, but unless the future is exactly like the past then it will not be as profitable when you actually trade it and will almost certainly be inferior to a much simpler system.

Good trading systems for beginners

The three characteristics I've listed above are important for all traders. But trading novices must consider some additional requirements. Firstly, the system should be relatively **simple to run**. An overly complicated set of rules will make it difficult to understand. You are more likely to ignore the rules if they are too complex. The Starter System I introduce later in the book is not as simple as many others, but it is as simple as it can be without becoming dangerous.

Secondly, if you are a newcomer to trading **you should not invest in fancy software or hardware** or cough up for expensive data feeds. You probably don't have much spare cash at your disposal, and what you have should be reserved entirely for trading, not spent on unnecessary technology. All the systems in this book can be traded with data that is available for free from many websites, and a simple spreadsheet.

Thirdly, like I just said, you probably don't have much cash for trading with. There is no point using a system which is designed to run with $100,000, if your trading account contains just $5,000. The Starter System can be traded with just $1,500 or £1,100.

Why you should avoid third party trading systems

This book is pretty long and will require some effort to understand. Why bother? Instead, get someone else to do the work for you. An *expert advisor* (EA) or *trading robot* is a computer algorithm that will do your systematic trading. Alternatively, you can try *copy trading*, where your account automatically duplicates another trader's buys and sells.

Unfortunately, it is very difficult to find a robot or EA whose track record can be trusted. The extraordinarily optimistic track records that can be found all over the internet are usually derived from back-testing and not real trading. Those back-tests are at best *over-fitted,* and many are completely fabricated. They have to be. Most system buyers will naively choose the system with the highest advertised return. You can't beat the fakers if you're honest, so to sell your system you have to heavily exaggerate.

Copy trading is slightly better, in that the track records you see are usually from real life trading. However, all the copy trading sites I've seen use poor scoring methods. These encourage copy traders to take large amounts of risk to reach the top of the leader board. Also, they don't properly account for different track record lengths. Copied traders may also set up multiple accounts, all trading differently. In the leader board you only see the one account that was successful by chance.

Many providers of trading systems have dubious relationships with brokers. They get kickbacks from the broker every time you trade. The more you trade, and the higher your leverage, the more the trading system provider earns. This makes it even less likely that an expert advisor or robot system will be worth buying.

PART TWO

Starting
to
Trade

CHAPTER FOUR

Concepts

Trading has its own jargon.

WHEN I FIRST STARTED TRADING professionally, I was working on the exotic interest rate desk of Barclays investment bank. It was a few weeks before the conversations about yards, gamma, Bermudan swaptions, and bookies made any sense. I had the same problem when I moved into hedge funds. What was a high-water mark, and how did it relate to the draw-down? How much is '2 and 20'?

Then I started trading my own money. I quickly found out that there was a whole new trading vernacular that I hadn't yet come across; novel terms included candles, Bollinger bands, Ichimoku, and Fibbonaci.[37]

In this chapter I explain some key ideas and terminology that you need to understand, before you begin trading with the Starter System, which I introduce in the next chapter.

Some definitions

An **instrument** is something you can trade, like the AUDUSD exchange rate or shares in Apple. A **product** is a specific way to trade a particular instrument, such as spread betting, CFD trading or futures. A **dated product** is an instance of an instrument expiring at a future date, such as June 2019 S&P 500 futures. Dated products include futures, quarterly spread bets, and CFDs based on futures. Margin

---

[37] A *yard* is traders slang for a billion. *Gamma* is a kind of risk that options traders are exposed to. *Bermudan swaptions* are a particular type of product that we traded. *Bookies* – a shortened version of bookmakers – was a derogatory term for a broker. You hit a *high watermark* when your fund's price hits a new peak. The *draw down* is the cumulative loss since you last reached a high watermark. '2 and 20' is a common fee structure in the hedge fund industry: a management fee of 2% which is paid regardless, plus 20% of any profits that you've made. A *candle* is a method for displaying a range of price movements on a chart. *Bollinger bands* are used to find the range of price changes, whilst *Ichimoku* and *Fibbonaci* are both psuedo scientific techniques for calculating key price levels (I don't use or recommend any of these methods).

accounts, spot FX, daily funded spread bets and cash CFDs do not have an expiry; they are **undated products**.

A **trading rule** is a systematic rule which determines how we trade. Initially, I will use one rule for deciding when to open positions, and a separate rule for closing them. A **stop loss** is a specific type of closing rule which, as the name suggests, is supposed to limit your losses. You would use a **position sizing rule** to calculate the size of your initial trade.

The total amount of cash you risk whilst trading is your **capital**. When you are trading you will be dealing with at least one type of currency. Your trading account will be denominated in your **home currency**: US dollars, British pounds, euros, or whatever. But you may be trading in products that have a different **instrument currency**, in which case you will use an FX rate to translate between currencies.

Risk and return concepts

Standard deviation

The most important factor to consider when trading is *risk*. It is also the second and third most important. We don't have much control over our profitability, but it is relatively easy to control our risk.

But what is risk? How do we define and measure it?

There are many different ways to measure risk, but I use a specific method known as the *standard deviation*. I will also use the term *volatility* interchangeably with risk and standard deviation. The standard deviation is a measure of the extent to which actual returns deviate from the average return over a certain period. For example, suppose that an instrument has daily returns of +6%, −4%, +6%, −4%. The average return is +1%, and all the returns are 5% away from that average (+6% is 5% above the average of +1%, and −4% is 5% below it). In this simple case, the daily standard deviation would be exactly 5%.

Notice that the standard deviation penalises unexpectedly good returns, as well as returns that are poorer than average. This might seem weird, since most people associate risk with the fear of losing money, not with unexpected gain. However, you should bear in mind that you cannot have upside risk without a high likelihood of downside risk. Even an exceptionally good trader can expect to lose money on around 46% of trading days.[38]

Daily profits are relatively small relative to risk, even for exceptional traders. An exceptional trader with a standard deviation of 2% a day could expect to make an

---

[38] Technical note: All calculations for the exceptional trader assume an annual Sharpe ratio of 2, daily standard deviation of 2%, and returns drawn from a Gaussian normal distribution.

average daily profit of about 0.25%. On a typical good day, their profits will be one standard deviation higher than average: **2% + 0.25% = 2.25%**. But on a typical bad day their profits will be one standard deviation lower than average: **2% − 0.25% = −1.75%**. Even for this exceptional trader the downside and upside risk are almost identical. Hence, it makes sense to think about volatility in both directions.

Another interpretation of the standard deviation is that it is **the amount you could expect to lose on an average losing day** (if we assume the average return is zero, which even for exceptional traders is a reasonable approximation).

In fact, we can be even more precise if we make another assumption. If we assume that returns follow a *Gaussian normal distribution*, then we can calculate exactly how frequently certain levels of returns are expected. A Gaussian normal distribution is sometimes called a Bell Curve, because it is shaped like a bell with a fat middle (values near the average are common) and thin edges (extreme values are uncommon). Feel free to consult Wikipedia if you need more information on this.

If returns are Gaussian, then they will have the following properties (where **m** is the mean return, and **s** is the standard deviation):

- 50% of the time above **m**, 50% of the time below **m**

- Around a third of the time (34.1%) they will be between **m** and **m + s**

- Around a third of the time (34.1%) they will be between **m** and **m − s**

- Around two-thirds of the time (68.2%) they will be between **m − s** and **m + s**

- 2.2% of the time they will be higher than **m + 2s**

- 2.2% of the time they will be lower than **m − 2s**

- Around 95% of the time they will be between **m − 2s** and **m + 2s**

Finally, a health warning. Returns in financial markets are notoriously badly behaved and do not fit neat statistical models. In particular, really bad days in the market are far worse and more common than predicted by the Gaussian model. Be cautious about taking the values above as gospel.

In this book I use annual standard deviations. A useful rule of thumb is that the annual standard deviation is about 16 times the daily standard deviation.[39] The standard deviation of an equity index, like the S&P 500, is about 16% a year. Hence the daily standard deviation is 16% ÷ 16 = 1%. You can find methods for calculating standard deviations in chapter six, and appendix C.

---

[39] Technical note: This is because standard deviation scales with the square root of time (if we make certain simplifying assumptions), and there are roughly 256 trading days in a year. The square root of 256 is 16.

Calculating the risk of a position

What sort of financial danger are we exposed to if we buy an S&P 500 futures contract, or go long a CFD, or place a spread bet at £1 a point? There is a simple formula to work this out:

FORMULA 1: ANNUAL RISK OF A POSITION

Annual risk = Notional exposure home currency × annual standard deviation % returns

I mentioned above that the standard deviation of the S&P 500 index was about 16% a year. With a notional exposure of $10,000 to the S&P 500, the annual risk is 16% × $10,000 = $1,600. Often to find out your risk you first have to convert the notional exposure into home currency. For example, if we were British, then we convert $10,000 into GBP. At a rate of 1.33 that works out to £7,519. Then we calculate the annual risk: 16% × £7,519 = £1,203.

That is all very interesting, but how do we calculate our notional exposure?[40]

---

[40] Technical note: Should we care about currency risk when speculating in an instrument that isn't denominated in our home currency? For example, if you buy US stocks as a GBP investor you are exposed to both US stock prices and also to the GBPUSD rate (if GBP appreciates, you will lose money). My own research indicates that currency risk forms only a small part of the overall risk of most investments. For traders using derivatives this is less important than for other traders, as they are only exposed to currency risk on their margin, not the entire position.

FORMULA 2: NOTIONAL EXPOSURE FORMULAS

FX	Your notional exposure is equal to the amount of FX that you have purchased. For example, consider a purchase of $10,000 USD using £7,518.80 GBP at a rate of 1 GBP = 1.33 USD. Our exposure is $10,000.
Futures	A futures contract is equivalent to a specific number of units in the underlying instrument. For example, a GBPUSD futures contract is £62,500 worth of GBP. A WTI crude oil contract is 1,000 barrels of oil. The value of a S&P 500 E-mini[41] futures contract is equal to $50 multiplied by the index price. These magic numbers (62,500, 1,000 and 50), are known as *futures multipliers*. To get the notional exposure in a futures trade you need to multiply the number of contracts you hold by the price, and the futures multiplier. So, for example, if you have 2 GBPUSD contracts, with a multiplier of 62,500 and the price is 1.33, then your exposure is: **Exposure = Number of contracts × multiplier × FX rate** **= 2 × 62,500 × $1.33 = $166,250**
Contract for difference (per contract)	A CFD contract has a given size, which reflects your exposure to the price changing by one unit. This is equivalent to the futures multiplier. Your exposure is the number of contracts, multiplied by the contract size and the price. For example, suppose you are long 2 contracts of GBPUSD, where the contract size is £10,000 and the FX rate is £1 = $1.33. Then your exposure is: **Exposure = Number of contracts × size × FX rate** **= 2 × 10,000 × 1.33 = $26,600**
Contract for difference (per point)	A CFD can also be expressed as a certain amount of money *per point*. The size of a point varies between instruments and brokers. For stock indices like the S&P 500, 1 point is usually a single index point. If the index changes from 2783 to 2784 that is a 1-point move. For FX, it's usually 1 basis point (1 ÷ 10,000 = 0.0001). If the GBPUSD rate changes from 1.3333 to 1.3334, that is a 1-point move. Your exposure will be equal to the amount per point, multiplied by the price, and divided by the size of a point. For example, suppose you have gone long GBPUSD at $2 a point, where the price (the FX rate) is 1.33 and 1 point is worth 0.0001. Then your exposure is: **Exposure = Amount per point × price ÷ point size** **= $2 × 1.33 ÷ 0.0001 = $26,600**

---

[41] So-called because there is a larger S&P 500 contract which is worth five times as much. But nobody trades that as virtually all the activity in this instrument has moved to the E-mini future. As I was completing this book in early 2019, a new S&P 500 micro future was launched which is worth one-tenth the value of an E-mini. The new future is still very illiquid, and at present is much more expensive to trade than the E-mini.

Spread bet (UK only)	Spread bets are very similar to CFDs using a bet per point, with the exception that it's often possible to bet in your home currency even on foreign instruments. So, a UK investor who wanted to bet on the US S&P 500, which is priced in USD with a current price of 2,700, and has a point size of 1, could bet £2 per point. Their exposure then would be the amount per point, multiplied by the price, and divided by the size of a point; i.e.: **Exposure = Amount per point × price ÷ point size** **= £2 × 2,700 ÷ 1 = £5,400**
Margin trade	Your notional exposure is equal to the value of the shares that you have bought or sold short. An investor who buys 10 shares of the SPY ETF (which tracks the S&P 500 index) at $274 a share has an exposure of: **Exposure = Number of shares × price** **= 10 × $274 = $2,740**

Risk-adjusted returns

Suppose you know two traders, Bill and Carol. Bill makes an average of 10% a year, whereas Carol makes just 8% a year. Who is the more successful trader?

The answer might seem obvious: surely, it's Bill?

Examining the track record of Bill and Carol more closely, you realise that Bill has a much riskier strategy. Some years he makes over 50%, whilst in others he incurs large losses. The standard deviation of Bill's returns comes out around 20% a year; whilst Carols more pedestrian trading produces a standard deviation of just 10% a year.

Given the choice I would invest in Carol, not Bill.

Why?

Well, suppose I had $1,000 to invest. If I put money into Bill's strategy, I earn 10% a year on average ($100), with a standard deviation of 20% ($200). But if I borrow another $1,000, I could invest a total of $2,000 in Carol's strategy. I would receive double her normal return of 8%, less the cost of borrowing the extra money. If I can borrow at 2% a year then I earn:

$$(8\% \times \$2,000) - (2\% \times \$1,000) = \$140 \text{ per year}$$

As a proportion of my original $1,000, I will receive 14% annually. The annual standard deviation of my returns is 10% × $2,000 = $200.

Using the same capital of $1,000, Carol's trading strategy now has the same standard deviation as Bill's ($200), but with a higher return ($140 rather than $100). After adjusting the strategies so they have the same risk, Carol is more profitable.

To properly compare trading strategies, we need to calculate a return that is adjusted for risk. A measure that does this is the *Sharpe ratio*.

FORMULA 3: SHARPE RATIO (SR)

$$SR = (r - b) \div s$$

Where **r** is the expected annual return of our trading strategy (without leverage), **b** is the annual interest rate we can borrow at[42] and **s** is the standard deviation of the trading strategy, before any leverage is applied.

So, Bill's Sharpe ratio is:

$$SR^B = (10\% - 2\%) \div 20\% = 0.4$$

This is lower than Carol's, which comes out at:

$$SR^C = (8\% - 2\%) \div 10\% = 0.6$$

Carol gets more return for the risk she takes, and hence has a higher Sharpe ratio.

The advantage of using the Sharpe ratio to compare strategies is that it isn't affected by leverage. For example, let us calculate the Sharpe ratio of Carol's strategy with a leveraged investment of $2,000 (a leverage factor of 2). I will earn 14% on my original investment, so **r** = 14%. The borrowing rate, **b** = 2%. Finally, if I apply a leverage factor of 2 it will double the standard deviation of Carol's strategy, **s** = 20%. Now I can recalculate the Sharpe ratio:

$$SR^C = (14\% - 2\%) \div 20\% = 0.6$$

This is the same as before. Let's unpick this calculation in more detail:

- With leverage factor **L**, we will earn **L × r** in returns, where **r** are the returns of the unlevered strategy.

---

[42] You might see this called the *risk-free rate* elsewhere.

- But we also have to pay to borrow, at a rate of **b**. With leverage factor **L** we will borrow **L −1** (remember that a leverage factor of 1 corresponds to no borrowing at all). So, we have to pay **(L − 1) × b** in borrowing costs.

- Hence, our net leveraged return after borrowing costs will be:

$$(\mathbf{L} \times \mathbf{r}) - (\mathbf{L} - \mathbf{1}) \times \mathbf{b} = (\mathbf{L} \times \mathbf{r}) - (\mathbf{L} \times \mathbf{b}) + \mathbf{b}$$

- The numerator (top part) of the Sharpe ratio equation is the net leveraged return minus the borrowing rate, i.e.,

$$[(\mathbf{L} \times \mathbf{r}) - (\mathbf{L} \times \mathbf{b}) + \mathbf{b}] - \mathbf{b} = (\mathbf{L} \times \mathbf{r}) - (\mathbf{L} \times \mathbf{b}) = \mathbf{L} \times (\mathbf{r} - \mathbf{b})$$

- This is identical to the leverage factor **L** multiplied by the numerator for the unleveraged Sharpe ratio (**r − b**).

- So, the numerator of the Sharpe ratio will double if leverage doubles, and so on.

- The denominator (bottom part) of the Sharpe ratio equation is the standard deviation. This will also double if leverage doubles, and so on. Mathematically the denominator will be **L × s**.

- Since both the numerator and denominator of the Sharpe ratio scale exactly with leverage, it is unaffected by the amount of leverage used. Or to put it mathematically, the **L** is cancelled out.

No matter what leverage I use, the Sharpe ratio will be the same. Hence, for traders who can use leverage, the Sharpe ratio is the most appropriate measure of risk-adjusted returns.

Knowing your expected risk-adjusted return is very important. As you will learn later in the book, traders with higher Sharpe ratios can safely use more leverage, and they can afford to pay higher costs.

Risk targeting

> "Hi guys and gals, i [*sic*] have a daily target of $1,000 per day, what is yours and [*why*] you have that target"

Posted on forexfactory.com

Inexperienced traders focus on *profits*. They want to make a certain amount of money on every trade, or set a target for each day, week, month or year.

Experienced traders target *risk*. They understand that returns are pretty random, particularly at shorter time intervals. But risk – the volatility of returns – is relatively predictable. If you know your expected risk, you have a good idea of how much you could reasonably expect to make or lose over a given time interval.

In this book, I specify target risk as an **annualised standard deviation**.

Instrument risk and leverage factor

What if you have a trading risk target of 25% a year, but are trading an instrument like German 2-year government bonds, whose risk, measured by the annual standard deviation of returns, is currently just 0.3%? You will need some leverage, but how much?

FORMULA 4: REQUIRED LEVERAGE FACTOR

Required leverage factor = Target risk ÷ instrument risk

To go from an instrument risk of 0.3% to get to a target of 25% a year you'll need a leverage factor of:

Required leverage factor = 25% ÷ 0.3% = 83.3

If you had $1,000 in capital, then your required exposure would be $83,300 in German 2-year bonds.

We won't always need to use leverage. A leverage factor of less than 1 would be required where the instrument risk is greater than your target. For example, suppose that you are trading a risky cryptocurrency with an instrument risk of 100% a year, and your own risk target is just 20%. The required leverage factor is 20% ÷ 100% = 0.2. With $1,000 in capital, your position would be just $200.

Getting the right level of risk

Most traders assume that you should always take more risk if you can. If you expect to earn 10% a year trading with no leverage (a leverage factor of 1), then surely it makes sense to use the maximum amount of leverage your broker will allow you: 30, 50 or even 200 times. But beware, even profitable traders can be wiped out if they use excessive leverage.

Consider this simple example: we have a trading strategy that earns 5% in year one, loses 10% in year two, and makes 20% in year three. What would have happened if we ran it at different degrees of leverage, assuming we can borrow money at 2% a year? Table 2 has the answer.

TABLE 2: SOME LEVERAGE IS GOOD. TOO MUCH IS BAD

Effect of increasing leverage factor on a hypothetical strategy.

	Leverage factor 1	Leverage factor 2	Leverage factor 3	Leverage factor 5	Leverage factor 8.5
Start with	$1,000	$1,000	$1,000	$1,000	$1,000
Year one +5%	$1,050	$1,080	$1,110	$1,170	$1,275
Year two –10%	$945	$842.40	$732.60	$491.4	$0
Year three +20%	$1,134	$1,162.51	$1,142.86	$943.49	$0
Total profit	$134	$162.51	$142.86	–$56.51	–$1,000
Total return	13.4%	16.25%	14.29%	–5.65%	–100%

In the table, columns show the growth of $1,000 at the end of each year given the relevant leverage factor, where leverage = 1 is no leverage; assuming a borrowing fee of 2% a year. The final row shows the total percentage growth in your account from the start of year one to the end of year three.

Leverage factor = 1

With no leverage (leverage factor 1) our initial $1,000 earns 5% in the first year, bringing us up to $1,000 × (1+0.05) = $1,050. In year two, we lose 10% of $1,050 and are down to $1,050 × (1–0.10) = $945. Things improve in year three, and we earn 20% on $945, giving us $945 × (1+0.20) = $1,134. Since $1.134 ÷ $1,000 = 13.4% we make a total of 13.4% over three years.

Leverage factor = 2

Applying a leverage factor of 2, we earn twice 5% in year one, less the interest we have to pay to borrow: (5% × 2) – 2% = 8%. So, we end up with $1,080 at the end of the first year. The loss of 10% in year two really hurts, since with leverage it becomes (–10% × 2) – 2% = –22%. We actually have less cash at this point than we had without leverage ($842.40 rather than $945). For year three, our return of 20% becomes 38% with leverage and, in total, after three years we end up with a return of 16.3%.

A little bit of leverage does indeed help. Doubling our leverage from 1 to 2 improves our returns a little, but does not double our profits.

Leverage factor = 3

For a leverage factor of 3, we have to borrow another $2,000 to have $3,000 to invest; we earn (5% × 3) – (2% × 2) = 11% in year one. After three years we end up with 14.3% more than we started with; less than the 16.3% we had with a leverage factor of 2. **Once leverage gets too high our total return starts to fall**.

Leverage factor = 5

With a leverage factor of 5, our total returns have turned negative, as we cannot recover from the amplified effect of losing 10% in year two.

Leverage factor = 8.5

With a leverage factor of 8.5, we end up completely broke. The modest loss in year two is magnified to the point where we lose everything. Even a profitable trading strategy can be wiped out if you use too much leverage.

So too much leverage is bad, but insufficient leverage means you will be leaving some profit on the table. What is the right level of leverage?

Fortunately, there is a precise formula for determining how much you should bet given your expected profits which is known as the *Kelly criterion*.[43] Under certain assumptions,[44] the Kelly criterion states that the optimal leverage factor f^* is:

FORMULA 5: OPTIMAL KELLY LEVERAGE FACTOR

Optimal leverage factor, $f^* = (r - b) \div s^2$

Where **r** is the expected annual return, **b** is the interest rate that you can borrow at, and **s** is the expected standard deviation of returns of the instrument you are investing in. You can now calculate the correct risk target. This will be equal to the risk of the instrument **s**, multiplied by the optimal leverage f^*:

FORMULA 6: OPTIMAL KELLY RISK TARGET

Optimal risk target $= s \times f^* = s \times (r - b) \div s^2 = (r - b) \div s$

You may recognise this from earlier – it's the Sharpe ratio from formula 3. **The optimal Kelly risk target is equal to your expected Sharpe ratio**.

Minimum trades and minimum capital

Minimum and incremental trades

When calculating what position to take, you will usually get a number with some pesky decimal places attached; the system might say, "Please buy 42.3442 shares in Google".

But you cannot buy less than one share of a company. Theoretically the minimum trade size in a margin account is a single share, but minimum commission levels make this uneconomic. For this reason, I recommend using a minimum of ten shares. Similarly, you cannot usually buy less than 1,000 units of foreign currency when FX trading. The minimum stake when spread betting is typically $1 or £1 a point, and nobody will let you buy less than one futures contract.

---

[43] John Kelly, 'A new interpretation of information rate', *Bell System Technical Journal*, (1956).

[44] Technical note: Returns need to be serially independent and drawn from a Gaussian normal distribution. Negative skew or high kurtosis will reduce the optimal leverage. Whilst these assumptions are not realistic for most trading strategies, in most they do not usually affect the level of optimal leverage to any significant degree. For FX carry, a strategy I will introduce in part three, which has modest negative skew, the optimal leverage is reduced by around 5%.

The *minimum trade size* is the smallest position you can possibly take in a given instrument and product. The *incremental trade size* is the smallest increase you can make to the minimum trade size.

In futures the minimum and incremental trade sizes are always the same: one futures contract. You have to buy a minimum of one contract, then if you want more exposure you buy another contract, and so on. In many cases FX, spread betting and CFD trading brokers operate a similar system. You might have to buy a certain round number of *lots* of FX, £ or $ *per point* of spread bet, or *contracts* of CFDs.

However, certain brokers are happy for you to make smaller incremental bets, over and above the minimum position. So, for example, my CFD broker has a minimum trade of ten contracts, each at £1 per point on the S&P 500. But they also allow one penny incremental increases to that trade size. My minimum trade size is £10 a point, but I can also place a trade for £10.01 or £10.02 per point.

The incremental trade size in a margin account is one share. Buying 11 or 12 shares is as economically viable as buying the minimum trade of ten.

Minimum required capital

An important implication of minimum position sizes is that there is a **minimum amount of capital required to trade a given instrument using a specific product**. We already saw this back in chapter two. To trade GBPUSD we used over £6,000 in capital for the futures trading example; the spread bet and the CFD for the same instrument came in at around £1,000 respectively, and we were able to trade spot FX with less than £100. Minimum capital requirements severely curtail the options that are open to traders who do not have six- or seven-figure account balances.[45]

Costs

> 'If you rationalise – hey, I am making profits, who cares if my trading costs are more than 40%. That would be like a pilot with 300 souls on board a flight across the Pacific ocean estimating their fuel based on a constant tailwind – when those headwinds show up, and they always do at some point – you crash."

> Excellent advice posted on elitetrader.com by 'comagnum'

Costs are a key factor to consider when trading but are usually over-looked by novice traders. They prefer to think about which model of Ferrari they will buy with all the money they are bound to make.

---

[45] I discuss exactly how to calculate the minimum capital required for a particular trading strategy in chapter five.

If you don't know your costs, then you cannot make sensible decisions about how often you should trade. Should you trade quickly, incurring large costs, but possibly making more money. Or trade more slowly to reduce your costs? Without estimating your likely costs, you cannot decide which instrument or product you should trade, which trading rule you should use, or how quickly you should cut losing trades.

Risk-adjusted costs

I calculate all costs in risk-adjusted terms: as an annual proportion of target risk. That's quite a mouthful! As an arbitrary example, if your target risk is 15% a year, and your annual costs are 1.5% of your capital, then your risk-adjusted costs will work out at 1.5% ÷ 15% = 0.10 = 10% of your target risk.

Why should you measure costs that way?

Because this measure of costs is indifferent to leverage. If you double your leverage, then you also double your costs. Your positions are twice as big relative to your capital, and therefore will cost you twice as much. But doubling your leverage will also double your risk. In the arbitrary example, with costs doubled to 3% a year and risk of 30%, your risk-adjusted costs will be unchanged: 3% ÷ 30% = 0.10 = 10%.

Regardless of your leverage, your risk-adjusted costs will be identical. This also makes it easier to compare costs between different instruments that have different levels of risk. This measure of costs can also be thought of in terms of risk-adjusted returns, as measured by the *Sharpe ratio*.[46] Dividing your costs by standard deviation will effectively tell you **how much of your pre-cost Sharpe ratio will get eaten up by costs.**

For example, suppose you are paying 2% costs with a risk target of 20%. Your risk-adjusted trading cost is 2% ÷ 20% = 0.10. You expect 0.10 units of your pre-cost Sharpe ratio to be paid out in costs. Let's check this. If you can make 10% in annual pre-cost return, with a borrowing rate of 2% and target risk of 20% then your pre-cost Sharpe ratio will be (from formula 3, page 61):

Sharpe ratio = (10% – 2%) ÷ 20% = 0.4

Now apply 2% costs. Your Sharpe ratio will be reduced to:

Sharpe ratio = (10% – 2% - 2%) ÷ 20% = 0.3

As expected, this is a reduction of 0.10 Sharpe ratio units.

---

[46] From formula 3 the Sharpe ratio is equal to your expected return, minus the interest rate you can borrow at; all divided by the standard deviation of your returns.

Cost calculations

There are two types of trading costs:

1. **Holding costs**: costs we have to pay whilst holding a position. These include the funding spread on any borrowing (for undated products: margin trading, spot FX, cash CFDs and daily funded spread bets), and the cost of rolling positions (for dated products: quarterly spread bets, futures, and instruments based on futures).[47]

2. **Transaction costs**: cost of opening and closing our positions. These comprise the trading spread, brokerage commissions, and any taxes we have to pay (like UK stamp duty on shares).

Let's look at these costs in turn.

Holding costs

We can work out the *risk-adjusted holding cost of an instrument*, by dividing holding costs with the instrument risk, measured in annual standard deviation terms.

FORMULA 7: RISK-ADJUSTED HOLDING COSTS

Risk-adjusted holding cost = Annual holding cost ÷ instrument risk

As an example, it costs around 0.033% a year to hold the US 2-year bond future, which has risk of around 0.54% a year. In risk-adjusted terms the holding cost is:

Risk-adjusted holding cost = 0.033% ÷ 0.54% = 0.061

How is this cost affected by leverage?

Let's find out. If your target risk was 20% a year, then using formula 4 (page 63) you need to apply a *leverage factor* of 20% ÷ 0.54% = 37.04. At a leverage factor of 37.04 it would cost you 37.04 × 0.033% = 1.22% of your capital every year to hold a position in the US 2-year bond future:

---

[47] Importantly the cost of carry is not equal to the holding cost (and if carry was positive, we would not automatically have negative holding costs). If holding costs were zero, we would earn carry that was equal in magnitude on long and short positions. The effect of holding costs is to reduce positive carry and increase negative carry. For example, if I can earn 5% from a deposit in one currency, and borrow at 1% in another currency, then my theoretical positive carry would be 4%, or –4% if I reversed the trade. But if my broker applies a financing spread of 0.5% then I will earn 4.5% on deposits, and borrow at 1.5%. My positive carry has been reduced to 3%, 1% lower than before, hence my holding costs are 1%. Similarly, the negative carry would be the difference between borrowing at 5.5% and depositing at 0.5%, or –5%; again, the holding costs have increased the negative carry by 1%.

Risk-adjusted holding cost = 1.22% ÷ 20% = 0.061

Holding cost as a proportion of risk is unchanged after applying all that leverage.

Transaction costs

Transaction costs should also be calculated as a proportion of risk.

FORMULA 8: RISK-ADJUSTED TRANSACTION COSTS

Risk-adjusted cost per transaction = Cost per transaction ÷ natural instrument risk

Again, let's look at an example. Suppose it will cost you 0.1% of your capital to trade your typical position in US 2-year bonds, with a target risk of 20% per year. Then the cost for each transaction, as a proportion of your risk, will be:

Risk-adjusted cost per transaction = 0.1% ÷ 20% = 0.005

To work out the annual cost we need an additional piece of information, which is the expected number of trades that will be executed each year.

FORMULA 9: RISK-ADJUSTED ANNUAL TRANSACTION COSTS

Risk-adjusted annual transaction costs = Risk-adjusted cost per transaction × # of trades per year

For example, if you do five trades per year, at a risk-adjusted cost of 0.005 per transaction then it will cost:

Risk-adjusted annual transaction cost = 0.005 × 5 = 0.025

Total annual trading costs are just the sum of transaction and holding costs:

FORMULA 10: TOTAL RISK-ADJUSTED COSTS

Total risk-adjusted cost = Risk-adjusted transaction cost + Risk-adjusted holding cost

For the simple example our total costs each year would be 0.061 in holding costs, plus 0.025 in transaction costs, for a total annual risk-adjusted cost of 0.061 + 0.025 = 0.086. Alternatively, you can think of this as giving up 0.086 of your Sharpe ratio in transaction costs every year. If your Sharpe ratio before costs was 0.4, then after costs it would be 0.4 – 0.086 = 0.314.

Appendix B, from page 293 onwards, explains in more detail how to calculate costs.

CHAPTER FIVE
Introducing the Starter System

I dabbled in shares during the tech bubble that ended in 2000, but my first encounter with serious trading was working for an investment bank as an options trader in 2002.

When I joined I had no idea how to trade.

I had spent several months on the bank's graduate training scheme, but this involved taking classes that were mostly completely irrelevant to life on the trading floor. The received wisdom was that trading was best learned by osmosis; sitting junior traders next to experienced veterans, in the hope they would eventually learn something useful. Until then, they could handle the senior traders' coffee orders.

I quickly learned the technical aspects of the job, such as how to work out a price for the products we were trading, and that my boss's preferred drink was a skinny latte with a double shot. But nobody taught me how trading decisions were made. I could not answer simple questions like: should I buy or sell? How big should my positions be? When should I close my trades?

At least initially, I could have really done with some kind of *system*. Something like: "If you see this pattern then buy. This one means sell. Here is the calculation you need to work out your positions. Finally, if this happens, then close your trade."

Then, when I had gained in confidence, I could have started to make my own decisions; gradually tweak the system, keeping the most important parts, and over-riding it where appropriate. Of course, to do that I would need to know which parts of the system were sacrosanct, and which could be safely ignored.

I am going to give you the help I never had: in this chapter, I'm going to introduce the Starter System. It is a complete system which tells you when to trade, how large your trades should be, and when you should close your trades. As you read through the rest of the book you will learn how and when to change it, and which parts are too important to change.

An overview of the system

The Starter System is a trading system which is as simple as possible and is designed to be suitable for beginner traders with minimal capital. Here are the main elements that it contains:

Instrument and product choice	The system is designed to trade a single instrument (e.g., GBPUSD), via a single type of leveraged product (e.g., spot FX).
Opening positions	The system uses a single rule for opening new positions.
Position sizing	A second rule decides on the size of position that should be opened.
Closing positions	Finally, a third rule determines when positions should be closed.

In this chapter I introduce each part of the system and explain how I designed it. The next chapter will show you how to actually implement and trade the system. Then, in the rest of the book, I explain how to adapt and improve the Starter System.

Which instrument and product to trade?

Do some instruments offer better returns than others?

Q: "What is the best market to learn to trade for a beginner?"

A: "The best market to learn to trade for a beginner I would say is definitely Forex. Not because it's the most liquid market in the world that runs 24/7 and all the big bucks are here, but because in my opinion it is way easier to trade than futures or stocks."

A: "All you need is to learn Forex trading and the rest of the markets will be like piece of cake for you. "

A: "Don't know a lot about futures trading. But can tell you something about Forex and Stocks. ... On Forex you can use leverage and make more money for less cost. Forex trading is faster, more risky, but may be more profitable."

Extremely poor advice in response to a question on quora.com

The point of trading is to make money. Specifically, we want to maximise the profits we can make, net of any costs we have to pay.

Like the posters quoted above, you probably assume that likely profitability is the most important factor when deciding which instruments to trade. To begin with, let's focus on trading profits before any holding or transaction costs have been paid: *pre-cost returns.* Figure 1 shows the back-tested pre-cost Sharpe ratio (SR) for the Starter System, across a large number of different instruments[48] which I currently trade in my own portfolio. The average SR is around 0.24, but there is a huge difference between various instruments.

FIGURE 1: BACK-TESTED PRE-COST SHARPE RATIO (SR) FOR THE STARTER SYSTEM

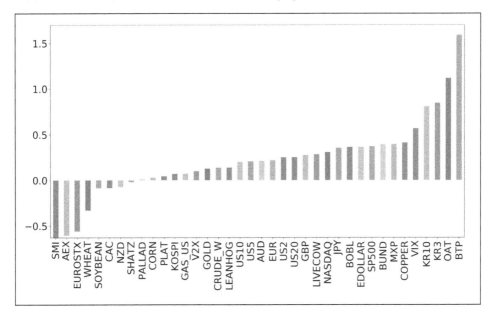

It's clearly a no brainer. We should all be trading Italian government bonds (BTP), or perhaps French bonds (OAT), or maybe Korean bonds (KR3 and KR10). Also, we should stay away from the Swiss and Dutch equity indices (SMI and AEX respectively). They are clearly a money loser. For what it's worth, most Forex markets (like the instrument labeled AUD, which is AUDUSD) fall somewhere in the middle.

But this ignores something very important: *statistical uncertainty.* The average performance of a trading system is a *statistical parameter,* which we can *estimate,* but which cannot be known exactly.

---

[48] Don't worry if you don't recognise all of the names or acronyms. They're just labels for different instruments, and you don't need to know which is which.

Statistical uncertainty of parameter estimates

Statistical uncertainty can be a difficult concept to get your head around. However, it's a key part of understanding how to trade properly, so it's vital that you grasp it.

Imagine that I am trying to sell you a trading system. I have traded it with my own money, and I have a back-test. Your first question should be, "How long is the back-test?" I admit to you that I have only a single day of back-tested trades.

Is one day long enough to prove that a particular trading system is worthwhile? Hopefully your instinctive answer is a firm no. Fortunately, I have another system which I have been trading for five years. Would you trust this system more than the other? Of course you would.

Longer track records give us more confidence, because we intuitively understand that the performance of a trading system isn't something that we can know precisely. With more evidence we can be more confident about the likely performance.

Statistical techniques allow us to go beyond this intuition and calculate how certain or uncertain we can be about the likely performance of a trading system given a track record or back-test. Consider a non-financial example. Imagine that I am standing outside a locked room full of people, and I am trying to work out the average height of everyone in the room. Before I arrived a certain number of people left the room, so they could be measured. The people who left the room were selected randomly, and in the jargon, they are my *sample*.

Suppose five people left the room, and I measure their heights. If I assume that these people are selected randomly, then my best guess for the average height of everyone left in the room will be equal to the average height of my sample. This is also known as my *central estimate* for the average height in the room.

However, I cannot be certain that my central estimate is accurate. The people in my random sample might be unusually tall or short. I can get a more accurate estimate by asking for a larger sample, but I can never be exactly sure of the average height of those left in the room.

Now let us relate this to trading systems. Imagine there is a mysterious black box on your desk. The box contains all the possible daily returns for a trading system, each written on a piece of paper. We cannot see inside the black box, which means we can never know the real properties of the system. In particular, we can only guess at what the future return or Sharpe ratio (SR) might be.

Whenever we run a back-test the black box spits out a stack of randomly selected daily returns, through a slot. For example, for a one year back-test we get about 250 returns. These returns are my *sample*. We can estimate the average and standard deviation across all those returns, and when combined with the interest rate we can borrow at, they can be used to calculate the SR. The Sharpe ratio we estimate from a back-test will be our best guess for what the true SR is for all the returns left inside the box; what we actually earn once we start trading. This is the *central estimate* of the SR.

However, we do not know if the random set of back-tested returns is representative of all the returns that are left in the black box. We might have got lucky, and pulled out some unusually good returns, or especially unlucky and got a bunch of bad returns. We have a good deal of uncertainty about how good or bad the returns really are. The longer the back-test, the less uncertainty we have, but we never know for sure what is left inside the box.

So, we can never say exactly what the SR is inside the black box, but we can use statistical techniques to quantify how uncertain we are.[49] Of course, there isn't really a black box that spits out paper, but the same techniques can be used to calculate how much confidence we should have in back tested returns, given the length and properties of a particular back test.

Figure 2 shows the effect of statistical uncertainty on our estimate of Sharpe ratio (SR) for different instruments. I have done this using a *box and whiskers plot*, which is a type of graph used to illustrate uncertainty.

FIGURE 2: ESTIMATES OF SHARPE RATIO FOR VARIOUS MARKETS

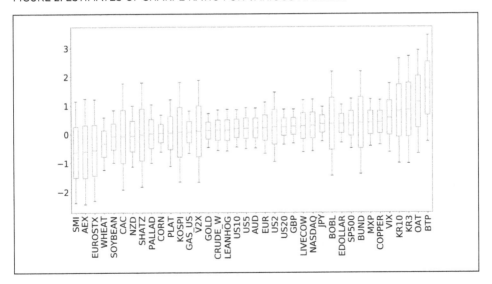

---

[49] Technical note: Specifically, if returns are independent and follow a Gaussian distribution, then the variance of the parameter estimate for Sharpe ratio is $(1+0.5SR^2) \div T$, where T is the number of observations.

In the middle of each vertical box is a horizontal line showing the *average* Sharpe ratio (SR) for a given instrument. These are identical to the values in figure 1. The other components of the plot show how confident we can be about these estimates of SR. There is roughly a two-thirds chance that the true SR lies within the *boxed* area (about 68% to be a little more exact). The statistical jargon for a range of uncertainty like this is a *confidence interval*. There is also a 95% chance that the true SR lies between the top and bottom ends of the lines extending from the box (these are the 'whiskers').[50]

Taking Italian BTP bonds as an example, there is a two-thirds chance the SR is between 0.64 and 2.5, and a 95% chance it is between –0.26 and +3.43. Where we have a longer back-test history we can be a little more confident about our results, and the confidence intervals will be narrower. For gold, whose back-test goes back several decades, there is a slightly narrower confidence interval: a 95% probability that the SR is between –0.46 and 0.72.

The key conclusion from figure 2 is that it is impossible to say, with any degree of certainty, that one instrument has performed better than another in their back-tested performance. It is possible that the best performing instrument (BTP) has a SR below –0.2, and equally possible that the worst (SMI) has a SR above 1.

Hence: we should ignore pre-cost returns when deciding which instrument to trade.

Sizing and costs

If we assume that all instruments have the same expected pre-cost performance, then **we should trade the instrument and leveraged product with the lowest expected costs.** Sadly, there is a snag with this approach. The cheapest instruments and products tend to require the largest amounts of capital.[51] Only very wealthy traders can use the very cheapest instruments. Regular people have to carefully consider what they can afford to spend on costs, given the limited cash they have available for trading.

---

[50] Using 68% and 95% confidence intervals might seem completely arbitrary, but these are the standard values used in statistics for these kinds of plots. They relate to the proportions of the most widely used statistical distribution, the 'Gaussian Normal', which we met in chapter four. The two intervals encompass the regions that are one standard deviation (68% confidence) and two standard deviations (95% confidence) around the central estimate. You might ask why there is no 100% confidence interval. In fact, we can never be 100% sure what the Sharpe ratio really is no matter how long the back-test is.

[51] The explanation for this is too large to fit into this footnote. If you are interested it is in appendix B, on page 300.

The one-third of costs rule: A speed limit on trading

Clearly it would be madness to spend all of your expected profits on trading costs. On the other hand, we have to spend *something*, otherwise we would not be trading at all. What is the correct proportion?

There is no single correct value, but my own rule is to **limit my costs to one-third of my expected return**. One-third might seem rather conservative, but there is considerable uncertainty about what our likely returns will be (look again at figure 2 if you don't believe me). If your returns are half what you expected, sticking to the one-third rule means that you are left with something after paying costs. Because trading faster costs more, this maximum cost level acts as a *speed limit* on our trading activity.

If both returns and costs are expressed in risk-adjusted terms, then this implies spending no more than one-third of our expected Sharpe ratio on costs.

FORMULA 11: SPEED LIMIT

Speed limit = Expected Sharpe ratio ÷ 3

The Starter System has an expected Sharpe ratio before costs of 0.24 (I'll explain why shortly), implying that our risk-adjusted costs should not exceed 0.08.

Speed limit = 0.24 ÷ 3 = 0.08 (maximum total risk adjusted costs per year)

One-third is an absolute maximum, but ideally you should spend less. For my own trading I spend about 5% of my expected pre-cost returns on costs: around one-sixth of the speed limit. However, I trade relatively cheap futures which are not accessible to those with less capital. If you are an FX, CFD or spread better you will have to spend a little more. Just don't break the speed limit.

In table 3, I analyse the average costs and minimum capital levels for different leveraged products. Ultra-cheap futures are only available to those with relatively deep pockets. Margin trading is also quite cheap. In theory, you can start margin trading with just a few thousand dollars, although many brokers require a minimum account value of five or ten thousand dollars.

If you can trade them, spread bets have an even lower capital entry level, but you need to be careful as many are too pricey to trade economically. Spot FX is the most democratic of all leveraged products, accessible to the very smallest traders, but also relatively expensive. With around eleven thousand dollars, or the equivalent in pounds, you can access CFDs. Although they are quite pricey, around a third of the CFDs I analysed are still cheap enough to trade the Starter System.

TABLE 3: CHEAPER PRODUCTS NEED MORE CAPITAL TO TRADE

Average minimum capital to run Starter System and average risk-adjusted trading cost, for each leveraged product type averaged across instruments.

	Average minimum capital ($)	Average minimum capital (£)	Average risk-adjusted trading cost
Futures	53,000	39,700	0.01
Margin trading	3,650	2,060	0.02
Quarterly spread bet / spread bet on future	*	2,000	0.06
Spot FX	760	560	0.07
CFD on future	*	8,300	0.09
Cash CFD	*	8,400	0.10
DFB spread bets	*	2,600	0.11

Using current exchange rates. Cost calculations using appendix B, and minimum capital calculations using formula 21.

* Not currently available to US traders.

Why is spot FX often expensive to trade?

Spot FX is the most accessible market for traders without much capital, but unfortunately it is often expensive. We can either day trade spot FX, closing our positions each day, or trade more slowly as in the Starter System. Both methods can have prohibitively high costs if you choose the wrong broker.

Day trading is not cost effective for many products, with the possible exception of the very cheapest futures markets (I explain why at the end of this chapter). Spot FX is no different, despite day traders avoiding the cost of overnight funding. Opening and closing a single trade every day in a relatively cheap market like AUDUSD would still cost around 0.35 a year in risk-adjusted terms. This is much higher than the expected Sharpe ratio of the Starter System, which comes in at 0.24 (I explain where this value comes from later).

Longer term trading in spot FX is a little cheaper, but still very expensive relative to other products. This is because the holding costs for FX are often very high. Many brokers charge at least 2% a year as a funding spread, which is the main holding cost for FX traders. Currencies have instrument risk of between 6% a year (for relatively stable developed market pairs like GBPUSD) and 15% (for emerging markets like USDMXN). On a risk-adjusted basis a holding cost of 2% translates to 2% ÷ 6% = 0.33 for a stable developed market pair, and 2% ÷ 15% = 0.13 for emerging markets. These are well above my speed limit of 0.08 units of risk-adjusted costs per year (calculated back a few pages back).

In their advertising, FX brokers are fond of trumpeting their tight spreads and generous levels of allowable leverage. But unless you are day trading, execution spreads make up only a fraction of total costs in FX, and excessive levels of permitted leverage are a curse, not a blessing. You should be looking for an FX broker who is happy to operate with a funding spread of 0.4% or lower, depending on how volatile the market is.

The FX broker I used to calculate the costs in this book has funding spreads between 0.25% and 0.5%, making FX trading just about viable.

Let us return to the problem we are trying to resolve: which instrument should we trade, and with which product?

The answer will depend on how much capital you have, and whether you are a UK trader, or based in the US. Table 4 shows the cheapest instruments and products for UK traders with up to £10,000 in capital.

TABLE 4: INDICATIVE COSTS FOR UK TRADERS WITH MINIMUM CAPITAL UP TO £10,000

	Minimum capital (£)	Risk-adjusted trading cost
Nasdaq equity index, Futures spread bet	5,500	0.015
S&P 500 equity index, Futures spread bet	1,800	0.015
FTSE 100 equity index, Futures spread bet	5,100	0.022
EURGBP FX, Forward spread bet	3,400	0.023
GBPUSD FX, Forward spread bet	3,900	0.026
NZDUSD FX, Forward spread bet	2,400	0.028
Gold, Futures spread bet	600	0.029
USDJPY FX, Forward spread bet	3,000	0.034
EURUSD FX, Forward spread bet	3,300	0.035
UK 10-year bond (Gilt), Futures spread bet	2,400	0.035
German 10-year bond (Bund), Futures spread bet	2,200	0.038
Euro Stoxx 50 equity index, Futures spread bet	1,400	0.040
AUDUSD Spot FX	550	0.045
EURGBP Spot FX	800	0.048
JPYUSD Spot FX	450	0.048
GBPUSD Spot FX	450	0.054
EURUSD Spot FX	450	0.058

Minimum capital has been rounded up. Cost calculations using appendix B, and minimum capital calculations using formula 21. To save space only instruments with risk-adjusted costs less than 0.06 per year are shown.

Table 5 shows the cheapest instruments and products for US traders with up to $20,000 in capital. Without access to spread bets there are more limited options for traders with less cash in their accounts.

TABLE 5: INDICATIVE COSTS FOR US TRADERS WITH MINIMUM CAPITAL UP TO $20,000

	Minimum capital ($)	Risk-adjusted trading cost
Corn, future	19,000	0.0037
Apple, Margin trade	4,400	0.016
Facebook, Margin trade	3,600	0.018
S&P 500 (SPY ETF), Margin trade	3,700	0.021
UK 10-year bond (Gilt), CFD on future	13,000	0.035
German 10-year bond (Bund), CFD on future	10,500	0.038
Euro Stoxx 50 equity index, CFD on future	6,500	0.041
AUDUSD Spot FX	800	0.045
EURGBP Spot FX	1,100	0.048
JPYUSD Spot FX	550	0.048
GBPUSD Spot FX	600	0.054
EURUSD Spot FX	550	0.058
European Volatility index, Future	5,300	0.064
WTI Crude oil, CFD on future	15,000	0.067
US 10-year bond, CFD on future	6,000	0.074
Eurodollar, future	11,000	0.074

Minimum capital has been rounded up. Cost calculations using appendix B, and minimum capital calculations using formula 21. Products with risk-adjusted costs greater than my speed limit of 0.08 per year have been excluded.

Dated versus undated costs

You may have noticed that the tables above contain relatively few *undated* products: daily funded spread bets, and cash CFDs (margin trades and spot FX are honourable exceptions). This isn't an accident – they are all more expensive than their *dated* counterparts (quarterly spread bets, futures, and products based on futures).

Why?

Undated products tend to have narrower spreads and hence lower transaction costs, but higher holding costs in the form of interest margins charged by brokers on funding. However, these holding costs can be avoided if positions are closed each day. Dated products have wider spreads, but lower holding costs. We expect undated products to make sense for people who trade very frequently, whilst slower traders should prefer dated products.

Let's consider some actual figures. Table 6 shows the total risk-adjusted costs at different trading frequencies for three different leveraged products, all trading the same underlying instrument: gold. I've also broken out the holding cost on the bottom row.

For fewer than 50 trades each year the dated CFD (based on the future) is cheaper than the undated cash CFD. For greater than 50 trades annually, their positions are reversed. But this is a moot point, because at that sort of trading frequency we are spending far too much on costs, well above my speed limit of 0.08 Sharpe ratio units.

TABLE 6: IF YOU TRADE QUICKLY, UNDATED PRODUCTS ARE RELATIVELY CHEAP – BUT STILL VERY EXPENSIVE

Risk-adjusted trading cost at different trading frequency for gold.

	Future	Dated CFD based on future	Undated Cash CFD
Day trading **	0.21*	1.06*	0.53*
200 trades per year	0.088*	0.43*	0.28*
100 trades per year	0.046	0.23*	0.18*
50 trades per year	0.024	0.13*	0.13*
25 trades per year	0.014	0.069	0.099*
10 trades per year	0.008	0.038	0.083*
5.4 trades per year***	0.006	0.028	0.078
Holding costs	0.003	0.017	0.073

* Exceeds the speed-limit of 0.08 risk-adjusted cost per year, formula 11

** Two trades every day, no positions held overnight

*** Trading frequency of Starter System

Cost calculations using appendix B

Gold futures are much cheaper than both types of CFD, but the minimum capital required is around $117,000 (£88,000). This is far too high for most traders. Incidentally, spread bets would have a similar cost to CFDs.

You may be surprised to see that the Starter System is only expected to do 5.4 trades on average each year. I discuss why I set up the system in this way later.

Table 7 shows the cheapest instruments and products for traders with very large amounts of capital; they are all futures.

TABLE 7: WEALTHY TRADERS PAY LOWER TRADING COSTS

Expected costs for UK / US traders with large amounts of capital.

	Minimum capital ($)	Minimum capital (£)	Risk-adjusted trading cost
Nasdaq equity index, future	216,000	162,000	0.0018
WTI Crude oil, future	109,000	82,000	0.0034
Corn, future	19,000	14,000	0.0037
FTSE 100 equity index, future	137,000	103,000	0.0038
S&P 500 equity index, future	178,000	133,000	0.0045
EURGBP FX, future	113,000	85,000	0.0055

Minimum capital has been rounded up. Cost calculations using appendix B, and minimum capital calculations using formula 21. To save space only the six cheapest instruments are shown.

The figures in this chapter are all indicative and are based on current market conditions and the costs currently charged by the brokers I use. If you are serious about trading, then you should recalculate and check them yourself, using the formulas in appendix B.

Product choice and tax for UK traders

All the cost figures I've shown here ignore the impact of taxes. Tax treatment in the US is fairly similar across different leveraged products; at least the differences aren't large enough that you should consider taxes when deciding which product to trade.

However, this isn't true on the other side of the Atlantic. UK traders who trade shares, futures, spot FX and CFDs have to pay Capital Gains Tax (CGT) on their profits above an annual threshold. At the time of writing the threshold is £11,700, and tax is charged at a rate of 10% or 20% (if you have other income it will probably be 20%). But UK spread betters will *usually* avoid paying any tax.[52]

As I explain later in this chapter, the sort of return you should expect on the Starter System is around 5% a year before costs. Unless you have hundreds of thousands of pounds in capital, it is unlikely you will be making £11,700 or more with the Starter System.

So, if you are a smaller trader you do not need to consider tax. When choosing how to trade a particular instrument, you can forget about futures, which have excessively high minimum capital requirements. CFDs and spread bets have roughly similar cost levels and spread bets usually have smaller minimum sizes relative to CFDs. So, in a fight between CFDs and spread bets, spread bets nearly always come out better.

But what about larger traders? Should they trade futures, which are cheap, or spread bets, which are exempt from CGT?

Let's look at a worked example for a gold trader with several hundred thousand pounds in capital (well above the minimum capital for gold futures, which is £88,000). For the Starter System, which is expected to trade 5.4 times a year, gold futures have risk-adjusted trading costs of 0.006, versus 0.029 for gold spread betting. To get the annual cost as a percentage of our capital we multiply these figures by the risk target of 12% (I explain where this comes from in a few pages). That translates to a cost of about 0.07% for futures (0.006 ×12% = 0.07%) and 0.35% for spread bets (0.029 ×12% = 0.35%).

The expected pre-cost return of the Starter System on both futures and spread bets is about 4.9% a year (again, this is calculated later in the chapter). So, a gold futures trader with £339,327 in capital can expect to make 4.9% − 0.07% = 4.83% a year after costs, or £16,383. After allowing for the tax-free allowance of

---

[52] If trading is your primary source of income and you make consistent returns then you *may* be liable to pay UK income tax on trading profits, and it's possible this could also apply to spread betting winnings. I should also point out that legislation is subject to change and interpretation, and I'm not a lawyer or an accountant.

£11,700 they pay tax on 16,383 – 11,700 = £4,682. CGT at a rate of 20% would cost 20% × 4682 = £937 leaving them with £15,446 in after tax profits.

A spread betting punter with the same capital would make 4.9% – 0.35% = 4.55%, or £15,446. They have no further tax to pay. You can see why I chose the rather odd figure of £339,327. This is the break-even point where the tax benefits of spread betting exactly match the hindrance of extra costs, at least in this example. With capital of less than £339,327 you are better off trading cheaper futures. With more than £339,327, the tax savings of spread betting give it the edge.

This break-even figure will vary depending on the level of taxes, the precise cost difference between products, and your expected returns. But clearly only extremely wealthy traders can benefit from the tax advantages of spread betting. Indeed, a trader with that sort of capital may struggle to find a broker willing to take his bets. This is doubly true if they are successful and trade relatively infrequently, making them both a large risk and an unprofitable customer.

Although my own trading account is relatively large, I still prefer futures to spread bets. Firstly, because my orders are passed through to the exchange, which is preferable for reasons I explained back in chapter two. Secondly, because costs are relatively predictable, but returns are not. This makes the tax advantages of spread betting more uncertain than the higher costs.

When should we open positions?

What makes a good opening rule?

To decide when we should open positions, we need a rule. Most people assume that finding the right opening rule is the only factor differentiating happy profitable traders from sad losers. Actually, this is not true, as you will discover in the rest of the chapter. Still, it's important to have a decent opening rule.

What makes a good rule?

Let's take a look at the some of the characteristics of good opening rules.

Objective	When trading systematically, rules must be purely objective so they can be coded into a formal algorithm. I am not a fan of subjective trading 'rules', where you have to squint at a chart and see if you can perceive a weird pattern such as a Morning star, Abandoned Baby, Descending Inverted Scallop, Shaved Bottom[53], or Vomiting Camel.[54]
Simple	Simpler rules have a better chance of working. They are less likely to be over-fitted and are easier to trade.
Explainable profits	There should be a reason why the trading rule worked in the past, not just an arbitrary pattern that just happened to be profitable in the back-test.
Intuitive behaviour	The pattern of buying and selling by a trading rule should make intuitive sense. If you ever think, "Why the heck does it want to buy now?", then you have the wrong rule.
Profitable back-test	It would be a bit crazy to trade a rule that has not worked in the past. This is no guarantee that it will work in the future, but it is a good start.

The Starter System opening rule: A moving average crossover

The rule we are going to use in the Starter System is a *moving average crossover*. Moving average crossovers are part of a larger group of trading rules known as *momentum*, or *trend following*, rules. I've chosen this rule because it is commonly used by many people, including myself and a substantial number of professional traders. Because it is so ubiquitous, your favourite trading software or charting website will probably calculate it for you. It is also easy to calculate with a spreadsheet.

These rules are *intuitive*: if something is going up we buy, expecting the upwards trend to continue. If the price is falling, we sell. They are *explainable*: there are several credible reasons as to why these rules might work.[55] They are *profitable*, with considerable evidence that momentum has worked in the past, both from back-tests[56]

---

[53] I am not making these up: all are charting patterns used by traders.

[54] This last pattern is a fake. It was made up by banking analyst Suvi Platerink to mock traders who use such techniques.

[55] Technical note: My favourite explanation of momentum returns comes from behavioural finance, specifically prospect theory. This explains why traders become more risk averse and wish to sell once the price has gone up. Conversely when the price has fallen, they become risk loving and are reluctant to sell. This leads to recent risers being undervalued, and recent fallers being overvalued.

[56] Several historical tests of momentum have been done, one which goes back 200 years, is by

and the successful track records of professional traders using this type of strategy. Finally, the rule is *simple* and *objective*. It can be calculated with a short formula and requires no subjective judgment.

Now for the rule.

First, I need to define a moving average. The moving average of an instrument price is the average price over the last *n* periods, where *n* is the *moving average length*. In this book I use daily prices, so *n* is in days. A moving average with length *n* (MA^n) is equal to the average over the last *n* prices at time *t* as follows:

FORMULA 12: MOVING AVERAGE

$$MA^n_t = \sum (P_t + P_{t-1} + P_{t-2} + ... + P_{t-n+1})/n$$

The following is the moving average crossover for a pair of speeds *f* (fast) and *s* (slow):

FORMULA 13: MOVING AVERAGE CROSSOVER (MAC)

$$MAC^{f,s}_t = MA^f_t - MA^s_t$$

When prices change, a faster moving average (small *n*) will react to the change quicker than a slower moving average (large *n*). Hence, in an uptrend the faster moving average will move higher than the slower, and in a downtrend their positions will be reversed. So, if the MAC is positive, we will be in an uptrend, and the rule will want to go long. When the MAC is negative, we are in a downtrend, and would be going short:

$MA^f > MA^s$; $MAC^{f,s} > 0$: Go long

$MA^f < MA^s$; $MAC^{f,s} < 0$: Go short

Figure 3 shows how a version of this rule worked in the 2008 financial crisis, trading the S&P 500 equity index. A clear sell signal is generated in June when the 16-day MA falls below the 64-day MA. Then in April 2009 a buy signal appears when the 16-day MA goes above the 64-day.

Christopher Geczy and Mikhail Samonov, 'Two Centuries of Price-Return Momentum', *Financial Analysts Journal*, (2016).

FIGURE 3: MOVING AVERAGES OVER THE FINANCIAL CRISIS

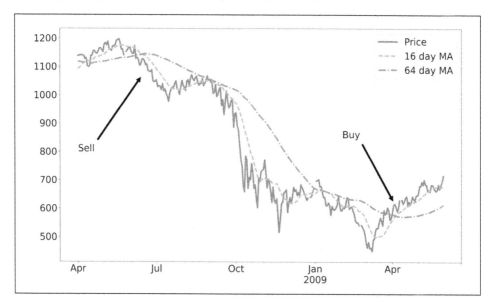

What crossover lengths?

How do we choose the right pair of moving average lengths, the optimal values of f and s?

As with selecting an instrument, the choice of crossover lengths will depend on both pre-cost returns and costs. Moving average crossovers with lower values for *f* and *s* will pick up more short-lived trends, but will trade frequently, giving them higher costs. Higher values of *f* and *s* will only detect a few slower trends but will be cheaper because they trade less often.

Firstly, let us examine pre-cost returns across a selection of crossovers.[57] Figure 4 shows the back-tested average Sharpe ratio for several crossovers, with the average taken across 37 instruments that I trade in my own portfolio. As I did with instruments in figure 2, I show the uncertainty of the Sharpe ratio estimates by displaying the values in a box and whiskers plot.

---

[57] You will notice that I fixed the ratio of the fast and slow moving averages at exactly 4 (so for example *f*=2 and *s*=8 which gives a ratio of 8 ÷ 2 = 4). This is to reduce the number of possibilities I had to consider. Any ratio between around 2 and 6 works equally well. You will also notice that the fast moving average length goes up in multiples of 2: *f*=2,4,8,16 and so on. Crossovers which use the missing intermediate values for the fast moving average (f=3,5,6,7,9...) end up being extremely similar to the crossovers I've shown here.

FIGURE 4: COMPARISON OF MOVING AVERAGE CROSSOVER LENGTHS

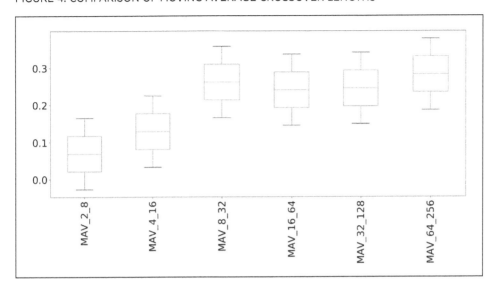

The rules go from relatively fast (lower values of *f* and *s* (on the left-hand side)) to relatively slow (higher values of *f* and *s* (on the right)). The rule I chose for the Starter System lies in the middle (MA_16_64). All the rules have very similar performance, shown by their overlapping boxes and whiskers, except for the very fastest rule (MAV_2_8), which is significantly worse than both MAV_8_32 and MAV_64_256.

With the possible exception of the very fastest rule – which looks significantly worse – there is no reason to pick one set of crossovers based on pre-cost returns.

Now let's consider costs: transaction and holding costs.

First, I calculated the number of trades done each year by the trading rule. The level of transaction costs will depend on the instrument and product: it will be the cost per trade, multiplied by the number of trades done each year. I also need to add on the holding cost, which is the same regardless of the trading rule that is used. Table 8 shows us the figures for each crossover, and for a selection of instruments and products.[58]

I have also included the 'speed limit' cost threshold for each trading rule: one-third of the average back-tested, pre-cost Sharpe ratio.

---

[58] I'll explain why I chose these particular products in the next chapter.

TABLE 8: FASTER CROSSOVERS ARE MORE EXPENSIVE, BUT IT DEPENDS ON THE PRODUCT

Estimated risk-adjusted trading costs for different length moving average crossovers.

Trading costs

	Average trades per year	1/3 of Pre-cost Sharpe ratio	Corn future	Euro Stoxx CFD on future	Gold quarterly spread-bet	AUDUSD spot FX	S&P 500 margin trade
MAC 2,8	39.1	0.023	0.021	0.139*	0.099*	0.069*	0.078*
MAC 4,16	19.1	0.043	0.011	0.080*	0.057*	0.055*	0.054*
MAC 8,32	9.4	0.087	0.006	0.051	0.037	0.048	0.030
MAC 16,64	5.4	0.080	0.004	0.041	0.029	0.045	0.021
MAC 32,128	2.3	0.082	0.002	0.030	0.022	0.043	0.013
MAC 64,256	1.1	0.094	0.002	0.027	0.019	0.042	0.010

* Product is too expensive to trade with rule (trading cost greater than speed limit: 1/3 of pre cost Sharpe ratio values shown in second column).

Values shown in body of table are total cost calculated as H + (TC×T) where T is the number of trades per year (first column), TC is the transaction cost per trade and H is the annual holding costs; all costs are risk-adjusted. Thus been estimated as an average over back-tests for all the instruments in my own data set. Costs calculated using the formulas in appendix B.

Corn futures are really cheap instruments which can trade all the crossovers, without spending too much on costs. However, we cannot trade the fastest crossover (2,8) using a Euro Stoxx 50 dated CFD. From the table it would cost 0.139 Sharpe ratio (SR) units to trade including holding costs, but from the second column, the most we should be prepared to spend on costs for the fastest crossover is 0.023, one-third of the pre-cost back-tested SR (which is 0.069). In fact, the two fastest crossovers (2,8 and 4,16) are too expensive for all the non-futures products.

You can now see why I've avoided choosing any of the faster crossovers. They would be prohibitively expensive, except for the very wealthiest traders who can trade futures. In contrast, MAC 16,64 is relatively affordable, with costs that are comfortably below the 'speed limit' of one-third of expected SR for all the instruments shown.

But why haven't I chosen either of the two slowest crossovers (32,128 and 64,256)? In figure 4 both have similar pre-cost performance to the crossover chosen for the Starter System (16,64), and they would be a little bit cheaper to trade.

I have two reasons for ignoring the very slowest crossovers. Firstly, for many instruments their performance will end up being similar to a static long position in the underlying instrument. One example: US bonds have mostly gone up in price over the last 40 years, so in the back-test for US 10-year bonds the MAV 64,256 crossover has been long around 72% of the time.

Secondly, with so few trades per year there is a risk that you will get bored. Some level of tedium is to be expected with system trading, but excessive boredom is problematic. Bored traders tend to end up ignoring their system and making their own trades. Hopefully the crossover MAV 16,64 is just active enough to keep you interested.

From figure 4, the **pre-cost Sharpe ratio of the Starter System using the MAV 16,64 crossover is 0.24** and, from table 8, **the expected number of trades per year is 5.4**. I will use these values throughout the rest of this chapter to calibrate the rest of the system (in fact, I have already used them to determine whether an instrument has a viable level of trading costs).

How large should positions be?

The next component of the system concerns *position sizing*. This is a vital part of any trading system. Many traders end up losing money because they take on too much risk. Even if a trading rule is 99% accurate, you will still eventually blow up your account if your position sizing is incorrect.

Calculating position sizes for a given trade is a two-step process.

Step one: determine the **required** *notional exposure* **in your home currency** for your chosen instrument. For example, we may want to take £7,500 of long exposure to the

Euro Stoxx 50 equity index. Our desired notional exposure is the same regardless of the product we are using.

Step two: calculate *what that exposure corresponds to in units of the relevant product*: how many futures or CFD contracts; or how many £ or $ per point of spread bets.

How do we determine our notional exposure?

The formula for working out the required notional exposure is relatively simple:

FORMULA 14: NOTIONAL EXPOSURE FROM RISK AND CAPITAL

Notional exposure = (target risk % × capital) ÷ instrument risk %

The *target risk* is **the annual standard deviation that you want on your account**. I explain how this is calculated in a moment. Your *capital* is the total amount of money you are currently risking, denominated in your *home currency* (the currency used to value your account). If you have made profits since you began trading, you may want to add these to your capital.[59] Any losses **must** be deducted. For most people capital will be equal to the current value of their trading account.

The *notional exposure* will also be in your home currency. Finally, the *instrument risk* is the annualised standard deviation of returns. I'll discuss how you can actually measure risk in chapter six.

As an example, suppose you have a risk target of 12% a year (I'll explain where this figure comes from shortly – page 99 if you're curious) and £10,000 in capital. For the S&P 500, which has instrument risk of 16% a year, your notional exposure target would be:

Notional exposure = (12% × £10,000) ÷ 16% = £7,500

This is a *leverage factor*[60] of £7,500 ÷ £10,000 = 0.75. Because this particular instrument has a higher risk than your target, you end up with a leverage factor of less than 1, with a notional exposure that is less than your capital. If the instrument risk was lower than the target, the leverage factor would be higher than 1.

How do we determine our target risk?

---

[59] It is not compulsory to add profits to your capital. For example, I regularly withdraw any profits that I make from my trading account and invest them elsewhere. This means I do not benefit from the compounding of returns in my account but it is safer.

[60] Another formula that will directly give you the required leverage factor (remember this is equal to notional exposure ÷ capital) is: Leverage factor = Target risk % ÷ instrument risk %.

Formula 14 is pretty simple, but determining the right level of *target risk* is a little more difficult. Target risk should be the set at the lowest, most conservative, value from the following list:

- maximum risk possible given leverage allowed by brokers or exchanges
- maximum risk possible given prudent leverage limits
- maximum risk given your own personal appetite for risk
- optimal risk level given the expected profitability of your trading system

Maximum risk possible given leverage limits

The maximum possible risk target given a particular leverage limit is:

FORMULA 15: RISK TARGET POSSIBLE GIVEN MAXIMUM LEVERAGE

Risk target = (Maximum leverage factor × instrument risk)

As an example, consider a margin trade in the SPY ETF, which tracks the S&P 500 index. The maximum leverage factor allowed for a margin account is usually 2, and the instrument risk is around 16% (annual standard deviation of returns). This implies that the maximum risk target will be:

Risk target = (2 × 16%) = 32%

Leverage is more generous in derivative markets. To trade the S&P 500 as a spread bet requires 5% margin with my current broker, equating to a maximum leverage of 100% ÷ 5% = 20, and a maximum risk target of:

Risk target = (20 × 16%) = 320%

As you might expect, margins tend to be higher for more volatile products and lower for safer products. My broker requires a 50% margin to trade spread bets on the cryptocurrency Bitcoin, which has instrument risk of around 100%. That equates to maximum leverage of 2, and a maximum risk target of 200%; not so different than the limit for S&P 500. Generally, for a given product the effect of margin and volatility will roughly cancel out, giving similar maximum risk targets across different instruments.

However, as I will explain, even a risk target of 32% is quite high for the Starter System. Unless you are an extremely aggressive trader, leverage limits will not cramp your style.

Risk possible given maximum prudent leverage

From 2011 to early 2015 the Swiss franc to euro exchange rate had extremely low risk, as the exchange rate was strictly controlled by the Swiss Central Bank. Many traders took advantage of the 200:1 leverage allowed by certain FX brokers, and speculated that the banks would continue holding the rate down. Unfortunately, the Central Bank changed their minds. They allowed the FX rate to move freely in January 2015, when it increased from 0.83 to over 1.00 in a matter of minutes. This wiped out the accounts of thousands of traders who used too much leverage.

Broker and exchange leverage limits are usually far too generous. Sensible people should set their own leverage limits that reflect the worst possible scenario. You should estimate (i) the worst possible loss on an instrument that could occur before you had a chance to close your position, and (ii) the highest bearable loss to your account. The maximum prudent leverage will then be:

FORMULA 16: PRUDENT LEVERAGE FACTOR

Prudent leverage factor = Maximum bearable loss ÷ worst possible instrument loss

Now you can calculate the maximum implied risk target:

FORMULA 17: MAXIMUM RISK TARGET GIVEN PRUDENT LEVERAGE

Prudent maximum risk target = Prudent leverage factor × instrument risk

For example, it is possible that the US stock market could crash 25% in a day, as it did in October 1987 (worst possible instrument loss = 25%), and suppose that you could not bear losing more than a third of your capital in one day (maximum account loss = 33.3%). The instrument risk of the US stock market is around 16% per year.

Prudent leverage factor = 33.3% ÷ 25% = 1.333

Prudent maximum risk target = 1.333 × 16% = 21.3%

Personal appetite for risk

Can you cope with seeing an annual standard deviation of returns of 24% on your account? Would you prefer 12%? You have probably responded with a shrug and a blank look. It's difficult for most people to relate to the rather abstract measure of risk which I use in this book.

It is easier to consider the likely losses you could expect to see when running the Starter System at a given risk target. Tables 9 through 11 show my calculations[61] for the probabilities[62] of suffering losses of various severities over different time horizons.[63]

TABLE 9: CHANCES OF A GIVEN DAILY LOSS WHEN RUNNING THE STARTER SYSTEM

Risk target	1% loss	2% loss	5% loss	10% loss	20% loss
6%	0.07%	*	*	*	*
9%	5.3%	0.07%	*	*	*
12%	14%	1.6%	*	*	*
24%	26%	10%	0.07%	*	*
48%	37%	26%	5.3%	0.07%	*
96%	43%	37%	21%	5.3%	0.07%
192%	46%	43%	34%	21%	5.3%

* Theoretically less than 0.01

---

[61] Health warning: Do not take these figures at face value. They make some assumptions about how likely different market returns are. Larger daily and monthly trading losses are more common in reality than the tables suggest. For example, the current instrument risk of the S&P 500 equity index is around 16% a year; according to the assumptions used to build these tables the chances of a 7% daily drop are extremely small; so small that such a drop should only happen once every 3.4bn years. But there have been six such falls in the last 40 years; four in 2008 alone!

[62] Technical note: The values in these tables have been calculated assuming that returns are drawn from a Gaussian normal distribution with a Sharpe ratio of 0.24 (the expected pre-cost return of the Starter System).

[63] You may be wondering why all the risk targets shown are multiples or fractions of 12%. 12% is the risk target I recommend using in the Starter System, for reasons I explain on page 99.

TABLE 10: CHANCES OF A GIVEN MONTHLY LOSS WHEN RUNNING THE STARTER SYSTEM

Risk target	2% loss	5% loss	10% loss	25% loss	50% loss
6%	7.3%	0.02%	*	*	*
9%	22%	3.6%	0.02%	*	*
12%	30%	11%	0.9%	*	*
24%	36%	22%	7.3%	0.02%	*
48%	42%	34%	22%	3.6%	0.02%
96%	44%	40%	34%	17%	3.6%
192%	46%	44%	40%	31%	17%

* Theoretically less than 0.01%

TABLE 11: CHANCES OF A GIVEN ANNUAL LOSS WHEN RUNNING THE STARTER SYSTEM

Risk target	5% loss	10% loss	20% loss	50% loss	75% loss
6%	11%	1.3%	*	*	*
9%	23%	11%	1.3%	*	*
12%	28%	18%	5.8%	0.02%	*
24%	33%	26%	15%	1.3%	0.06%
48%	37%	33%	26%	11%	4.1%
96%	39%	37%	33%	23%	16%
192%	40%	39%	37%	31%	27%

* Theoretically less than 0.01%

As an example of how to use these tables, suppose you are worried about a loss of 10% over a year. From table 11 (annual losses), the odds of losing 10% vary between 1.3% (with a risk target of 6%) and 39% (with a target of 192%). With a risk target of 24% you expect to lose 10%, or more, about 26% of the time: one out of every four out of years. If you are uncomfortable with that, then you should choose a lower risk target.

My own personal tolerance for risk translates to a risk target of 24%, but you should make your own personal judgment.

Optimal risk level given system profitability

How much risk should we take given our expected profitability? We need to use the *Kelly Criterion* formula from the previous chapter. There I showed you that under Kelly the **optimal risk target is equal to your expected Sharpe ratio (SR)**. For the Starter System the expected SR is 0.24 (from page 92), equating to a risk target of 24%. If you use a higher or lower risk target, then you make less money in the long run.[64]

However, most professional traders are wary of using the optimum risk determined by the Kelly criterion. There are several reasons for their caution. Firstly, the Kelly criterion makes assumptions about the statistical distribution of returns which are rather unrealistic.

Secondly, there is a great deal of uncertainty about the real Sharpe ratio of any trading system. Look back at figure 4 (page 90), which shows that there is a reasonable chance[65] the back-tested SR of the Starter System is actually less than 0.15, which would require a risk target below 15%. A risk target of 24% could be far too high. Also, back-tested returns cannot precisely forecast what we will earn in the future.

Finally, the SR of 0.24 is a pre-cost return. Using more expensive products to trade will bring the SR down substantially.[66] With my speed limit we're allowed to spend a third of our expected pre-cost SR on trading costs: up to 0.08. This would leave us with a SR of just 0.16.

Most professional traders use a conservative version of the Kelly criterion known as *half Kelly*. Under half Kelly we use half the Sharpe ratio as our risk target:

FORMULA 18: PRUDENT 'HALF KELLY' RISK TARGET FROM SHARPE RATIO

Prudent risk target = Expected Sharpe ratio ÷ 2

For the Starter System, with a Sharpe ratio of 0.24, that implies a **risk target of 12%**.

---

[64] In fact, if you use a risk target that's more than double your expected Sharpe ratio you'll end up expecting to lose money, no matter how good your opening rule is.

[65] From figure 4 there is a 95% chance that the SR is between 0.15 and 0.34; hence there is a 5% chance the SR is outside of this range, implying a 2.5% chance the SR is below 0.15. All this assumes that a trading system continues to work as well in the future as it did in the past.

[66] Strictly speaking, we should use a risk target based on the expected after costs Sharpe ratio, which would be different for each product. However, this would make the book much more complicated, and using half Kelly is sufficiently conservative assuming you stick to the speed limit for trading costs.

Determining the correct risk target

Let's put together the various figures I've calculated for a hypothetical S&P 500 ETF margin trade to see what the correct risk target should be in this example:

- Risk possible given maximum leverage allowed by brokers: **32%** per year (calculated on page 94). This varies by instrument.

- Risk possible given maximum prudent leverage: **21.3%** per year (see page 95). This varies by instrument, and also depends on your appetite for losses.

- Your own personal appetite for risk: I've used my own figure of **24%** (page 98). This is different for individual traders.

- Optimal and prudent risk level given the expected profitability of your trading system: half the Sharpe ratio **12%** (page 98). This depends on the trading system you are using.

The lowest and most conservative risk target from this list is the final figure based on expected profitability: 12%. Most of the time the expected Sharpe ratio will determine the leverage target you should use, unless you have a relatively conservative attitude to risk, or a broker who is unusually stingy with leverage limits.

You should run the Starter System with an annual risk target of 12%. This might seem low, but risk targets for leading hedge funds typically range between 10% and 20%, and the profitability of these funds is expected to be much higher than that of the Starter System.

How much money could the Starter System make?

I can now work out the expected profitability of the Starter System. If we rearrange the Sharpe ratio formula 3 (page 61):

$$SR = (r - b) \div s$$

We can use it to work out the expected return:

FORMULA 19: EXPECTED RETURN FROM SHARPE RATIO

$$r = (SR \times s) + b$$

Where **SR** is the Sharpe ratio, **r** is the average return, **b** is the rate we can borrow at and **s** is the standard deviation. The expected Sharpe ratio without costs **SR** = 0.24, the risk target I just calculated **s** = 12%, and **b** the rate we can borrow at is currently around 2.0%. So, our pre-cost expected return is:

$$r = (0.24 \times 0.12) + 0.02 = 4.9\%$$

With a really cheap instrument we get an after-cost return which is pretty close to 4.9%. The most expensive instruments that I recommend trading would take away a third of our Sharpe ratio, leaving us with a post-cost expected return of:

$$r = (0.24 \times [1 - \tfrac{1}{3}] \times 0.12) + 0.02 = 3.9\%$$

An expected return between 3.9% and 4.9% may not seem very exciting. It is tempting to increase the risk target, apply more leverage and achieve a higher return. But this would be dangerous. You would need much higher performance expectations before it is safe to use a higher risk target.

Have some patience! The Starter System is designed to help you learn the principles of good trading. Improvements that I will introduce in parts three and four will substantially improve these expected returns.

Beware of systems with extremely high advertised returns, these can only be achieved by taking far too much risk, or by creating track records that are over-fitted or entirely fabricated.

From notional exposure to position size

Once you have determined the risk target, and calculated your required notional exposure using formula 14 (page 93), you need to work out the size of your trade. This depends on the type of product:

FORMULA 20: POSITION SIZES FROM NOTIONAL EXPOSURE

FX	Your notional exposure is equal to the amount of FX that you have purchased. For example, suppose you are trading AUDUSD; a purchase of AUD 10,000 will require $7,100 USD at a rate of 1 AUD = 0.71 USD. Our exposure is A$10,000 in the *instrument currency*. For a US investor that would be in $7,100 in *home currency*, and for a UK investor around £5,600 (depending on the AUDGBP exchange rate).
Futures	To get the notional exposure in a futures trade, you need to multiply the number of contracts you hold for a given date by the price and the futures multiplier. So, we'd buy or sell the following number of contracts: **(Exposure home currency × FX Rate) ÷ (Multiplier × price)** Where the FX rate is the exchange rate between our home currency and the instrument currency. Suppose you are a very large trader with a very fat wallet who had a target exposure of long £2,000,000. For S&P 500 contracts the multiplier is 50 and the current price is 2,700. The home currency is GBP and the instrument currency USD, so we need the GBPUSD rate which is currently 1.33. So, the number of contracts to buy is: **(Exposure home currency × FX Rate) ÷ (Multiplier × price)** **= (2,000,000 × 1.33) ÷ (50 × 2,700) = 19.7** Of course, you cannot actually buy 19.7 contracts; instead round this to 20 contracts.
Contract for difference (per contract)	A CFD bet is often sized as a certain number of contracts. Your exposure as an amount per point can be calculated as follows: **(Exposure home currency × FX Rate) ÷ (price × contract size)** Let's look at an example of the S&P 500 with a contract size of 5. To bet £30,000 on the S&P 500 priced at 2,700 with an exchange rate of 1.33 GBP per USD we buy the following number of contracts: **(Exposure home currency × FX Rate) ÷ (price × contract size)** **= (30,000 × 1.33) ÷ (2,700 × 5) = 2.96 contracts** We round this to 3 contracts unless our broker allowed fractional contracts.

Alternatively, a CFD can also be expressed as a certain amount of money per point. The size of a point varies between instruments and brokers. Your exposure as an amount per point can be calculated as follows:

(Exposure home currency × FX Rate × point size)
÷ price

For an FX trade a point is usually 0.0001, so to get $100,000 of exposure on the GBPUSD FX rate with a price of 1.3300 we bet the following number of dollars per point:

Contract for difference (per point)

(Exposure home currency × FX Rate × point size)
÷ price

= (100,000 × 1 × 0.0001) ÷ 1.33 = $7.52 per point

A broker might require us to round this and bet $8 or $10 per point. Notice that in this example, the home currency is the same as the instrument currency so the FX rate is 1.

For stock indices like the S&P 500, 1 point is usually a single index point. If the index changes from 2,783 to 2,784 that is a 1 point move. To bet £7,500 on the S&P 500 priced at 2,700 with an exchange rate of 1.333 GBP per USD we bet the following number of dollars per point:

(7,500 × 1.33 × 1) ÷ 2,700 = $3.69 per point

If our broker only allows whole dollar bets then we bet $4 per point.

We'd use the same formula as for CFDs to calculate the bet per point:

(Exposure home currency × FX Rate × point size)
÷ price

Unlike CFDs it's often possible to bet in your home currency even on foreign instruments. Where we are betting in our home currency the FX rate would be 1. To bet £7,500 on the S&P 500 priced at 2,700 we'd bet

Spread bet (UK only)

the following number of pounds per point:

(Exposure home currency × FX Rate × point size)
÷ price

= (7,500 × 1 × 1) ÷ 2,700 = £2.78 per point

My broker has a minimum bet of £1 per point but allows incremental amounts of £0.01 on top of this. Other brokers may restrict bets to round amounts of £1 per point, so this would be rounded to £3 per point.

The notional exposure is just the share price multiplied by the number of shares held; multiplied by the FX rate if we're dealing in a foreign currency. So, to find the number of shares to hold we use the following formula:

(Exposure home currency × FX Rate) ÷ price

Margin account

Where we are betting in our home currency the FX rate would be 1. To bet $10,000 on the S&P 500 SPY ETF priced at 274 we'd buy or sell short the following number of shares:

(Exposure home currency × FX Rate) ÷ price

= ($10,000 × 1) ÷ 274 = 36.496

It's impossible to buy a fraction of a share so we'd round this to 36 shares.

Minimum required capital

We can now calculate the *minimum capital*, a concept I introduced in chapter four. This figure is necessary to decide which instrument and product we can trade. First, I use the position sizing formula (formula 14):

Notional exposure = (target risk % × capital) ÷ instrument risk %

Substituting in the minimum notional exposure and minimum capital, and then rearranging:

FORMULA 21: MINIMUM CAPITAL

Minimum capital = (Minimum exposure × instrument risk %) ÷ target risk %

Where the *minimum notional exposure* is the exposure of the *minimum trade*, calculated using the formulas for notional exposure starting on page 59.

Minimum capital and the siren call of leverage

Minimum capital is an annoying concept, since it often prevents traders from trading the products they want, or even trading at all. Looking at formula 21 there are three ways that minimum capital levels can be reduced:

1. Finding an instrument with a lower minimum exposure.
2. Finding an instrument with lower instrument risk.
3. Increasing the target risk.

Options 1 and 2 are fine, in theory. In reality, as I have already discussed, you will probably end up paying higher costs for instruments that have higher minimum capital.

Option 3 is the dangerous one. It is particularly dangerous because a trader using the Starter System will usually be using much less leverage than the brokers permitted maximum. I suggest using a leverage factor of 1.25 to trade Euro Stoxx 50 CFDs, but my broker has a maximum of 20 (for retail customers: professionals can use even more). I could use a target risk that is ten times higher (120%), and still end up with a leverage factor that is well below the maximum (12.5, much less than 20). Even better, I would only need one-tenth of the minimum capital: just $645.

But remember once more the formulas used to determine the appropriate target risk:

- Risk possible given maximum leverage allowed by brokers: sure, no problem here.

- Risk possible given maximum prudent leverage: with leverage of 12.5 a 4% move would wipe out half your capital. Moves that size are not uncommon in the equity markets.

- Your own personal appetite for risk: Look again at tables 9 to 11 and decide whether you are comfortable with a 120% risk target. I wouldn't be.

- Optimal and prudent risk level given the expected profitability of your trading system: half the Sharpe ratio. You would need a Sharpe ratio of 2.4 to justify a risk target of 120%. This is much better than almost any other trader on the planet[67] can expect to achieve when trading a single instrument!

Please do not be lured down this path by the brokers. Stick to the risk target I recommend and keep your leverage down.

---

[67] As you'll see later in the book diversifying your trading across multiple instruments can easily improve your expected Sharpe ratio (SR) by a factor of 2.5. A fund making a SR of 2.4 on an individual instrument would have an overall SR across all of their instruments of 2.4 × 2.5 = 6. This is very high. Some professional traders will occasionally make this level of return for short periods, but very few have consistently made that kind of Sharpe ratio. The elite firms which manage to do this employ extremely sophisticated technology which is not accessible to amateur traders.

Here are some examples showing how minimum capital is calculated, using the target risk of 12% for the Starter System, and my current estimates of instrument risk:

AUDUSD FX	Your notional exposure is equal to the amount of FX that you have purchased. Micro lots are the smallest practical FX trade that most brokers will let you do. A micro lot for AUDUSD will have a value of $1,000 (equivalent to $0.1 per pip). With instrument risk of 8.7%: **Minimum exposure = $1,000** **Minimum capital = ($1,000 × 8.7%) ÷ 12%** **= $725 or £540**
Corn futures	To get the notional exposure in a futures trade you need to multiply the number of contracts you hold for a given date by the price and the futures multiplier. Corn futures currently have a current price of $379, instrument risk of 11.9%, a multiplier of 50, and the minimum trade is one contract: **Minimum exposure = 1 × 379 × $50 = $18,950** **Minimum capital = ($18,950 × 11.9%) ÷ 12%** **= $18,792 or £13,906**
Gold spread bet	Your exposure will be equal to the minimum bet per point, multiplied by the price, and divided by the size of a point. For gold the minimum bet is £0.50, the current price is 1,268, a point is worth 1 price unit, and the instrument risk is 11%: **Minimum exposure = £0.50 × 1,268 ÷ 1 = £634** **Minimum capital = (£634 × 11%) ÷ 12% = £581**
Euro Stoxx CFD (per contract)	Your exposure will be equal to the number of contracts, multiplied by the contract size and the price. For Euro Stoxx the minimum trade is one contract, the contract size is €2, the current price is 3,391, and the standard deviation is 9.6%: **Minimum exposure = 1 × €2 × 3,391 = €6,782** **Minimum capital = (€6,782 × 9.6%) ÷ 12%** **= €5,426, equal to £4,475 or $6,452**
Euro Stoxx CFD (per point)	Your exposure will be equal to the minimum bet per point, multiplied by the price, and divided by the size of a point. For Euro Stoxx the minimum bet per point is €2, the current price is 3,391, a point is worth 1 price unit, and the standard deviation is 9.6%: **Minimum exposure = €2 × 3,391 ÷ 1 = €6,782** **Minimum capital = (€6,782 × 9.6%) ÷ 12%** **= €5,426, equal to £4,475 or $6,452**
S&P 500 Margin trade, using SPY ETF	Your exposure is equal to the number of shares multiplied by the price. For the SPY ETF I assume that the minimum trade is buying ten shares, with a price of $274, and standard deviation of 16%: **Minimum exposure = $274 × 10 = $2,740** **Minimum capital = ($2,740 × 16%) ÷ 12%** **= $3,653**

Position sizing and minimum capital requirements

Remember from earlier in the chapter that we use the current value of our account for calculating trade sizes. This can lead to problems for smaller traders who start with only just enough capital.

Suppose you started trading US Eurodollar futures with $12,000. According to my calculations these currently require a minimum capital of $11,000. You start with $1,000 more than you need. Sadly, in this particular example things don't go well. After a few losing trades you're down to $10,900. This is insufficient to meet the minimum capital requirement.

You have three options to deal with this problem. Firstly, **you can ignore it and carry on trading**. This means that you will have too much risk relative to your current capital. If you make further trading losses your account will be emptied: quickly. **Don't do this.**

Secondly, you can **add money to your account** to replenish your losses and get you back to $11,000. **I really don't recommend this**. Topping up your account when you lose money is like repeatedly pushing coins into a slot machine. It probably won't end well.

The third option is to **increase your starting capital**. Then you can lose some money but still continue trading. For example, if you initially had $22,000 in your account then you could continue to trade Eurodollar futures until you had lost half your money. **I recommend starting with twice the minimum capital** for your preferred instrument – more if possible.

A fourth option is to **switch to trading a different instrument** with lower capital requirements, once you're below the minimum level for the instrument you initially selected. That might make sense if the alternative instrument is still cheap enough to trade.

When should positions be closed?

Too many traders fall in love with a position and then refuse to close it. If you *never* close positions then you are investing, not trading. There is nothing wrong with investing – I do it myself – but this is a book about trading. Other traders will close their trades prematurely, before any potential profits have been realised. Deciding when to close your positions should not be down to personal whims and fancies. It should be subject to the same level of discipline as deciding when to open positions.

What type of closing rule?

There are a number of different methods that traders typically use for closing positions:

Using the opening trading rule (Used in part four of this book)	We wait for our opening trading rule to produce the opposite signal of whatever trade we currently have on (i.e., the rule wants to go short when we're long, and vice versa).
	This is sometimes called 'Stop and Reverse', because if the trading rule says we should close a trade ('stop') it will always want us to put the opposite trade on immediately ('reverse').
	This is a valid method, but I won't use it in this chapter as it is relatively difficult and time consuming to implement. But I will use it in part four of the book, when I explain how experienced traders can improve upon the Starter System.
Using some other trading rule AVOID	Some traders use a separate trading rule to decide when to close positions. They might use moving average crossovers to open positions, but then close them using an entirely different kind of rule.
	I'm very sceptical of trading systems that are constructed like this, as the interaction of opening and closing rules can get rather complicated and unintuitive. It also means we have more decisions to make when designing our systems, which leads to dangerous *over-fitting*.
Time based exit AVOID	We always close our position after a given period of time.
	I don't recommend this method. It's difficult enough to forecast the direction of a future price move, without also trying to predict exactly when it will happen.
'Stop profit' AVOID	Here, we determine how much money to make on each trade and then close the position when we reach the target.
	It makes no sense to use 'stop profit' with the trend-following opening rule used by the Starter System. If prices are trending, we wouldn't want to close our trade until the trend had exhausted itself, and it is difficult to forecast when that will occur in advance.
	Stop profits are also dangerous if used without a stop loss and using both together is unnecessarily complicated.
Fixed 'stop loss' AVOID	We decide how much money we can afford to lose on each trade, and then close our position when the price reaches that level.
	It makes no sense to use a fixed stop loss with a trend-following opening rule. Imagine a situation like this: we managed to catch a profitable trend, stayed in the trade during the trend, but then didn't close out once the trend had reversed. Instead we close our position once the price had gone down past its original level, turning a profitable trade into a loss.

Trailing 'stop loss' (Used in the Starter System)	This is similar to the fixed stop loss, except that the stop loss level is adjusted.
	We calculate how big the *stop loss gap* should be – the maximum amount of money we can lose relative to the *high watermark* of each trade – and then close our position when we reach that level. The high watermark is the price where we have made maximum profits (the maximum daily closing price since entry if we're long, or the minimum daily closing price when short).
	Trailing stop losses make a lot of sense for trend-following strategies like the rule used in the Starter System. They allow us to stay in a trend until it has exhausted itself and began to reverse. Trailing stop losses are also familiar to many traders.
	You should use them for the Starter System.

How do we determine the right stop loss level?

Do you prefer your stops tight or loose? A *tight* stop loss implies the price barely has to budge from its recent high (or low if you're short) before the trade gets closed. Tight stops keep losses small, but you will be prematurely stopped out of many trades that could have been profitable. With a *loose* stop you will see larger losses before the rule closes each trade, but by sticking with the position and not getting shaken out by small price fluctuations there might be a better chance of making money.

Which is better?

Some traders use fixed stop loss gaps:

"I always close my position when the price has retraced by $1"

Paraphrased from an anonymous trading blog

But more sensible people understand that setting stop losses is a little more complicated than that.

There are a number of factors that traders usually consider when setting their stop losses. Typically, these include:

1. The size of their account (smaller accounts need tighter stops, because small movements in price have a large effect on a small account).

2. The size of their position (larger positions need tighter stops, because smaller movements in price quickly get magnified into large losses).

In fact, **these are both completely irrelevant.**

If you use account size when setting stop losses, then smaller traders end up with tighter stops than the larger traders. As a result, smaller traders will trade more frequently than those with more capital, regardless of whether that makes sense or not for a given instrument. This is nonsensical: **the market doesn't know or care how big your account is, or how large your positions are.**

But surely it is dangerous to ignore the size of your account and position size when setting stop losses?

In fact, if you have used a position sizing rule, then the risk of your trade will already have been calculated taking account size into account. It is then unnecessary to consider account size or position size when setting your stop loss.

These are the three factors that actually matter when determining stop losses:

1. The current risk of the instrument.

2. Interaction with the opening rule.

3. Trading costs.

It is fairly obvious why instrument risk is important when setting stop losses. It would make no sense to use the same stop loss on both US 2-year and 10-year bonds. US 2-year bonds have about one-quarter the volatility of 10-year bonds. A stop that is correct for 2-year bonds will be far too tight for ten years.

A stop loss gap that is fine for quiet and peaceful periods will be far too tight when things get crazy. By regularly re-estimating instrument risk we can ensure the stop loss is appropriate for the market environment. If you use the current level of instrument risk to calculate your stop, then you will have wider stop losses when markets are jumpier. The position sizing rule will automatically calculate smaller positions when risk is higher, so you do not need to worry about the risk of losing more money if you widen your stops when instrument risk goes up.

So, you should set your *stop loss gap* as a **fraction of the relevant instrument's current volatility**, i.e., as a fraction of *instrument risk*, measured as an **annual standard deviation of returns**.

But what fraction should you use? A small fraction such as 0.1 will give a very tight stop, whilst a large fraction like 1.0 translates to a relatively wide stop. For example, consider the S&P 500 with instrument risk of 16% a year. A fraction of 0.1 translates to a stop loss gap of 0.1 × 16% = 1.6%. A move of that size can easily happen over a few hours. Conversely a fraction of 1.0 produces a stop loss gap of 1.0 × 16% =16%. Normally it takes several months for the price to move that much.

To make this decision we need to consider the remaining factors from the list above: **the interaction of the stop loss with our opening trading rule**, and **trading costs**.

It would be nuts to use a wide stop loss with a relatively fast pair of moving average crossovers, like MAC 2,8. We would end up opening a position based on a trend that was just a few days old, and then stay in the trade for months. Equally, it makes no sense to use a tight stop loss with a slow pair of crossovers. Imagine – you wait patiently for weeks, until the market shows a clear trend, before placing your trade. Then just a few hours later you are stopped out when the price moves slightly against you.

Trading costs are also important when setting the stop loss volatility fraction. With tighter stop losses we trade more frequently, which will result in costs that are too high for most instruments and products. However, I calibrated the opening rule with costs in mind. So, we don't need to explicitly consider costs again, as long as the closing stop loss rule is properly aligned with the opening rule.

To calibrate the stop loss fraction, I did some back-testing. I estimated the average length of time that different levels of stop loss fraction[68] held a position. I then matched these fractions to the moving average crossover (MAC) rule with the most similar trading frequency. The results are in table 12. For the Starter System, which uses the MAC 16,64 crossover pair, the table implies we should use a **stop loss fraction of 0.5**.

TABLE 12: FASTER TRADING RULES NEED TIGHTER STOP LOSSES

Trades per year for different stop loss fractions, matched to opening trade rule with different crossover speeds.

Stop loss closing rule: Fraction of volatility	Stop loss closing rule: Average trades per year	Momentum crossover opening rule	Momentum crossover opening rule: Average trades per year
0.025	97.5	*	*
0.05	76.5	*	*
0.1	46.9	MAC 2,8	39.1
0.2	21.4	MAC 4,16	19.1
0.3	11.9	*	*
0.4	7.8	MAC 8,32	9.4
0.5	**5.4**	**MAC 16,64**	**5.4**
0.6	4.0	*	*
0.7	3.1	*	*
0.8	2.4	MAC 32,128	2.3
0.9	2.1	*	*
1.0	1.7	*	*
1.2	1.3	*	*
1.4	1.1	MAC 64,256	1.1
1.5	1.0	*	*

[68] Technical note: To separate the effect of the opening rule, I used a random opening rule which entered long trades with 50% probability with an equal chance for short trades. I then measured the trading frequency across 37 different futures contracts and took a weighted average.

* None of the crossover pairs I use have the same trading frequency as the stop loss fraction shown in this row.

All values calculated from back-testing different MAV opening rules and stop loss fractions over the instruments in my data set. Row in bold is Starter System.

Stop loss calculations

Instrument risk is usually measured as an annualised standard deviation of percentage returns. When calculating your stop loss gap it's better to measure the instrument risk in *price units* rather than *percentage units*. This is because we need to set our stop level, and thus our stop loss gap, in price units.

FORMULA 22: PRICE UNIT VOLATILITY

Instrument risk in price units = Instrument risk as percentage volatility × current price

FORMULA 23: STOP LOSS GAP

Stop loss gap = Instrument risk in price units × stop loss fraction

- **If we are long**, to calculate the *stop loss level* we subtract the stop loss gap from the *high watermark*. This is the highest daily closing price since the trade was opened. If at any point the daily closing price falls below the stop loss level, we close the position. The stop loss will always be lower than the current price (until it is hit). If the price is going up, then the stop loss level will be going up.

- **If we have a short position,** then everything is reversed. We close our positions if the price trades *above* the stop loss level. The high watermark will be the *lowest* daily price we've seen. We *add* the stop loss gap to the high watermark to get the stop loss level. If the closing price goes below the lowest daily price we have seen, then the stop loss will be moved down. The stop loss will always be higher than the current price (until it's hit). If the price is falling, then the stop loss level will also be falling.

FORMULA 24: STOP LOSS LEVEL

> **Stop loss level (when long) = Highest price since trade opened – stop loss gap**

> **Stop loss level (when short) = Lowest price since trade opened + stop loss gap**

Let's suppose we go long gold at $1,300 per ounce, with instrument risk of 11% a year. First, convert the instrument risk into price units (formula 22):

> **Instrument risk in price units = 11% × $1,300 = $143**

Next, we multiply this by the stop loss fraction (0.5), to get the stop loss gap in price units (formula 23):

> **Stop loss gap = $143 × 0.5 = $71.50**

Finally, as we are long gold, we subtract the stop loss gap from the *high watermark* to get the stop loss level. As we have just opened the trade this will be the level that we purchased at, $1,300 (formula 24):

> **Stop loss level = $1,300 – $71.50 = $1,228.50**

Our *stop loss level* will be set at $1,228.50. If the daily closing price falls below this level, we will close the position. But, if the daily closing price of gold goes higher than $1,300, then we increase our stop loss level appropriately. For example, if the price goes to $1,350 then we change our stop loss level to $1,350 − $71.50 = $1,278.50.

What proportion of my capital is at risk on each trade?

"Career day traders use a risk-management method called the 1 percent risk rule, or vary it slightly to fit their trading methods."

Some potentially dangerous advice from a trading blog

Many traders recommend setting a fixed percentage of your capital that should be at risk on each trade. Values between 1% and 5% are typical. However, in the Starter System we put on a position of a given size to target a certain level of risk, and then close it once a stop loss has been triggered. Why the difference?

Actually, the Starter System method is indeed equivalent to setting a percentage of capital at risk. Suppose we have a position in an instrument that had the same risk as the risk target for the Starter System: 12% a year. As instrument risk and target risk are equal, we would use a leverage factor of one, creating a notional exposure equal to our account value. The stop loss on this trade would be set at half the annual risk: 6%. So, in theory, 6% of our capital is at risk on this trade.[69]

We would get exactly the same result if the risk of the instrument was different. If the risk was doubled, we would deploy half our capital in the trade and the stop loss would be twice as large, which exactly offsets the change in position size. There would still be 6% of our capital at risk.

I can write this as a general formula:

FORMULA 25: PERCENTAGE OF CAPITAL AT RISK ON EACH TRADE

Capital at risk per trade % = Risk target % × stop loss fraction

Capital at risk per trade % = 12% × 0.5 = 6%

Although 6% might seem quite high, it is actually relatively small because the Starter System trades very slowly. Allegedly, more conservative figures of 1% or 2% for capital at risk are used by traders like the blogger above, who trade dozens or even hundreds of times a year. If I was trading that quickly with the Starter System I would have a lower stop loss fraction, and hence a much smaller proportion of capital at risk.

From table 12 earlier, if you were trading a hundred times a year then a stop loss fraction of 0.025 is appropriate. The capital at risk per trade would be 12% × 0.025 = 0.3%. Someone trading at least twice a day – 500 times per year – would risk even less. Risking 1% on each trade as a day trader sounds conservative, but 1% is actually far too high.

In summary, **it makes no sense to set an arbitrary constant percentage of capital at risk without considering your risk target, and how long you're going to be holding positions for.** This is why I prefer to specify risk separately as (a) a risk target, and (b) a stop loss fraction. The former can be set according to the criteria I laid out earlier in the chapter, whilst the latter is determined by how quickly you can trade given the costs of your system.

---

[69] Actually, it's unlikely we'd close our position exactly at the stop loss level so it's probably a bit more than 6%. But this is also true if you set your position size as an explicit fraction of your capital.

How to implement stop losses

There are three principal methods for implementing stop loss rules:

DIY stop loss **RECOMMENDED**	Monitor the price yourself and close your position when the price hits your stop. (This is sometimes called a *mental stop loss.*) There is no guarantee that you will close your trade exactly at the stop. I use an automated algorithm to monitor my own positions and close them when required. If you aren't a technology wizard, you can sign up to the free price alert services offered by most brokers and many financial websites. Because the Starter System holds positions for many weeks, don't panic if you can't close your position immediately. In fact, because we use daily prices for the Starter System, **you only close a position when the closing price for the previous day has passed through a stop level.**[70]
Leave order with broker (without guarantee) **NOT RECOMMENDED**	Let your broker take the strain and leave a stop order with them. This does sound appealing, though you might still need to update the stop level yourself when prices move, if the broker won't do that automatically. As with DIY stop losses, there is no guarantee that your trade will be closed exactly at the stop level. But there are two more serious disadvantages: Firstly, with a DIY stop loss you have more control over how it's implemented. I recommend that you only close a trade if the daily closing price hits the stop. But with a broker stop there is no discretion. They will trigger the stop if the price touches it, even for just a fraction of a second. Secondly, by setting a stop order you are giving your broker some valuable information. An unscrupulous broker could use that information against you.[71] Of course, there are times when you might not have any choice but to use broker stop losses. If you want a relaxing vacation, and don't have an automated trading system, then it makes sense to leave stop loss orders with your broker before going on holiday.

---

[70] This means you'll keep a position open if a price briefly hits a stop during the day and then bounces back before the close.

[71] As you may remember from chapter two, many brokers don't pass through your order to the market, and they control the price that you trade at. As such, they could briefly push the price beyond your stop level, trigger your stop, and make an easy profit. If you don't believe this really happens, then offer to buy any experienced OTC trader a few drinks. By the end of the evening you will have heard countless stories about broker misbehaviour related to stop losses.

Guaranteed stop loss **AVOID**	You can ask your broker for a *guaranteed* stop loss. Effectively, you are buying insurance against your closing trade going badly wrong. Just like other types of insurance you have to pay for the privilege, as there is usually a charge associated with guaranteed stops.[72]
	Personally, I wouldn't bother with guaranteed stops. The risk limits on the Starter System are set sufficiently low that you should not worry about exiting your trades exactly at the stop. Also, guaranteed stops are not always honoured. Brokers usually have sufficient wiggle room in their terms and conditions to get out of their guarantees if they really want to.

When do we re-enter the trade after a stop has been triggered?

If we close a trade after a stop loss, when should we re-enter it?

There are two possibilities:

Our opening rule wants to open a position in the opposite direction	**We should immediately open a new trade in the new direction required by the rule.**
	For example, suppose we are long, and hit a stop loss, and now the opening rule thinks we should go short. We should close our long trade and open a new short trade immediately.
Our opening rule wants to open a position in the same direction	**We should ignore the opening rule. Do not open a new position until the opening rule has changed its mind and wants to open a trade in the opposite direction.**
	For example, suppose we are long, and hit a stop loss, but the opening rule still thinks we should remain long. We should close our long trade immediately. Then we should wait until the opening rule is indicating that we should go short before opening a new trade.
	Why do this? Well, we use stop losses to limit our exposure in situations when a trend has reversed. If we re-open the same trade as before, then we leave ourselves open to further losses should the price continue to move against us. We would probably end up closing the new trade after a few days, incurring both a further loss and unnecessary trading costs.

---

[72] For example, it costs an extra 0.3 of a point to place a guaranteed stop on gold spread bets with my broker. That might not sound very much, but it's enough to almost double the annual risk adjusted trading cost of the Starter System, from 0.028 up to 0.057. That is too high a price to pay for peace of mind. If your leverage isn't excessive you shouldn't need to use guaranteed stop losses.

Why is day trading so dangerous?

I've mentioned several times in this book that I'm not a fan of day trading – a type of trading where you have no active positions at the end of each day. This is a controversial and unpopular view. Closing out your positions before the end of each day sounds superficially appealing for several reasons:

- You trade more often: more chances to make money.

- If you are trading undated products like spot FX, you avoid paying funding costs.

- It is safer, as you are not exposed to the market moving overnight. You cannot close positions in the middle of the night.

- You take less risk. Day traders frequently risk 1% or less on each trade compared to the 6% at risk in the Starter System (calculated on page 113).

These arguments are all deeply flawed.

In theory, trading quickly is indeed more profitable. If you increase your frequency of trading by a factor of four, then this will double the maximum Sharpe ratio you can theoretically achieve.[73]

However, this calculation ignores two key problems. Firstly, this is only a theoretical result. In reality, you are unlikely to see these sorts of improvements. Look again at figure 4 on page 90. Here the two fastest moving average crossover rules actually had worse performance than the slower versions.

Secondly, if you increase your frequency of trading, you will definitely pay higher costs. At a minimum, day trading involves doing two trades per day (an open, and a close). This will cost a fortune. For example, two trades a day in a gold spread bet works out at a risk-adjusted annual cost of 1.07, whilst for a Euro Stoxx 50 CFD it is 1.50. Whilst day traders can indeed avoid overnight funding costs on undated products, any saving is completely wiped out by the extra transaction costs.

Futures are the cheapest product, but most of these are still too expensive for day trading. For example, day trading corn futures still costs a pricey 0.12 in risk-adjusted costs each year. There are a few instruments where day trading futures is feasible. Day trading the Nasdaq future would cost around 0.034 annually in risk-adjusted trading costs. But the minimum capital for Nasdaq futures is over $200,000!

---

[73] Technical note: This result is from the fundamental law of active management framed by Grinold and Kahn. The law states that the information ratio is proportional to the square root of the number of uncorrelated bets (the information ratio is similar to the Sharpe ratio, but is adjusted for a benchmark rather than the risk-free rate). If we trade four times more often then we increase the number of uncorrelated bets by a factor of four, hence doubling the information ratio.

Remember, I impose a speed limit on trading costs: you should never pay more than a third of your expected pre-cost Sharpe ratio out on costs. This works out at a speed limit of 0.08 in annual risk-adjusted costs for the Starter System. Hence, for day trading to make sense you need to either:

- Trade only very cheap futures like the Nasdaq. These require huge amounts of capital.

- Increase the speed limit up to a higher proportion of your expected Sharpe ratio: perhaps a half, or even higher. This would make day trading feasible on most futures like corn, but this does not help traders who can't afford the minimum trade sizes. It is extremely risky given the uncertainty of expected Sharpe ratios. **Don't do this**.

- Improve your pre-cost Sharpe ratio, so it is at least three times the cost of day trading.

Is it realistic to improve your pre-cost Sharpe ratio to the point when you could safely day trade? Consider AUDUSD spot FX, which is accessible to smaller traders and whose risk-adjusted cost when day trading is a relatively low 0.35 per year. To ensure you were under the speed limit – a maximum one-third of pre-cost returns paid out in costs – you need to be generating a pre-cost Sharpe ratio of 3 × 0.35 = 1.05. This is extremely optimistic. Only a few elite professional traders can confidently expect to make that kind of return when trading a single instrument.[74]

Now, let us consider the alleged lower risk of day trading. Although you miss out on overnight moves as a day trader, you are still exposed to intra-day moves. Markets tend to move more during the day than overnight, as there is more news flow and trading activity during the day creates its own volatility. Also remember that the Starter System carefully calibrates position size, and thus risk, based on expected market volatility. Since instrument risk is estimated based on daily closing prices it will account for both intra-day and overnight market movements.

It is true that you cannot close positions overnight, but this should only be a concern for traders who are taking on far too much risk. Prices frequently gap up or down during the day. When gaps occur you would be unable to get out at your stop loss level, even though the market is open.

A day trader will have a smaller amount of capital at risk on each trade, but as they trade more often this doesn't necessarily make them any safer. Consider a trader

---

[74] As you'll see later in the book, diversifying your trading across multiple instruments can easily improve your expected Sharpe ratio (SR) by a factor of 2.5. A fund making a SR of 1.05 on an individual instrument would have an overall SR across all of their instruments of 1.05 × 2.5 = 2.625. This is very high. Some professional traders will occasionally make this level of return for a year or two, but very few have consistently made that kind of Sharpe ratio.

trading the Starter System who does six trades in a particular year (remember the average is 5.4), each risking 6% of their capital (I calculated this figure back on page 113). We will compare them to a day trader risking 'only' 0.5% of their capital but opening and closing positions every day: roughly 250 times a year.

Let's suppose both traders are unlucky and lose money consistently for two months straight – about one-sixth of a year. The slower trader will expect to do a single trade and will lose **6%** of their account. The day trader will lose on 250 ÷ 6 = 41.7 occasions. Losing 0.5% of your capital 41.7 times equates to a loss of around 0.5% × 41.7 = **21%**. The smaller position size of the day trader is actually much riskier than the Starter System.

To have the equivalent amount of risk, the day trader will need to have an extremely small position size (around 0.14%), and hence a much lower risk target. With a lower risk target comes another problem – higher requirements for minimum capital. The day trader risking 0.14% of their capital will need more than forty times as much capital as is required in the Starter System.

Some day traders claim they can improve their returns by trading selectively. A day trader might only trade on 50 days of the year when they see the 'best' opportunities. This will reduce their costs somewhat; though they will still be many times higher than the costs of the Starter System. But it will also reduce their opportunities to make money relative to the Starter System, which is in the market the entire time. I am extremely sceptical that it's possible to choose certain trades with a high enough success rate for selective trading to make sense.

If day trading is so difficult, why is it so heavily promoted by self-proclaimed internet trading experts? Well, most of these 'experts' are earning kickbacks from brokerage firms, and brokerage firms love day traders as they generate much higher profits. Brokers also do their bit by creating nice mobile apps and websites that make day trading child's play. Don't be taken in by the hype – avoid day trading like the plague!

CHAPTER SIX

Trading the Starter System

T HE PREVIOUS CHAPTER DISCUSSED THE design of the Starter System. In this chapter I explain how you actually trade it.

It is always easier to understand something when you're shown how it's done. So, this chapter includes specific examples for each of the leveraged products I'm covering in this book: stock margin trading, spot FX, futures, CFDs, and spread bets. I explain how I calculated the initial trades that were appropriate when I started writing this chapter in June 2018, and how trading subsequently panned out over the rest of the year.

Warning: the calculations in this chapter may seem rather lengthy and time consuming. But don't forget that you will be doing them with a spreadsheet. Spreadsheets for all the calculations in this book are available from the book's website.

That doesn't mean you can quickly skim through the boring bits in each chapter, as it is really important to grasp the details behind the spreadsheet. Traders make money by having an edge, and one of your edges will be putting in the hard work of understanding how the system is put together. Also, if you don't understand the system, then you won't be able to develop as a trader and start adapting the calculations to use in your own unique trading strategies.

Before you start trading

Writing your trade plan

Firstly, you need to determine how much capital you have to trade with. You will need at least $1,500 or £1,100 to trade the Starter System (I explain why in a couple of pages). If you have more, wonderful. You will have a wider choice of instruments you can potentially trade. **But only put money in your trading account you can afford to lose, and NEVER trade with borrowed money**. Trading with leverage is dangerous enough without putting your credit rating, or your house, at risk.

I suggest you put all your trading capital into your brokerage account. If you do this, then, unless you are extremely unlucky, you won't need to pay margin calls when using the Starter System, since it keeps leverage well below maximum allowable limits. Keeping some of your capital outside your account might seem a prudent way to protect yourself from broker bankruptcy, but it will mean you might face margin calls. Once you start replenishing your trading account with extra cash it can be difficult to stop, even after you've drained your notional pot of trading capital. If all your capital is in your account, then hopefully you won't be tempted to pony up more funds if you start making losses.

Before you transfer cash to your broker, it's important to be clear what the rules of your trading system will be. Together these rules make up the *trade plan*. For the Starter System the trade plan is:

TRADE PLAN

Instrument	Trade a single instrument. Choose the cheapest instrument and product you can, given the capital you have available.
Opening rule	Moving average crossover: 16-day moving average minus 64-day moving average. • If 16-day moving average > 64-day moving average: go long • If 16-day moving average < 64-day moving average: go short Do not open a new trade in the same direction as a recently closed trade. Wait until the opening rule has changed direction.
Position sizing	Use formula 14: **Notional exposure = (target risk % × capital) ÷ instrument risk %** Where target risk = 12% and instrument risk is measured as annual standard deviation of returns.
Closing rule	Trailing stop loss, with a stop loss gap set at 0.5 multiplied by the risk of the instrument, measured in annual standard deviation of returns (price units). See formulas 23 and 24.

Choose instrument and product to trade

First you need to choose your instrument and product. As I explained in chapter five, you should always choose the cheapest product and instrument that you can afford, given the minimum capital requirement. Table 13 shows the instruments I'm going to use for examples in this chapter.[75]

TABLE 13: COSTS AND MINIMUM CAPITAL FOR EXAMPLE INSTRUMENTS AND PRODUCTS AS OF JUNE 2018

	Recommended instrument	Minimum capital $	Minimum capital £	Risk-adjusted trading cost
Futures spread bet	Gold	773	581	0.029
Future	Corn	18,792	13,906	0.0037
CFD on future	Euro Stoxx 50	6,452	4,475	0.041
Spot FX	AUDUSD	725	540	0.045
Margin trading	S&P 500 SPY ETF	3,653	2,747	0.021

Costs calculated according to method in appendix B. Minimum capital calculated using method in chapter five.

Before trading you should calculate your own figures for risk-adjusted trading cost, using the formulas in appendix B, with your own brokers commission, trading spread and funding spread. You should also recalculate the minimum capital, using formula 21 (page 103). To do these calculations you also need the *instrument risk*. I discuss how to estimate risk later in the chapter.

In this chapter, I'm going to use the following minimum capital in my examples. Each trade will live in a separate notional trading account, with capital as follows:

• Gold futures spread bet £1,200

• Corn future $40,000

---

[75] The SPY ETF tracks the S&P 500 US equity index and is highly liquid. It is comparable in costs and minimum capital to large cap stocks like Facebook, although Facebook currently has a slightly lower minimum capital level and cost level. I've chosen this ETF rather than any individual share as it's possible to get much longer data history for the S&P 500, which makes it more suitable for back-testing.

- Euro Stoxx 50, CFD on future $13,000

- AUDUSD spot FX £1,100

- S&P 500 margin trading of the SPY ETF $7,100

These values are double those in table 13, as per my recommendation from chapter five to use twice the minimum capital, and have also been rounded up. Here capital is only specified in GBP or USD, however traders in other countries can also use the Starter System, as long as the relevant products are legal.

Get relevant instrument parameters

To translate the exposure you need for a given instrument into contracts or a bet per point, you will need the appropriate position sizing parameters for the instrument you're trading:

FX	• Currency the exchange rate is normally specified in (so, for example, is it AUDUSD or USDAUD?) • Minimum exposure
Futures	• Currency future is traded in • Futures multiplier (value of a 1 point move in price)
CFD (contracts)	• Currency contract is priced in • Size of contract (value of a 1 point move in price) • Minimum number of contracts
CFD (per point)	• Currency contract is priced in • Point size (fraction of a price unit that we bet on) • Minimum bet per point
Spread bet (per point)	• Currency contract is priced in • Point size (fraction of a price unit that we bet on) • Minimum bet per point
Margin trade	• Currency share is priced in • Minimum viable trade size

Table 14 shows the relevant parameters for each of the example products, as currently provided by my brokers.

TABLE 14: TRADING PARAMETERS FOR EXAMPLE PRODUCTS

	Recommended instrument	Currency	Futures multiplier	CFD contract size	CFD or spread bet point size	Minimum position size
Futures spread bet	Gold	GBP	-	-	1	£0.50 per point
Future	Corn	USD	$50	-	-	1 contract
CFD on future (per contract)	Euro Stoxx 50	EUR	-	€2	-	1 contract
CFD on future (per point)	Euro Stoxx 50	EUR	-	-	1	€2 per point
Spot FX	AUDUSD	USD	-	-	-	$1,000
Margin trading	S&P 500	USD	-	-	-	10 shares *

The minimum is actually one share, but the costs are prohibitive unless at least ten shares are traded.

Tasks on day one

In this section, I describe the tasks that need completing on your first day of trading, using the four example instruments. All the example calculations here were done on 19 June 2018, when I began writing this chapter.

Get a price series and last price

You need a history of daily closing prices[76] for your chosen instrument for the opening and closing rules. This history should include the previous day's closing price, which you will use to calculate your position size and stop loss level. Fortunately, there are many websites with free daily closing prices,[77] and you can also get prices from your broker. Most websites allow you to download historic prices into a .csv file, which you can then transfer into a spreadsheet for further calculations.

To calculate instrument risk, you will require at least 20 trading days of daily prices, excluding weekends and market holidays. For the opening trading rule, you need at least 64 days of daily prices.

Once you have a spreadsheet of historic prices, you can add each days new closing price as an additional row. If you miss a few days then you just need to return to your source of historic prices and grab the missing prices.

The wacky world of back-adjusted prices

Most of the examples in this chapter are for **dated products**, where we trade an instrument with a specific expiry date. This is because dated products are almost always cheaper to trade than their undated cousins.

However, this gives us a problem, which is best illustrated with an example. Suppose we're using a dated instrument to trade gold, where there is normally a new dated instrument every two months. Imagine that it's May 2020, the current dated bet expires in mid-June 2020, and we've been trading the current incarnation of gold for a month.

Instead of the 64 days of closing prices that are required to calculate our opening trading rule, we only have a month (about 20 days). To solve this problem, we need to *stitch* together the prices of previous dated gold expiries to create one long series of prices. Prior to the prices we have for June 2020 expiry, there will be prices for April 2020, February 2020 and so on. Then, every time we start trading a new dated expiry, we can just glue the prices on to our existing series.

However, this solution brings its own problem, which becomes clear if we look at the current price of gold for different expiries. As I write this chapter the gold

---

[76] Some instruments have both *closing* and *settlement* prices, some have just one or the other. There is a subtle difference between these two types of price. The closing price is usually the price at which the last trade of the day was done, whilst the settlement price is averaged over a short time period before the exchange closes. Where you have the choice, you should use the settlement price, as it is based on multiple trades. This makes it more reliable.

[77] Appendix A includes links to sources of data. To name just two websites that are active and free at the time of writing: quandl.com and barchart.com

contract dated April 2020 is trading at 1,342.3, and for the June 2020 contract the price is 1,349.3. This is a 7-point difference. If I was to stitch together the April and June prices, then the price of gold in my spreadsheet will apparently jump by 7 points in one day.

But in reality, gold hasn't actually gone up in value by 7 points. This artificial jump will make our estimate of natural instrument risk a little higher than it should be, and will occasionally make us open trades we shouldn't, or close positions that should have been left alone.

There are a couple of ways we could deal with this problem. One approach is to **use the underlying price of gold** – the *spot price* or *cash price*. This isn't ideal, because we aren't actually trading spot gold, as would be the case for an undated product. Using the spot price will distort our data.[78] It's also hard to get the spot price for many instruments, like bond futures and certain commodities. I wouldn't recommend this, unless you're really short of time and there is actually a spot price available.

A better option is to apply a *back-adjustment* to our futures price series which will remove the jumps. The simplest method of back-adjustment is known as *Panama adjustment*.[79] Using Panama back-adjustment when I stitched the gold price I'd add 7 points to all my previous prices upon switching to the June expiry.[80] The price for April 2020 gold on the switch date would be adjusted from 1,342.3 to 1,349.3. It would then be exactly the same as the June 2020 price on the switch date, and there would be no spurious price change.

You can do back-adjustment yourself in your price spreadsheet, using the method in appendix C, on page 307. Alternatively, some websites[81] will provide back-adjusted price series, though you usually need to pay for this data.

Once you have your back-adjusted price series you should use it all the time: for measuring instrument risk, the opening trading rule, and for stop loss calculations.

---

[78] Technical note: Specifically, the effects of carry (contango and backwardation) will be removed from the price. If we take bond futures as an example, these tend to be in permanent backwardation with the spot price above the future. This means that going long the future and regularly rolling it will earn an additional return which translates into an upward drift in the stitched price. This in turn introduces a long bias into a trend following system which uses the stitched price rather than the spot price. Removing this bias by replacing the stitched price with the spot price will reduce back-tested performance and will also reduce future performance if bonds continue to attract a risk premium.

[79] Apparently, the adjustments made to prices are evocative of ships rising up or down in the locks of the Panama Canal. There are other more complex methods for back adjusting prices, but I prefer the relative simplicity of the Panama method.

[80] I'll explain later in the chapter when you should switch from one dated product to the next.

[81] At the time of writing quandl.com provide this data, but at a premium price.

FIGURE 5: PRICE OF AUDUSD FX AS OF JUNE 2018 – NOT BACK-ADJUSTED AS THIS IS AN UNDATED PRODUCT

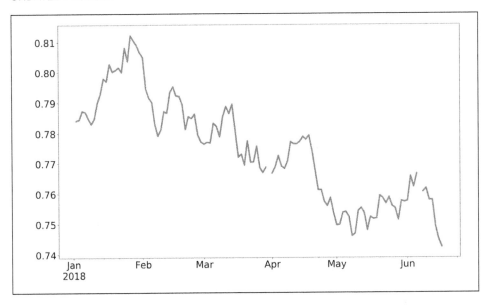

FIGURE 6: BACK-ADJUSTED PRICE OF EURO STOXX 50 AS OF JUNE 2018

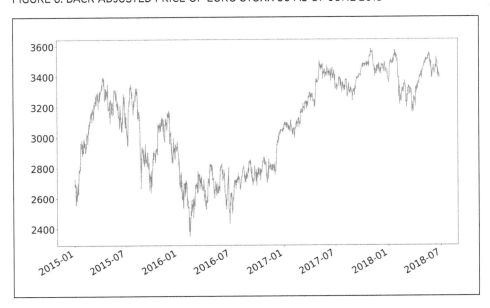

FIGURE 7: BACK-ADJUSTED PRICE OF CORN AS OF JUNE 2018

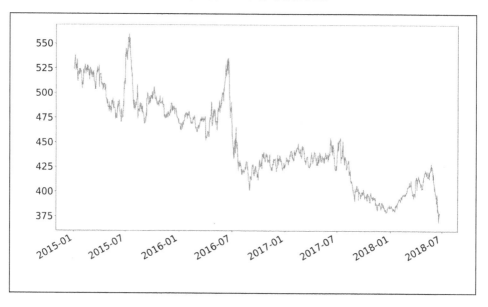

FIGURE 8: BACK-ADJUSTED PRICE OF GOLD AS OF JUNE 2018

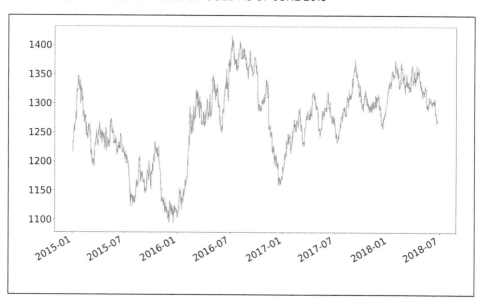

FIGURE 9: PRICE OF S&P 500 AS OF JUNE 2018 – NOT BACK-ADJUSTED AS WE ARE USING AN UNDATED PRODUCT

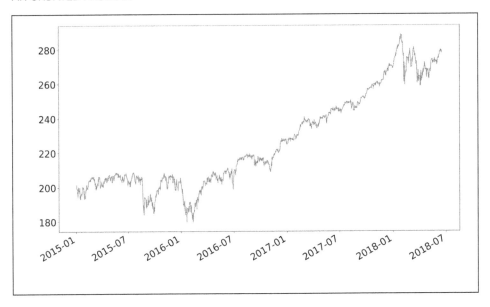

TABLE 15: PRICES OF EXAMPLE INSTRUMENTS ON DAY ONE OF TRADING (19 JUNE 2018)

	Recommended instrument	Price
Futures spread bet	Gold	1,268
Future	Corn	379
CFD on future (per contract)	Euro Stoxx 50	3,391
Spot FX	AUDUSD	0.744
Margin trading ETF	S&P 500	276

Notice that the price of the SPY ETF is quoted at one-tenth of the S&P 500 index level, which on this particular day was 2,760.

Measure instrument risk

Once you have your price series you need to measure the *instrument risk*: the annual standard deviation of its percentage returns. This is required to decide trade size, to work out stop loss levels, and also to manage existing positions. There are a few different methods you can use, listed here in order of my personal preference:

Calculate your own standard deviation (My favourite method)	You can calculate the standard deviation figure yourself, using the method described in appendix C, on page 313.
	Important: If you are using back-adjusted prices then you need to make sure the calculation corrects for this. Appendix C explains how.
Use a provided standard deviation	Some websites provide a calculation of standard deviation for a given instrument. Just make sure that it's an annual figure. If your website provides you with a daily risk figure, then multiply it by 16 to get the annualised equivalent.[82] Also ensure you are dealing with a percentage standard deviation, rather than one expressed in price units. If it is in price units, you need to divide it by the current price to get a percentage.
Use a provided Average True Range, and convert it to standard deviation	Average True Range (ATR) is a common measure of risk that is freely available on many websites. According to my research if you multiply the ATR[83] by 14, then this is a good approximation for the annual standard deviation.
Eyeball the chart (My least favourite method)	You can try to estimate risk just by looking at the chart. So, for example, if the price looks like it moves by about 3 points a day, and the current price is 300, then the daily standard deviation will be about $3 \div 300 = 1\%$ per day. The annual standard deviation will be about $1\% \times 16 = 16\%$ per year.

---

[82] There are roughly 251 trading days in a year, depending on where and what you are trading. But as standard deviation scales with the square root of time it's easier to pretend there are exactly 256 days, since the square root of 256 is 16.

[83] Technical note: Without making assumptions about the ratio of intraday and overnight volatility it isn't possible to calculate the relationship between standard deviation and ATR with an explicit formula. This figure was derived by taking an average of the ratios of each risk measure across 37 different futures contracts.

TABLE 16: VOLATILITY FOR EXAMPLE INSTRUMENTS ON 19 JUNE 2018

	Recommended instrument	Annual standard deviation (instrument risk)	Daily standard deviation	ATR
Futures spread bet	Gold	11.0%	0.69%	0.79%
Future	Corn	11.9%	0.74%	0.85%
CFD on future (per contract)	Euro Stoxx 50	9.6%	0.60%	0.69%
Spot FX	AUDUSD	8.7%	0.54%	0.62%
Margin trading	S&P 500	16.0%	1.0%	1.14%

All values estimated from daily closing prices.

Check opening rules

As we don't have a position when we start trading, our next task is to check if one should be opened. We need to calculate the value for the moving average crossover: the difference between a 16-day and a 64-day moving average (formula 13, page 88). I explain how to do this using a spreadsheet in appendix C.

Alternatively, some charting websites will calculate the crossover for you. Make sure that you're looking at daily closing prices if you use the value provided by a website. Most websites default to showing only today's price movement in five-minute increments, and others like to show prices as bars or candles which also include the open, high and low prices for the day. The website will probably not be using back-adjusted prices, which isn't ideal, but using a website saves a great deal of time.

Remember: if the 16-day is higher than the 64-day go long, and if the 16-day is lower than the 64-day go short. If you've had a position before which has just been closed, then don't open up a new position in the same direction as the previous one. Wait until the moving average crossover has reversed direction. See the flowchart below:

FLOWCHART: TRADE DECISION MAKING

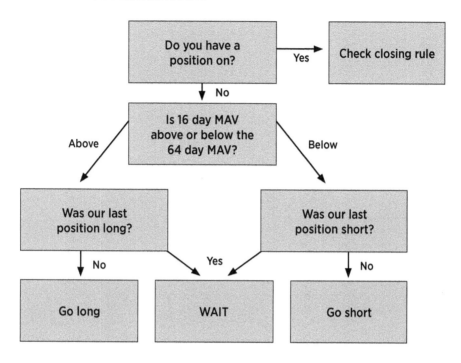

The following charts show the price and moving averages for our five contracts from the beginning of 2018 to June.

FIGURE 10: AUDUSD

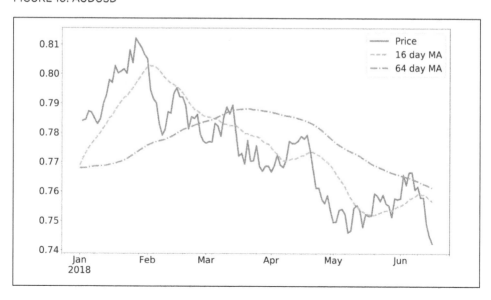

FIGURE 11: EURO STOXX 50

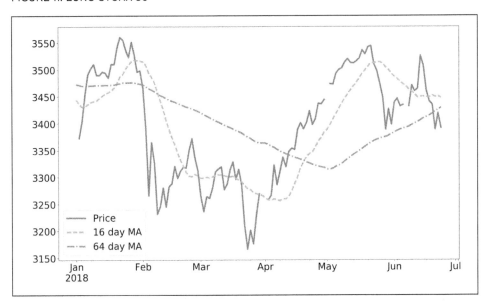

FIGURE 12: CORN (FUTURES PRICES)

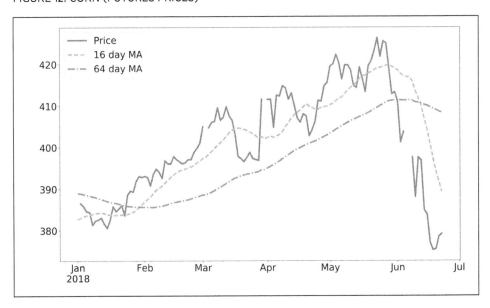

FIGURE 13: GOLD

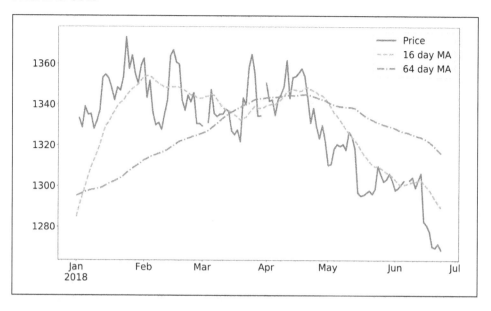

FIGURE 14: S&P 500 ETF PRICE

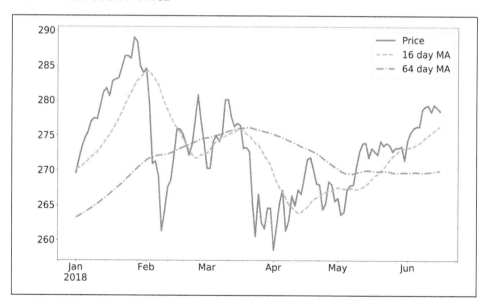

Note: Figures 10 to 14 show that when I wrote this chapter in late June 2018 the opening rule was *long* S&P 500 and Euro Stoxx, but *short* AUDUSD, gold, and corn.

Position sizing

Before a position is opened you need to work out how large it should be. This is a two-step process.

Step 1

The first step is to work out the required notional exposure, using formula 14:

Notional exposure = (target risk × capital) ÷ instrument risk %

TABLE 17: NOTIONAL EXPOSURE FOR INITIAL TRADES IN JUNE 2018

	Recommended instrument	Instrument risk (A)	Capital (B)	Notional exposure (B × 12%) ÷ A
Futures spread bet	Gold	11.0%	£1,200	£1,309
Future	Corn	11.9%	$40,000	$40,336
CFD on future	Euro Stoxx 50	9.6%	$13,000	$16,250
Spot FX	AUDUSD	8.7%	£1,100	£1,517
Margin trading	S&P 500	16.0%	$7,100	$5,325

Instrument risk from table 16. Notional exposure calculated with formula 14 using 12% target risk, and rounded to nearest $1 or £1.

Table 17 shows the notional exposure calculations for the initial example trades, using the appropriate capital. Before trading in real life, you will also need to check that the resulting leverage factors don't breach any margining limits set by the brokers or exchanges. Note that for subsequent trades, I will need to change the capital figure to reflect any profits or losses that have been made, and any changes in estimated instrument risk.

Step 2

Step two is to calculate how large your position should be in the appropriate units for each product. You need to calculate the required number of contracts or bet per point, using formula 20. All the prices I'm using here come from table 15, the relevant product parameters are in table 14, and I am using the prevailing FX rates as of 19 June 2018.

Gold: Spread bet on future	**Spread bet per point = (Exposure home currency × FX Rate × point size) ÷ price** For gold, the FX rate is 1 (since you can bet in pounds per point and your capital is in £), the point size is 1 and the price is 1,268. **Spread bet per point = (£1,309 × 1 × 1) ÷ (1,268) = £1.032 per point** The minimum bet per point is £0.50 and I can bet in 1p increments beyond this: the bet is **short gold at £1.03 per point**.
Corn: Futures	**Futures contracts = (Exposure home currency × FX Rate) ÷ (price × contract multiplier)** For corn, the FX rate is 1 (since the example capital is in dollars), the price is 379 and the multiplier is $50. **Futures contracts = ($40,336 × 1) ÷ (379 × $50) = 2.13** This needs to be rounded: **go short 2 contracts of corn futures**.
Euro Stoxx 50: CFD per contract	**CFD contracts to bet = (Exposure home currency × FX Rate) ÷ (price × contract size)** For Euro Stoxx, the FX rate to convert dollars into euros is currently 0.86, the contract size is €2 and the price is 3,391. **CFD contracts = ($16,250 × 0.86) ÷ (3,391 × 2) = 2.06 contracts** I have to round this to **long 2 contracts of Euro Stoxx**.
Euro Stoxx 50: CFD per point	**CFD bet per point = (Exposure home currency × FX Rate × point size) ÷ price** For Euro Stoxx, the FX rate to convert dollars into euros is currently 0.86, the point size is 1 and the price is 3,391. **CFD bet per point = ($16,250 × 0.86 × 1) ÷ 3,391 = €4.121 per point** The minimum bet is €2 per point and you can bet in one cent increments beyond this, so the required position is **long €4.12 per point of Euro Stoxx**.

	FX exposure = Exposure home currency × FX Rate
AUDUSD: **Spot FX**	The AUDGBP rate on 18 June was 1.781 (note, we're using this and not the AUDUSD rate as our home currency is GBP). We'd go short (buy USD, sell AUD) £1,517 × 1.781 = A$2,701.78 Depending on your broker you might have to round this to A$2,700 (smallest increment $100) or A$3,000 (smallest increment A$1,000). For my broker I have to round it to **short A$2,700**.
S&P 500: Margin trading	**Number of shares = Exposure home currency × FX Rate ÷ price** For the S&P 500 ETF with a price of $276, the FX rate is 1, so the number of shares is: **Number of shares = $5,325 × 1 ÷ 276 = 19.3 shares** I round this to **long 19 shares**.

Which dated position?

In this chapter I've recommended that you use dated products like futures, or spread bets and CFDs based on futures, rather than their more costly, undated brethren. But with dated products you need to decide which expiry date to trade. The appropriate strategy depends on the instrument you are trading.

Equity index Government bonds FX Metals	For these instruments **only the nearest contract** is usually liquid enough to trade.
Volatility (VIX, VSTOXX)	Volatility indices usually have good liquidity for six months or so ahead. However, the nearest contracts have a tendency to move very sharply in a market crash. To avoid this, **I usually hold the second monthly contract**. For example, if it's currently June 2018, then I avoid the July 2018 contract and instead trade the contract expiring in August 2018.
Short-term interest rate futures (e.g., Eurodollar, Short Sterling)	Interest rate futures have plenty of liquidity for several years ahead. But the nearest contracts currently have relatively low risk; this is potentially dangerous, makes them more expensive to trade and increases the minimum capital required. It's also expensive to roll interest rate futures, and holding a position further out reduces the frequency of rolls that are required. **I prefer to trade the contract that is around three years out**. For example, if it's June 2018, then I'd hold June 2021.
Seasonal commodities with forward liquidity	Crude oil that is being delivered in chilly December has different price attributes from crude oil in summery June (if you live in the Southern Hemisphere, swap these two adjectives round). Like crude oil, most commodities have a seasonal component. To cope with this, I prefer to stick to **holding commodities for a fixed month in the year**. For simplicity, I always hold the nearest December crude oil future. If it was June 2018, then I'd hold December 2018.
Seasonal commodities without forward liquidity	Not all commodities have enough liquidity for the strategy of holding a fixed month. For example, I would ideally trade Natural Gas as a seasonal commodity, but **only the nearest contract is normally liquid enough**. If it was June 2018, then I'd hold July 2018.

For CFDs, or spread bets based on futures, the broker may limit the number of expiry dates you can trade. They often restrict you to the nearest expiry date, even if other dates are available and liquid in the futures market. Try and get as close as you can to the ideal contract.

For our example products, when I was writing this chapter in June 2018, I chose to trade these dates:

- Corn future:
  - This is a seasonal commodity with forward liquidity, so I choose to stick to trading December; in June 2018, I was holding **December 2018**.

- Gold spread bet, based on future:
  - My spread betting broker only offers the next date that the futures expire, which, for gold in June 2018, was **August 2018**.

- Euro Stoxx, CFD based on future:
  - Only the next dated product is liquid, which for Euro Stoxx, in June 2018, was **September 2018**.

- AUDUSD Spot FX and S&P 500 margin traded ETF:
  - Both are undated products so there is **no expiry date**.

Calculate stop losses

The next part of the trading process is to calculate your stop losses. First the stop loss gap:

- Take the current instrument *risk*. This is expressed as an annual percentage standard deviation.

- Multiply the instrument risk by the current price: this will give you the *standard deviation in price points* (see formula 22).

- Multiply the standard deviation in price points by the trailing stop loss factor, which is 0.5 for the Starter System (see formula 23). This equals the *stop loss gap*: the amount a price needs to move before your position is closed. **The stop loss gap will remain fixed throughout the life of the trade.**[84]

Now work out the stop levels (formula 24):

- If **long**, your stop loss level will be equal to the initial entry price *minus* the stop loss gap.

- With a **short** position your stop loss level is the entry price *plus* the stop loss gap.

It is most likely you will have to round your stop loss levels. If after rounding you find that the stop loss has come out a 'round number', then you should adjust it. Increase the stop level slightly if you are long; reduce it slightly if you are short. Inexperienced

---

[84] This rule is here to keep the Starter System simple. In theory we should adjust both stop loss gap and position size when instrument risk changes, but for the vast majority of traders this is unnecessary work which adds no significant value. I discuss more complicated position management rules in chapter ten.

traders tend to set stop losses at round numbers, and you want to avoid having a stop at exactly the same level as many other traders. This is especially important if you have left your stop loss orders with your broker.

For example, if your stop level for corn (where we are short) came in at $400 exactly, you would reduce it to $399.99 or slightly lower. If the stop for Euro Stoxx 50 (a long position) was 3,200, then you would increase it slightly to 3,200.01 or even a little higher.

The opening stop loss calculations for the chapter examples are shown in table 18. Notice that the stop loss level is above the initial price for my short positions, and below the initial price for the longs in Euro Stoxx 50 and S&P 500.

TABLE 18: INITIAL STOP LOSSES FOR EXAMPLE INSTRUMENTS

	Position	Instrument risk (A)	Initial price (B)	Annual standard deviation, price points (C = A × B)	Stop loss gap (D = 0.5 × C)	Initial stop loss level B + D (short) B – D (long)
Gold	Short	11.0%	1,268	139.48	69.74	1,337.74
Corn	Short	11.9%	379	45.10	22.55	401.55
Euro Stoxx 50	Long	9.60%	3,391	325.54	162.77	3,228.23
AUDUSD	Short	8.7%	0.744	0.0647	0.0324	0.7764
S&P 500	Long	16%	276	44.16	22.08	253.92

Instrument risk (A) from table 16. Prices (B) from table 15.

Trade

Now it is time to actually trade.

Some advice on how to place orders and reduce trading costs is given in appendix B. Table 19 shows the *trade log* for the initial trades. You should keep your own log, either on paper or in a spreadsheet. I will update this log after each subsequent trade.

TABLE 19: TRADE LOG AFTER INITIAL TRADING

	Trade date in 2018	Dated expiry	Trade	Size	Price	Commission
Gold spread bet	19 June	Aug 2018	Short	£1.03 per point	1,268	0
Corn future	19 June	Dec 2018	Short	2 contracts	379	$2
Euro Stoxx 50 CFD (per contract)	19 June	Sep 2018	Long	2 contracts €2 each	3,391	0
Euro Stoxx 50 CFD (per point)	19 June	Sep 2018	Long	€4.12 per point	3,391	0
AUDUSD spot FX	19 June	N/A	Short	A$2,700	0.744	0
S&P 500 ETF margin trade	19 June	N/A	Long	19 shares	276	$1

Table includes commissions, but not spread costs, since the price shown reflects the effect of paying the spread. No commissions are payable for spread bets, CFD, and spot FX.

Tasks on subsequent days

Because the Starter System trades quite slowly, it is suitable for *daily trading*.[85] Daily trading is ideal for traders who have other things to do besides trade. It also means that you can use daily closing prices, which can be obtained for free, rather than expensive intraday data. In this section, I discuss the daily tasks required when running the Starter System.

---

[85] To be clear: this means trading at most once a day. This is not the same as day trading, where you always close your positions before the end of each day! As I've already mentioned you should avoid day trading: you will trade too quickly, and your trading account will be emptied quickly.

Get, and record, the value of your account

You need to snapshot the current value of your account[86] to size positions on any new trades. It's also useful to record your daily profits and losses so that you can evaluate your trading performance.[87]

Get an updated price series and measure instrument risk

Follow the process discussed earlier in this chapter (pages 124 and 129 respectively).

Monitor stop loss gaps

This also needs to be done daily.

- Firstly, work out when the most profitable price point of your existing trade was – the *high watermark*. If long, take the *highest* daily closing price achieved since you entered the trade. With a short position use the *lowest* closing price. For dated products high and low watermarks should ideally be calculated using the back-adjusted price, as this can be directly compared to the price of the current dated instrument that you are trading.

- If you are long your stop loss price will be equal to the high watermark price point *minus* the stop loss gap. With a short position your stop loss is the high watermark price *plus* the stop loss gap (see formula 24).

- Traders using stop loss orders left with their broker, and whose stop level has changed, will need to update their orders (some brokers will do this for you, but it's worth checking they have done it correctly).

- Traders using DIY stop losses should compare the last closing price[88] to their stop loss level. If long, then a closing price below your stop loss is a breach; if you're short then it's a price higher than your stop. If the closing price has breached the stop loss then you must close your position. **You must close it immediately, even if the price has recovered and your stop loss is no longer being breached**.

Table 20 shows the values I calculated on one particular day – 18 September 2018 – when all four of the initial trades were still open. For the short positions all prices are below the relevant stop loss level, and for the long positions the current price is above the stop. Hence all these positions can be kept open.

---

[86] This is the value of all the open positions in your account, plus any unused cash. Some brokers describe this as the net liquidation value.

[87] I'll explain how you can do this properly in chapter eleven.

[88] Or settlement price. Where both closing and settlement prices are available, make sure you are consistent with your choice of which to use.

TABLE 20: UPDATED STOP LOSSES FOR EXAMPLE INSTRUMENTS (18 SEPTEMBER 2018)

	Position	High-water mark (B)	Stop loss gap (D)	New stop loss level B + D (short) B − D (long)	Current price
Gold	Short	1,174	69.74	1,243.74	1,203
Corn	Short	343	22.55	365.55	343
Euro Stoxx 50	Long	3,528	162.77	3,365.23	3,367
AUDUSD	Short	0.71	0.0324	0.7424	0.7214
S&P 500	Long	291.5	22.08	269.42	290.91

High-water mark (A) based on most profitable price level between 18 June and 18 September. Stop loss gap (D) from table 18. Current price on the 18 September 2019.

Rolling of dated positions

When trading the Starter System, you should expect to hold positions for a couple of months or so, though some trades will be stopped out quickly and others will last longer. Sooner or later you will find yourself holding a position in a dated product that is about to expire. At that point you will need to *roll* into the next dated product: closing your current date and opening the same position in the next date. The new contract date you select should be the one you'd choose if it was a brand-new trade, using the guidelines I outlined earlier in this chapter (see page 137).

There is a cost to rolling, which is built into the calculations for holding costs in appendix B. However, it is worth trying to reduce that cost if you can. If you are trading futures, you would ideally use a *spread order*. This is a single order consisting of both a closing and an opening trade, which will be cheaper to execute than two separate orders. In some instruments the spread market isn't very liquid, and you'll need to do the roll as two individual orders. When CFD and spread betting, some brokers will charge half the normal spread, while others will make you pay the full cost. You should take this into account when choosing your broker.

In futures you will have to organise your own rolls. If you don't roll futures trades with enough time left before the expiry date, then the broker will sometimes automatically close them.[89] But they won't open the new trade for you. Fortunately, most CFD and spread betting brokers will automatically roll trades if you request it in advance.

Here are the rolls I did for the example trades in this chapter, before the end of 2018:

Corn: Future	I was originally short December 2018 futures. Corn is a seasonal commodity and I want to keep the exposure in the winter month of December. I decided to roll this nice and early[90] into December 2019, on 26 September, using a spread order.
Gold: Spread bet on future	I started out short August 2018 gold. On 26 July 2018 I closed this position as the underlying futures contract was nearing expiry, and rolled into December 2018, which was the next liquid contract.
Euro Stoxx 50: CFD	Initially I was long September 2018 Euro Stoxx. I had to roll out of this on 19 September as it was about to expire. The next liquid contract was December 2018. I closed the long position by selling September 2018 and opening a new long in December 2018.
AUDUSD: Spot FX	As an undated trade no rolling is required.
S&P 500 ETF: Margin trade	As an undated trade no rolling is required.

I have added these trades to the trade log, in table 21. There is a new column 'P&L' which shows the profit or loss for the trade (losses are shown as negative values). This is calculated in price points; I will convert these into real money later in the chapter.

---

[89] This depends on whether the futures are *cash settled* (if the position expires you get paid your accrued profits or losses) or *physically settled* (if long you receive actual bushels of corn or bars of gold; if short you have to deliver them), and whether the broker allows physical settlement (most brokers do not allow physical settlement except for certain FX futures, as most retail traders do not have the garage space to store the 5,000 bushels of corn represented by one corn future).

[90] One advantage of futures is that you usually have more flexibility about when to roll and which contract to hold, compared to CFDs and spread bets. The reasons for this early roll will become apparent in chapter eight.

TABLE 21: TRADE LOG AFTER ROLLS

	Trade date in 2018	Dated expiry	Trade	Size	Price	P&L	Comm.
Gold spread bet	19 June	Aug 2018	Short	£1.03 per point	1268		0
	26 July	Aug 2018	Close	£1.03 per point	1228.1	39.9	0
	26 July	Dec 2018	Short	£1.03 per point	1237.4		0
Corn future	19 June	Dec 2018	Short	2 contracts	379		$2
	26 Sep	Dec 2018	Close	2 contracts	362.75	16.25	$2
	26 Sep	Dec 2019	Short	2 contracts	397		$2
Euro Stoxx 50 CFD (per contract)	19 June	Sep 2018	Long	2 contracts at €2 each	3391		0
	19 Sep	Sep 2018	Close	2 contracts	3365	-26	0
	19 Sep	Dec 2018	Long	2 contracts	3346		0
Euro Stoxx 50 CFD (per point)	19 June	Sep 2018	Long	€4.12 per point	3391		0
	19 Sep	Sep 2018	Close	€4.12 per point	3365	-26	0
	19 Sep	Dec 2018	Long	€4.12 per point	3346		0

'Comm': commissions. Excludes spread cost, since the price shown reflects the effect of paying the spread. No commissions are payable for spread bets, CFD, and spot FX. P&L is profit or loss in price points for closing trades only.

Trading diary

This section shows the trades that I subsequently did in each example instrument.

10 October 2018: first two stop losses are hit

Table 22 shows the state of my stop loss calculations on the 10 October 2018. This was an interesting day in the markets – the S&P 500 dropped nearly 100 points, and there were sharp movements in markets across the globe. Both my corn and Euro Stoxx stop losses were triggered.

TABLE 22: UPDATED STOP LOSSES FOR EXAMPLE INSTRUMENTS (10 OCTOBER 2018)

	Position	High-water mark (B)	Stop loss gap (D)	New stop loss level B + D (short) B – D (long)	Current price
Gold	Short	1,174	69.74	1,243.74	1,220
Corn	Short	343	22.55	365.55	401 *
Euro Stoxx 50	Long	3,528	162.77	3,365.23	3,330 *
AUDUSD	Short	0.704	0.0324	0.7364	0.7056
S&P 500	Long	294	22.08	271.92	277

* Stop loss triggered. High-water mark (B) based on most profitable price level between 18 June and 10 October. Stop loss gap (D) from table 18. Current price on 10 October 2019.

I immediately closed both my corn and Euro Stoxx positions.

Next, I need to check to see if the opening rule has reversed its position, to see if a new trade is justified. Figure 15 shows that the opening rule for corn doesn't want a long position, so for now I won't be buying any corn. The trading plan forbids me from opening another short position in the same direction as the one I've just closed. In figure 16 the moving average crossover for Euro Stoxx has been short for several weeks.[91] A new short trade is required here.

---

[91] This is potentially confusing. If the opening rule has been short for weeks, why have we only just closed the trade? It's because the opening rule and closing rule are different: the Starter System uses a moving average to open trades, and a stop loss to determine when to close a trade or not. In part four of the book, I'll explain how you can use the opening rule to close as well as open trades.

FIGURE 15: CORN DOESN'T WANT A LONG POSITION

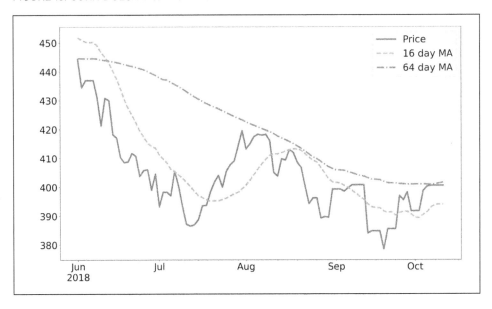

FIGURE 16: EURO STOXX OPENING RULE HAS BEEN SHORT FOR WEEKS

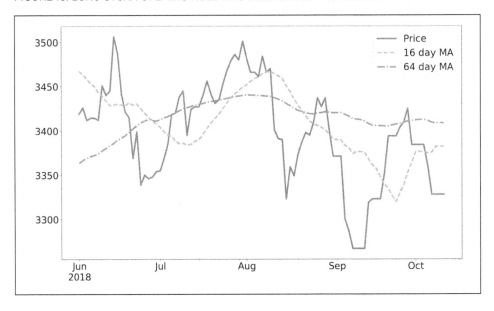

TABLE 23: TRADE LOG AFTER CLOSING CORN AND EURO STOXX POSITIONS, AND OPENING NEW EURO STOXX TRADE

	Trade Date in 2018	Dated expiry	Trade	Size	Price	P&L	Comm.
Corn future	19 June	Dec 2018	Short	2 contracts	379		$2
	26 Sep	Dec 2018	Close	2 contracts	362.75	16.25	$2
	26 Sep	Dec 2019	Short	2 contracts	397		$2
	10 Oct	Dec 2019	Close	2 contracts	401	−4	$2
Euro Stoxx 50 CFD (per contract)	19 June	Sep 2018	Long	2 contracts at €2 each	3,391		0
	19 Sep	Sep 2018	Close	2 contracts	3,365	−26	0
	19 Sep	Dec 2018	Long	2 contracts	3,346		0
	10 Oct	Dec 2018	Close	2 contracts	3,330	−16	0
	10 Oct	Dec 2018	Short	1 contract at €2	3,329		0
Euro Stoxx 50 CFD (per point)	19 June	Sep 2018	Long	€4.12 per point	3,391		0
	19 Sep	Sep 2018	Close	€4.12 per point	3,365	−26	0
	19 Sep	Dec 2018	Long	€4.12 per point	3,346		0
	10 Oct	Dec 2018	Close	€4.12 per point	3,330	−16	0
	10 Oct	Dec 2018	Short	€2 per point	3,329		0

'Comm': commissions. Excludes spread cost, since the price shown reflects the effect of paying the spread. No commissions are payable for spread bets, CFD, and spot FX. P&L is profit or loss in price points for closing trades only.

To work out how large the new Euro Stoxx trade needs to be, I need to know the current capital available for that trade. And to work that out, I need to calculate the size of the loss made on the initial trade. Table 23 shows an updated trade log for corn and Euro Stoxx. This also includes the new trade on Euro Stoxx.

I made losses on both Euro Stoxx trades: 26 points on one and 16 points on the next, for a total of 42 points. For the per contract CFD, where the position size was two contracts at €2 per contract, that works out at:

$$2 \times €2 \times 42 = €168 = \$191$$

There were no commissions or holding costs. For the CFD betting per point, where the position size was €4.12 per point, the loss is:

$$€4.12 \times 42 = €173 = \$197$$

The capital for Euro Stoxx has fallen from \$13,000 to \$12,809 (per contract) or \$12,803 (per point). All the relevant calculations for the new short trade in Euro Stoxx are shown below.

TABLE 24: EXPOSURE SIZING FOR OCTOBER 10 EURO STOXX TRADE

	Instrument risk (A)	Capital (B)	Notional exposure (B × 12%) ÷ A
CFD on future (per contract)	20.4%	$12,809	$7,534
CFD on future (per point)	20.4%	$12,803	$7,531

Instrument risk (A) as of 10 October. Capital (B) includes original $13,000, less the loss on the first trade. Notional exposure calculated using formula 14 and risk target of 12%.

	CFD contracts to bet = (Exposure home currency × FX Rate) ÷ (price × contract size)
Euro Stoxx 50: CFD per contract	The FX rate to convert dollars into euros is currently 0.88, the contract size is €2, and the price is 3,330.
	($7,534 × 0.88) ÷ (3,330 × 2) = 0.995 contracts
	I have to round this to **long 1 contract**.
	CFD bet per point = (Exposure home currency × FX Rate × point size) ÷ price
Euro Stoxx 50: CFD per point	The FX rate to convert dollars into euros is currently 0.88, the point size is 1 and the price is 3,330.
	($7,531 × 0.88 × 1) ÷ 3,330 = €1.99 per point
	The minimum bet is €2 per point, so the required position is **long €2 per point**.

TABLE 25: INITIAL STOP LOSS FOR OCTOBER 10 EURO STOXX TRADE

	Position	Instrument risk (A)	Initial price (B)	Annual standard deviation, price points (C = A × B)	Stop loss gap (D = 0.5 × C)	Initial stop loss level (Short, so: B + D)
Euro Stoxx 50	Short	20.4%	3,330	679.32	339.66	3,669.96

Instrument risk (A) and initial price (B) as of 10 October.

24 October 2018: hit a stop in S&P 500

The market takes another tumble on 24 October, and my stop level of $271.92 in S&P 500 is hit. I get taken out at $265 per share. Looking at the opening rule in figure 17, I need to open a new short trade straight away.

FIGURE 17: S&P 500 OPENING RULE IS ALREADY SHORT

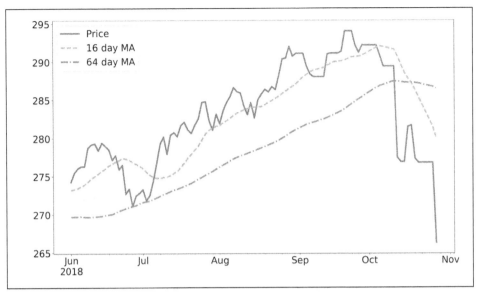

Next, we need to see how much capital is available. Table 26 shows the updated trade log. Again, this includes the new short trade, which I'll do the calculations for in a moment.

TABLE 26: TRADE LOG FOR S&P 500; OLD TRADE HITS STOP, NEW TRADE PUT ON

	Trade date in 2018	Dated expiry	Trade	Size	Price	P&L	Comm.
	19 June	N/A	Long	19 shares	276		$1
S&P 500 ETF margin trade	24 Oct	N/A	Close	19 shares	265	−11	$1
	24 Oct	N/A	Short	17 shares	265		$1

'Comm': commissions. Excludes spread cost, since the price shown reflects the effect of paying the spread. P&L is profit or loss in price points for closing trades only.

I've lost $11 per share for a net loss of:

$$11 \times 19 = \$209$$

As my position ($5,244) was smaller than my account size ($7,100), I didn't have to pay any financing costs; but I did have to cough up two lots of commission at $1 per trade, leaving me with a total loss of $211. Out of my original $7,100 capital, $6,889 is left.

My calculations for the new short trade are shown below.

TABLE 27: NOTIONAL EXPOSURE FOR NEW S&P 500 TRADE

	Recommended instrument	Instrument risk (A)	Capital (B)	Notional exposure (B × 12%) ÷ A
Margin trading	S&P 500	18.5%	$6,889	$4,469

Instrument risk (A) as of 24th October. Capital (B) includes original $7,100 less loss on original trade. Notional exposure calculated using formula 14 and risk target of 12%.

	Number of shares = Exposure home currency × FX Rate ÷ price
S&P 500: Margin trading	For the S&P 500 ETF with a price of $265, the FX rate is 1, so the number of shares is: **$4,469 × 1 ÷ 265 = 16.86 shares** I round this to **17 shares**.

TABLE 28: INITIAL STOP LOSS FOR NEW S&P 500 TRADE

	Position	Instrument risk (A)	Initial price (B)	Annual standard deviation, price points (C = A × B)	Stop loss gap (D = 0.5 × C)	Initial stop loss level (Short so: B + D)
S&P 500	Short	18.5%	265	49.03	24.51	289.51

Instrument risk (A) and initial price (B) as of 24 October.

26 October 2018: A new trade in corn

I had to wait over two weeks before the opening rule has reversed its opinion on corn, as figure 18 shows. It is time to open a new position, again in the December 2019 contract.

FIGURE 18: FINALLY TIME TO GO LONG CORN

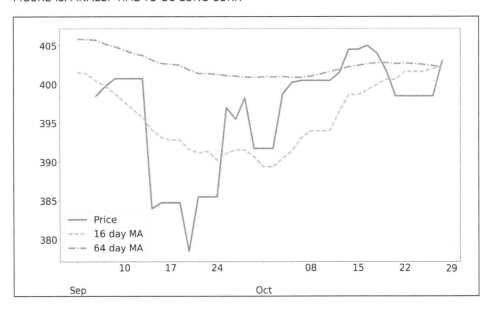

First, we need to calculate the amount of capital available for the trade. Table 29 shows the updated trade log for corn.

TABLE 29: TRADE LOG FOR CORN, INCLUDING NEW TRADE

	Date in 2018	Dated expiry	Trade	Size	Price	P&L	Comm.
	19 June	Dec 2018	Short	2 contracts	379		$2
	26 Sep	Dec 2018	Close	2 contracts	362.75	16.25	$2
Corn future	26 Sep	Dec 2019	Short	2 contracts	397		$2
	10 Oct	Dec 2019	Close	2 contracts	401	−4	$2
	26 Oct	Dec 2019	Long	1 contract	403		$1

'Comm': commissions. Excludes spread cost, since the price shown reflects the effect of paying the spread. P&L is profit or loss in price points for closing trades only.

The previous corn trade made 16.25 − 4 =12.25 points. Since each contract price point is worth $50 (see table 14) that works out to:

$$12.25 \times \$50 \times 2 = \$1,225$$

After subtracting $8 in commissions, that leaves me with $1,217. The position and stop loss calculations on this new trade are shown below.

TABLE 30: EXPOSURE SIZING FOR 26 OCTOBER CORN TRADE

	Recommended instrument	Instrument risk (A)	Capital (B)	Notional exposure (B × 12%) ÷ A
Future	Corn	16.5%	$41,217	$29,976

Instrument risk (A) as of 26 October. Capital (B) includes original $40,000 plus profits from first trade. Notional exposure calculated using formula 14 and risk target of 12%.

**Futures contracts = (Exposure home currency ×
FX Rate) ÷ (price × contract multiplier)**

Corn:
Futures

For corn, the FX rate is 1 (since the example capital is in dollars), the price
is 403, and the multiplier is $50.

($29,976 × 1) ÷ (403 × $50) = 1.488

This needs to be rounded: **go long one contract of corn futures**.

TABLE 31: INITIAL STOP LOSS FOR 26 OCTOBER CORN TRADE

	Position	Instrument risk (A)	Initial price (B)	Annual standard deviation, price points (C = A × B)	Stop loss gap (D = 0.5 × C)	Initial stop loss level (Long, so: B – D)
Corn	Long	16.5%	403	66.5	33.25	369.75

Instrument risk (A) and initial price (B) as of 26 October.

8 November 2018: trading activity summary

I could not keep these example trades going forever, or this book would never have
been finished. I decided to close all the remaining trades on 8 November. Below are
the calculations for my profit and loss in the various notional trading accounts.

Gold

TABLE 32: FINAL GOLD TRADE LOG

	Trade date in 2018	Dated expiry	Trade	Size	Price	P&L
	19 June	Aug 2018	Short	£1.03 per point	1,268.0	
Gold spread bet	26 July	Aug 2018	Close	£1.03 per point	1,228.1	39.9
	26 July	Dec 2018	Short	£1.03 per point	1,237.4	
	8 Nov	Dec 2018	Close	£1.03 per point	1,224.2	13.2

There are no commissions. Excludes spread cost, since the price shown reflects the effect of paying the spread. P&L is profit or loss in price points for closing trades only.

On gold, I made a total of 39.9+13.2 = 53.1 points. At £1.03 per point, with no commissions or holding costs, that works out to a profit in the gold account of:[92]

£1.03 × 53.1 = £54.69

---

[92] Remember the account we are using to trade gold with is a GBP account, and we are betting on the price in £ per point (even though gold is priced in dollars). Hence no FX conversion is needed.

Corn

TABLE 33: FINAL CORN FUTURE TRADE LOG

	Trade date in 2018	Dated expiry	Trade	Size	Price	P&L	Comm.
	19 June	Dec 2018	Short	2 contracts	379		$2
	26 Sep	Dec 2018	Close	2 contracts	362.75	16.25	$2
Corn	26 Sep	Dec 2019	Short	2 contracts	397		$2
future	10 Oct	Dec 2019	Close	2 contracts	401	−4	$2
	26 Oct	Dec 2019	Long	1 contract	403		$1
	8 Nov	Dec 2019	Close	1 contract	402	−1	$1

'Comm': commissions. Excludes spread cost, since the price shown reflects the effect of paying the spread. P&L is profit or loss in price points for closing trades only.

The first corn trade, closed on 10 October, made $1,217. The second trade lost a single price point. Since each contract price point is worth $50 (see table 14) that works out to a loss of:

$$-1 \times \$50 \times 1 = -\$50$$

After subtracting $2 in commissions, that makes a loss of $52. The total profit for corn is $1,217 − $52 = **$1,165**

Euro Stoxx 50

TABLE 34: FINAL TRADE LOG FOR EURO STOXX CFD

	Trade date in 2018	Dated expiry	Trade	Size	Price	P&L
Euro Stoxx 50 CFD (per contract)	19 June	Sep 2018	Long	2 contracts at €2 each	3,391	
	19 Sep	Sep 2018	Close	2 contracts	3,365	−26
	19 Sep	Dec 2018	Long	2 contracts	3,346	
	10 Oct	Dec 2018	Close	2 contracts	3,330	−16
	10 Oct	Dec 2018	Short	1 contract at €2	3,329	
	8 Nov	Dec 2018	Close	1 contract at €2	3,202.5	26.5
Euro Stoxx 50 CFD (per point)	19 June	Sep 2018	Long	€4.12 per point	3,391	
	19 Sep	Sep 2018	Close	€4.12 per point	3,365	−26
	19 Sep	Dec 2018	Long	€4.12 per point	3,346	
	10 Oct	Dec 2018	Close	€4.12 per point	3,330	−16
	10 Oct	Dec 2018	Short	€2 per point	3,329	
	8 Nov	Dec 2018	Close	€2 per point	3,202.5	26.5

There are no commissions. Excludes spread cost, since the price shown reflects the effect of paying the spread. P&L is profit or loss in price points for closing trades only.

For the per contract CFD trade the loss on the first trade, closed on 10 October, was $191. The next trade was up 26.5 points. With a position size of one contract at €2 per contract, that works out at a profit of:

1 × €2 × 26.5 = €53 = $60

I converted the euros into dollars, as this is a dollar trading account. There were no commissions or holding costs. The total return for Euro Stoxx is −$191 + $60 = −$131; a loss of **$131.**

For the CFD betting per point, the loss on the first trade was $197. The next trade also made 26.5 points with a bet of €2 per point, making a profit of:

€2 × 26.5 = €53 = $60

The total loss is −$197 + $60 = **$137**

AUDUSD

TABLE 35: FINAL TRADE LOG FOR AUDUSD SPOT FX TRADE

	Trade date in 2018	Dated expiry	Trade	Size	Price	P&L
AUDUSD spot FX	19 June	N/A	Short	A$2,700	0.744	
	8 Nov	N/A	Close	A$2,700	0.7254	0.02

There are no commissions. Excludes spread cost, since the price shown reflects the effect of paying the spread. P&L is profit or loss in price points for closing trades only.

In the AUDUSD account my initial entry price was 0.744. I sold A$2,700 which bought:

2,700 × 0.744 = US$2,008.80

I closed the trade at 0.7254, at which level my original US$2,008.80 was worth:

2008.8 ÷ 0.7254 = A$2,769.23

This gives me a profit of:

A\$2,769.23 – A\$2,700 = A\$69.23 = £38.46

This is converted into pounds, as this is a GBP account. There are no commissions, but as an undated trade there were funding costs. I borrowed my AUD at an interest rate of 2%, and earned 2.25% in USD; hence I earned an extra 0.25% a year which over the life of the trade equates to A\$2.64 = £1.47. The total profit for AUDUSD is £39.93.

S&P 500

TABLE 36: FINAL TRADE LOG FOR S&P 500 MARGIN TRADING

	Trade date in 2018	Dated expiry	Trade	Size	Price	P&L	Comm.
	19 June	N/A	Long	19 shares	276		$1
S&P 500 ETF margin trade	24 Oct	N/A	Close	19 shares	265	−11	$1
	24 Oct	N/A	Short	17 shares	265		$1
	8 Nov	N/A	Close	17 shares	280	−15	$1

'Comm': commissions. Excludes spread cost, since the price shown reflects the effect of paying the spread. P&L is profit or loss in price points for closing trades only.

For the S&P 500 account, I lost $211 on my initial trade. The second trade on 24 October was also closed for a further loss, this time of $15 per share:

−15 × 17 = −$255

Commissions cost me another $2. As I was short, I also had to pay a borrowing fee of 0.25% a year: $0.47. Sadly, my broker didn't pay me any interest on the cash I realised from selling short. The loss on the second trade works out to:

−$255 – $2 – $0.47 = −$257.47

That makes the total loss on S&P 500 trading −$211 – $257.47 = **−$468.47**

TABLE 37: SUMMARY OF TRADING PROFIT AND LOSS

	Capital	P&L	% P&L
Gold spread bet	£1,200	+£54.69	+4.6%
Corn future	$40,000	+$1,165	+2.9%
Euro Stoxx 50 CFD (per contract)	$13,000	–$131	–1.0%
Euro Stoxx 50 CFD (per point)	$13,000	–$137	–1.0%
AUDUSD spot FX	£1,100	£39.93	+3.6%
S&P 500 ETF margin trade	$7,100	–$468.47	–6.6%

Table 37 summarises the profits, and losses, across the different trading accounts. If I count the two types of CFD as a single instrument, then the final score is three wins and two losses. Of course, this is far too short a period to draw any conclusions about the likely profitability of the Starter System. More importantly, the size of the losses and gains is roughly what I'd expect, given the risk target and time period.

In practice, someone actually using the Starter System would only have traded one of these instruments in a single account. I will discuss how to trade multiple instruments in part three.

Time saving tips

Performing the daily tasks to run the Starter System is less time consuming than working as a day trader and being chained to a desk. With practice, running the system only takes a few minutes each day, except for the occasions when you are actually trading. But if you're really short of time even that might seem too much of a commitment. Here are some tips for reducing your workload further.

Use the power of the internet

Many providers of free price data provide free tools for charting moving average crossovers. You can use these to see if an opening position should be established. This is quicker than doing it yourself, although it won't be quite as accurate as using your own back-adjusted price series and a spreadsheet to calculate the crossovers.

Make your broker do some of the work

I am not a fan of leaving stop loss orders with your broker, but they are a time saving aid. If a broker will execute your stops, then you don't need to check the price level every day. Alternatively, you can subscribe to a brokers alert service that sends an email or SMS text message when a stop loss level has been reached. You can then close the position yourself using a mobile trading app.

Leave less urgent matters to the weekend

Most part-time traders will have more spare time at the weekend. As the Starter System trades relatively slowly, there are quite a few tasks you can safely postpone to Saturday or Sunday:

- Checking and recording your account value.

- Download the last week of prices.

- Estimate the instrument risk.

- Update the stop loss gap calculation for any positions that you might open next week.

- Update any exchange rates you need to work out position sizes.

- Calculate the size of positions needed if you were to open a position next week.

- Decide which dated position you'd own if you were to open a position and evaluating whether a current position needs to be rolled.

That leaves the following tasks to complete on weekdays:

- Check to see if any trades require opening (which can be done using free internet price charts) or closing (which can be done using alert services).

- Do any opening trades that are required, using pre-calculated position sizes.

- Do any rolling trades that are required.

- Update stop loss levels (and any stop loss orders left with your broker) using your pre-calculated stop loss gaps, if the price makes a new daily high (for long positions) or low (for short positions).

Summary

That is the end of part two of the book. Congratulations for getting this far! You know how to use a trading system to trade a single instrument, using a single opening rule. Once you have practiced trading the Starter System and are comfortable with it, you will probably want to start improving it. Part three of the book explains how to do this by **diversifying** the system: adding more instruments and more trading rules.

PART THREE
Diversifying

CHAPTER SEVEN
Adding New Markets

I OPENED THIS BOOK WITH a quote from legendary investor, Warren Buffett. Here is another of his gems:

> "Diversification is protection against ignorance. It makes little sense if you know what you are doing."

Many traders concur with Mr Buffett[93] – diversification is a dirty word. In their opinion you should become an AUDUSD FX trader, or a crude oil trader, and stick to that. Trying to trade AUDUSD *and* crude oil is a waste of time. This attitude stems from days of old, when professionals traded exclusively 'on the floor' in physical, rather than electronic, exchanges. Exchange floors were split into *pits*, each trading a different instrument, and traders were fiercely loyal to their own pit.

Today's trading gurus still claim that you should find an instrument that 'suits your trading style', build up 'expertise' in that particular market, and then trade it exclusively. I don't agree with these self-proclaimed experts. For traders like myself, who use a systematic approach, diversification makes a huge amount of sense. In this chapter, I will explain why, how, and when you should diversify your trading across different instruments.

Advantages and disadvantages of diversification

In the Starter System we picked a single instrument to trade, but it was impossible to predict *which* instrument would be the most profitable. From figure 2 (way back on page 76), there is no robust historical evidence to say that any one instrument performed better than another.

But choosing one instrument is risky. The Starter System looks for *trends* in markets and it's unlikely that all the worlds markets will simultaneously have profitable trends. If we are unlucky, we could pick an instrument that turns out to be a poor

---

[93] Although, to be fair, this quote was aimed at stock investors rather than traders.

performer, like the S&P 500 margin trade in the previous chapter. By trading a variety of instruments simultaneously you will be in a better position to catch any trends wherever, and whenever, they appear.

For this reason, large systematic hedge funds are constantly looking for ways to diversify the set of instruments they trade. When I was working at AHL, I recruited Ben – a smart young graduate. Soon after Ben joined, I assigned him his own project: adding a large batch of new instruments to one of our flagship funds. Ben wasn't too happy and probably thought this boring and mechanical task was a waste of his undoubted academic abilities.

I said: "You probably don't appreciate this right now, but this project will add more value to this company than pretty much anything else". I was right. Over the next few years the fund went on to win several awards for outstanding performance, much of it thanks to those extra markets.

Why diversification works: the maths

Let's suppose you're trading the Euro Stoxx 50 equity index, which is the instrument I recommended for CFD traders in chapter six. Another CFD that's available with a reasonable minimum capital and isn't too expensive are US 10-year bonds.

Why would it make sense to trade both of these instruments, rather than just one? If there is no evidence that one instrument is better for trading than another, then how can trading two instruments improve your expected returns? In fact, **you should not expect diversification to improve returns. Diversification is good because it reduces risk**.

Risk is reduced because the returns from trading US 10-year bonds will be different from those earned in the Euro Stoxx. Some days your 10-year bond trading will be profitable and the Euro Stoxx will lose money, whilst on other days, Euro Stoxx will beat bonds. Trading both instruments will reduce the variability of returns in your trading account. To confirm this, I back-tested the returns of the Starter System trading both instruments. I found that the risk of the entire trading account came out significantly lower than the 12% risk target: 9.2% a year.

Lower risk is nice to have, but the risk of the Starter System is already fairly modest. Most traders would prefer to stick to the original risk target and swap the diversification for higher returns. **This is done by applying more leverage and running the trading strategy for each instrument at a higher risk target.**

To do this you should increase the risk target on each individual instrument by a multiplying factor, which in this case is 12% ÷ 9.2% = 1.304. This factor is the *instrument diversification multiplier (IDM)*. The IDM exactly compensates for the reduction in expected risk which comes from trading both instruments.

Now we have:

- Euro Stoxx trading strategy, with a target risk of:

  IDM × risk target = 1.304 × 12% = 15.6%

- US 10-year bond trading strategy, also with a target risk of 15.6%

Using formula 19 (page 100) I can work out the expected pre-cost return of each instrument:

r = (SR × s) + b

Where **SR** is the Sharpe ratio, **r** is the average return, **b** is the rate we can borrow at and **s** is the standard deviation. From chapter five the expected Sharpe ratio without costs for one instrument[94] **SR** =0.24, the risk target including the diversification multiplier **s** = 15.6%, and **b** the rate we can borrow at is currently around 2.0%. The pre-cost expected return on each instrument is:

r = (SR × s) + b = (0.24 × 15.6%) + 2% = 5.7%

If we expect both instruments to provide the same expected return, then we will also make 5.7% on the trading account as a whole. The individual instruments have risk of 15.6%, but what is the expected risk for the whole account? Thanks to the power of diversification the risk will be lower by a factor of (9.2% ÷ 12%). The risk for the entire account is:

15.6% × (9.2% ÷ 12%) = 12%

So now we have:

- Euro Stoxx CFD trading, with a target risk of 15.6% and an expected return of 5.7%.
- US 10-year bond CFD trading, also with a target risk of 15.6% and an expected return of 5.7%.
- Entire trading account, achieving a target risk of 12% and an expected return of 5.7%.

Back in part two, on page 100, I calculated that the Starter System is expected to make 4.9% before costs. Adding the extra instrument has increased the expected return from 4.9% to 5.7% without changing the account level target risk, which remains at 12%.

---

[94] See page 92.

The extra leverage added by the IDM has converted the risk reduction into improved expected profits.[95]

Diversify or trade a cheaper instrument?

The calculations above are done on a pre-cost basis. But adding more instruments will probably increase your costs. Rather than choosing a cheap instrument with higher minimum capital, you will have to opt for two instruments with lower minimum capital, that are likely to be more expensive. If you have enough capital is it better to diversify, or to cut costs by trading a single cheaper instrument?

Let's find out with an example. Before reading this chapter a US CFD trader with $25,000 would have looked at table 5 (chapter five, page 82) and decided they should trade German 10-year Bonds (known as 'Bunds' by professional traders). Bunds have a lower cost than both the Euro Stoxx and the US 10-year bond CFD products. But they need $10,500 in capital; and ideally twice that: $21,000. Alternatively, with $25,000 the trader could trade Euro Stoxx (requires $6,500 minimum, and ideally $13,000) *and* US 10-year bonds (ideally needs $12,000).

Which is the better option? We start with formula 19 (page 100):

$$r = (SR \times s) + b$$

Where **SR** is the Sharpe ratio (0.24 for the Starter System), **s** is the standard deviation (12% for one instrument), **r** is the average return, **b** is the rate we can borrow at (I assume 2%). Subtracting costs, I get the formula for post-cost returns:

FORMULA 26: EXPECTED POST-COST RETURNS

$$r = (SR \times s) + b - (c \times s)$$

Where **c** is the expected cost in risk-adjusted returns (equivalent to Sharpe ratio units). To translate risk adjusted costs into annual returns I multiply by the standard deviation.

Trading only Bund CFDs with **c** = 0.038:

$$r = (0.24 \times 12\%) + 2\% - (0.038 \times 12\%) = 4.42\%$$

Now for the diversified CFD account with two instruments: Euro Stoxx and US 10-year. For Euro Stoxx (**c** = 0.04) with **s** = 15.6% (because of the diversification multiplier):

---

[95] Because a diversified system has a higher expected return for the same level of risk, it will also have a higher expected Sharpe ratio. As we saw in part two (page 98) a higher Sharpe ratio means that it is safe to set a higher risk target for the account as a whole. I will discuss how we can quantify this effect later in the chapter.

r = (0.24 × 15.6%) + 2% – (0.04 × 15.6%) = 5.12%

For US 10-year bonds (c = 0.074) also with s = 15.6%:

r = (0.24 × 15.6%) + 2% – (0.074× 15.6%) = 4.59%

To calculate the return of the whole account we take a weighted average. The weights are the proportion of account value in each instrument:

r = 5.12% × (13,000 ÷ 25,000) + 4.59% × (12,000 ÷ 25,000) = 4.87%

This is significantly higher than the 4.42% return obtained by trading Bund CFDs, even though Bunds are cheaper than both Euro Stoxx and 10-year bonds. In general, **diversification is nearly always better than using a larger account to trade a cheaper instrument.**

Why diversification works: the evidence

Some of you may be unconvinced by the fancy maths above. Good! Cynicism is a very desirable quality in any trader. Let's look at some evidence which, as usual, is drawn from a back-test. It will tell us what happened in the past, but not what will occur in the future.

When looking at back-tests it's important to use as many different instruments as possible; this is so we know that the results aren't just a fluke, and also that the author hasn't just cherry-picked their favorite. It's also important to check the statistical significance of the results, just like I did back in chapter five when deciding which instrument and opening rule to use.

The results are in the box and whiskers plot shown in figure 19. On the extreme left-hand side, you can see that the Sharpe ratio (SR) of the Starter System for a single instrument, with returns averaged across all the instruments in my data set, comes out at 0.24. As in previous figures, (i) the line in the middle of the box shows the average, (ii) there is a two-thirds chance the true SR is inside the box between 0.17 and 0.31, and (iii) the whisker lines outside the box show there is a 95% chance the SR is between 0.1 and 0.39.

So, if I chose one instrument at random, and trade the Starter System with it, then on average I expect to have a Sharpe ratio of 0.24, with a 95% chance the SR was between 0.10 and 0.38.

FIGURE 19: ADDING INSTRUMENTS SIGNIFICANTLY IMPROVES RETURNS – AVERAGE SHARPE
RATIO WITH ERROR BARS AS INSTRUMENTS ARE ADDED TO A TRADING STRATEGY

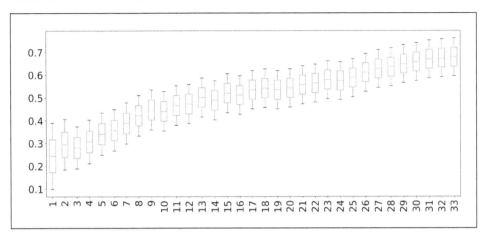

What performance can I expect from trading two instruments? Moving rightwards to the next box, if I add another random instrument the average SR leaps to around 0.3. Adding further instruments continues to increase the expected back-tested performance of the trading system,[96] and once I have a dozen instruments the SR is significantly better than the SR for a single instrument.

This is very clear evidence that diversifying across different instruments will improve the Sharpe ratio, and thus our returns.

If you are able to trade 15 or more instruments you can expect to double your SR. There is no other change you can make to the Starter System which will deliver such an improvement, as you'll realise once you have read the rest of the book.

In fact, this evidence actually undersells diversification. Rather than picking instruments at random, as I did here, we can deliberately choose instruments that bring the maximum amount of diversification into our portfolio. This will produce even higher improvements in Sharpe ratio. I'll discuss how this is done later in the chapter.

---

[96] Sometimes the average performance goes down slightly when an instrument is added. The average returns depend on exactly which instruments are drawn randomly, and sometimes we are unlucky and happen to get a set of instruments whose returns is slightly worse. But this slight degradation in performance isn't significant or meaningful.

The bad news: more capital required

The good news: adding more instruments to your portfolio is undoubtedly the most reliable way to improve your profitability. The bad news: you need more money. Your cash will be shared out between different instruments, and each one needs to have the minimum level of capital for that product.

Let's return to the example of trading two CFDs: Euro Stoxx, and US 10-year bond. The respective minima are $6,500 and $6,000.[97] With the usual rule that you should use twice the minimum capital, the total capital required is:

$$($6,500 × 2) + ($6,000 × 2) = $25,000$$

This is considerably more than the $13,000 you'd need to trade only Euro Stoxx (twice $6,500), or $12,000 for US 10-year bonds (twice $6,000).

Don't worry: **when trading multiple instruments, you can safely ignore my recommendation to use double the minimum capital required**. That rule made sense in the Starter System with a single instrument. Without it, if you lost money you could end up without enough capital to meet the minimum trade size requirement. But if you're trading two instruments, and you lose some money, then you have another fall-back option: **go back to trading a single instrument.**

Suppose you are trading Euro Stoxx and US 10-year bonds with CFDs, but only using the minimum capital for each: $6,500 and $6,000 respectively, totaling $12,500. You are then unlucky with your first trade and have just $11,000 left. This isn't enough to continue trading both instruments, but you can revert to trading a single instrument: Euro Stoxx. Of course, if you continue to lose money and end up with less than $6,500 you will have to stop trading completely (or switch to another instrument with lower minimum capital).

This approach is equally valid regardless of whether you start with three, four, 40, or 400 instruments. I discuss which order you should discard instruments later in the chapter.

More bad news: time commitment

Another disadvantage of trading multiple instruments is that it will take up more time. I automate my trading, so diversification is easy; the computer does the extra work with no complaints. But even if you are running your trading manually off a spreadsheet and some free internet data, it's still relatively easy to trade more instruments without too much additional effort. With practice, and correctly set up spreadsheets, it should

---

[97] Table 5, page 82.

only take a few minutes to process each additional instrument – especially if you follow the time saving tips from chapter six.

The theory of diversification

Which instruments should you add?

I'm going to assume that you are already trading a Starter System with a single instrument, chosen using the criteria in chapter five: **the cheapest instrument for which you can meet the minimum capital requirement**. Having done that, which instrument will come next?

The instrument you choose needs to satisfy the following criteria. Two of these should be familiar from the Starter System, but the third is new:

1. The additional instrument must be **cheap enough to trade** (under my speed limit:[98] maximum risk-adjusted cost of 0.08, and ideally lower).

2. You must be able to meet the **minimum capital requirements** for both the first and the second instrument (though you do not need double the minimum capital).

3. The choice of instrument should **maximise diversification**. You get more diversification by adding instruments that **are as different as possible from the instruments you already have.**

Back in chapter one I discussed the various different *asset classes* that instruments belong to: FX, shares, bonds and so on. Adding a new asset class is the most diversifying thing you can do. If you're already trading Euro Stoxx CFDs, then adding another equity index like S&P 500 won't provide much diversification benefit – the instruments are just too similar. Instead, you should choose an instrument from another asset class.

But which asset class should you add?

Table 38 will help.

---

[98] Page 78.

TABLE 38: APPROXIMATE CORRELATIONS OF TRADING STRATEGY RETURNS

	Bonds	STIR	Equities	Vol.	FX	Comm.	Crypto.
Bonds	1	0.4	0.1	0.1	0.1	0	0
STIR	0.4	1	0.1	0.1	0.1	0	0
Equities	0.1	0.1	1	0.5	0.1	0	0.1
Volatility	0.1	0.1	0.5	1	0.2	0	0.1
FX	0.1	0.1	0.1	0.2	1	0.2	0.1
Commodities	0	0	0	0	0.2	1	0
Crypto.	0	0	0.1	0.1	0.1	0	1

STIR: Short-term interest rates. Vol: Volatility. FX: Foreign exchange. Comm.: Commodities. Crypto.: Cryptocurrency

Correlation values are long-run averages derived from back-tested results.

Table 38 shows the *correlation* between Starter System trading strategies for instruments from different asset classes. Correlation is a measure of diversification. Lower values for correlation mean more diversification.[99]

To use this table, start by selecting the row which relates to the instrument you currently have in your Starter System. Now, going along the row look for the lowest correlation values. These are the asset classes which you should consider adding next.

Once you've decided the possible asset class(es) the other two criteria come into play: cost and minimum account size. You need to pick the cheapest instrument you can, given the capital you have available.

What if you want to add additional instruments? For example, suppose you've already got the Euro Stoxx and US 10-year bonds in your trading account, but still have surplus capital? You just repeat the process as before, although now when you examine table 38 you would look at both the equities and bonds rows. You'd probably not want to add STIR (correlation of 0.4 with bonds), or volatility (correlation of 0.5 with equities), but anything else would do just fine.

---

[99] If you are familiar with correlations, you may be surprised to see how low these values are. However, they are the correlations of *trading systems* for particular instruments, not the correlations of returns in the *actual instruments*. The correlation of trading systems for a given pair of instruments is nearly always much lower than the correlation of the underlying returns.

You can then proceed to add instruments from other asset classes until you run out of money to allocate or run out of asset classes to add.[100]

Diversification for CFD traders

In theory CFD traders have access to a wide variety of asset classes, although not all instruments will be cheap enough to trade or have achievable levels of minimum capital.

TABLE 39: INDICATIVE COSTS AND MINIMUM CAPITAL FOR CFD TRADERS

	Product	Asset class	Minimum capital £	Minimum capital $	Risk-adjusted trading cost
Gilt	CFD on future	Bonds	£7,800	$13,000	0.038
US 10-year	CFD on future	Bonds	£4,500	$6,000	0.074
Nasdaq	CFD on future	Equities	£162,000	$220,000	0.015
Euro Stoxx	CFD on future	Equities	£4,800	$6,500	0.040
USDMXP	CFD on spot FX	FX	£171,000	$230,000	0.065
Gold	CFD on future	Commodities	£30,000	$40,000	0.028
Crude oil	CFD on future	Commodities	£11,000	$15,000	0.067

Minimum capital has been rounded up. Cost calculations using appendix B, and minimum capital calculations using formula 21 (page 103). Where possible, the cheapest (lowest risk-adjusted cost) and most accessible (lowest minimum capital) instrument are shown for each asset class. Only instruments with trading costs less than 0.08 are shown.

Table 39 has my recommended menu of options for CFD traders. Like all menus, there are choices for the well-heeled, but also some cheaper dishes. Where possible, I include two instruments for each asset class. For wealthy traders, I've shown the cheapest instrument in the relevant asset class. There is also a more democratic choice: the instrument with the smallest minimum capital that meets my speed limit (risk-adjusted cost of 0.08 or less per year). Not all asset classes are included, and not all

---

[100] Incidentally, don't feel you have to trade every asset class, even if you have the capital to do so. Never add an instrument which is too expensive to trade (risk-adjusted costs greater than one-third of the expected Sharpe ratio: 0.08 for the opening rule specified in the Starter System). You may have good reasons for avoiding other asset classes entirely, for example, I don't trade cryptocurrencies.

asset classes have two options. This is because I've excluded all instruments that cost more than my speed limit.

As usual, the figures in these tables reflect current market conditions, and you should recalculate them using the methods in appendix B before you make your own decisions.

For the CFD examples in this chapter, we began with the Euro Stoxx used in chapter six which is in the third row (equities) of table 38. Looking along the equity row, the volatility asset class (e.g., VIX) comes in at 0.5, most other assets measure 0.1 and commodities have a correlation estimate of 0. Ideally then you'd choose a commodity as your next instrument; failing that, something from another asset class – except volatility – would suffice.

Looking at table 39, possible commodities for CFD traders include crude oil, but that has a relatively high minimum capital: $15,000. If that is too rich for your taste then you should opt for another asset class, as long as it isn't volatility. The US 10-year bond has a minimum capital of just $6,000, so that would be a good choice for your second instrument if you haven't got the capital for crude oil. With sufficient capital you could trade all three: Euro Stoxx (equities), US 10-year bonds (bonds), and crude oil (commodities).

Based on my calculations, there aren't any further asset classes which a CFD trader should consider adding.[101]

Diversification for spread betters

The Starter System begins spread betting with a commodity: gold. Looking across the sixth row (for commodities) of table 38, all asset classes apart from FX have a correlation of zero.

---

[101] Okay in theory you could add the MXPUSD CFD, but the minimum capital requirement is so large that, if you could afford it, you would be better off trading futures.

Leveraged Trading

TABLE 40: INDICATIVE COSTS AND MINIMUM CAPITAL FOR SPREAD BETTERS

	Product	Asset class	Minimum capital £	Minimum capital $	Risk-adjusted trading cost
Gilt	Spread bet on future	Bonds	£2,400	$3,300	0.035
US 10-year	Spread bet on future	Bonds	£1,500	$2,100	0.074
Nasdaq	Spread bet on future	Equities	£5,500	$7,400	0.015
Euro Stoxx	Spread bet on future	Equities	£1,400	$2,000	0.040
EURGBP	Spread bet on forward	FX	£3,400	$4,600	0.023
NZDUSD	Spread bet on forward	FX	£2,400	$3,300	0.028
Gold	Spread bet on future	Commodities	£600	$800	0.028

Minimum capital has been rounded up. Cost calculations using appendix B, and minimum capital calculations using formula 21 (page 103). Where possible the cheapest (lowest risk-adjusted cost) and most accessible (lowest minimum capital) instrument are shown for each asset class. Only instruments with trading cost less than 0.08 are shown.

From table 40, the Euro Stoxx spread bet would be an excellent choice for a second asset: equities and commodities have a correlation of zero in table 38, and it has a relatively low minimum capital (£1,400). With more capital you might consider adding the Nasdaq equity index, which is amongst the cheapest instruments shown in table 40.

What if we had the cash to add a third instrument?

With a commodity and an equity, we look again at table 38. There are no strikingly high correlations between commodities, equities, and other asset classes, with the exception of the 0.5 correlation between equities and volatility, and the 0.2 correlation of FX and commodities. So, we have a strong preference to avoid volatility and a slight prejudice against FX. I would add a bond – gilts if you have sufficient capital, or US 10-year bonds if your account value can't stretch to that.

For a fourth spread bet, I'd add an FX rate such as EURGBP or NZDUSD.

Diversification for futures traders

I recommended in chapter six that futures traders use corn as their first instrument. Looking across the sixth row (for commodities) of table 38, all asset classes apart from FX have a correlation of zero.

TABLE 41: INDICATIVE COSTS AND MINIMUM CAPITAL FOR FUTURES TRADERS

	Product	Asset class	Minimum capital $	Minimum capital £	Risk-adjusted trading cost
UK 10-year	Future	Bonds	$65,000	£49,000	0.014
US 5-year	Future	Bonds	$14,500	£10,600	0.069
Eurodollar	Future	STIR	$11,000	£8,100	0.074
Nasdaq	Future	Equities	$216,000	£162,000	0.002
Euro Stoxx	Future	Equities	$34,000	£25,000	0.024
VIX US Vol.	Future	Volatility	$70,000	£52,000	0.042
European Vol.	Future	Volatility	$7,300	£5,400	0.064
EURGBP	Future	FX	$113,000	£85,000	0.006
MXPUSD	Future	FX	$30,000	£23,000	0.013
Crude Oil	Future	Commodities	$109,000	£82,000	0.003
Corn	Future	Commodities	$19,000	£14,000	0.004
Bitcoin	Future	Crypto	$223,000	£168,000	0.007

Minimum capital has been rounded up. Cost calculations using appendix B, and minimum capital calculations using formula 21 (page 103). The cheapest (lowest risk-adjusted cost) and most accessible (lowest minimum capital) instrument are shown for each asset class.

If you are a futures trader who is short of capital then, after examining table 41, you should first add European volatility. Volatility is highly correlated with equities, so for the next instrument I suggest US 5-year bonds. Bonds and short-term interest rate futures (STIR) have a high correlation, so the fourth asset class should be FX. MXPUSD is a good choice. Then I would include a STIR market, and only Eurodollar meets my speed limit. Finally, you should add an equity market; Euro Stoxx has the lowest minimum capital requirement.

Wealthier futures traders can focus on minimising trading costs. The Nasdaq equity future is ultra-cheap and would be the second instrument I would add after corn. Equities and volatility are correlated, so we have to look elsewhere for our third instrument. EURGBP is an ultra-cheap FX instrument that is a worthy addition to the portfolio. A cheap bond future like UK 10-year is next. Bonds and STIR are highly correlated so, for the next instrument, I would suggest an unorthodox choice: Bitcoin (unless, like me, you are violently opposed to trading cryptocurrencies on principal).

There are only two asset classes left, and the correlation of Bonds and STIR (0.4) is lower than the correlation of equities and volatility (0.5). So, I would choose a STIR market next, and only Eurodollar meets the speed limit. Finally, I would add a volatility market – the VIX is the cheapest.

Diversification for margin traders

How can margin traders diversify across different asset classes, when they can only trade shares? Trading in both Facebook and Apple provides precious little diversification, as they are both US technology stocks. However, there is the option of buying exchange traded funds (ETFs), and there are ETFs available for many different asset classes including bonds, currencies, volatility, and commodities.

There is a varied and ever-changing number of ETFs available on the market. For this reason, I haven't included specific examples in this chapter.

Diversification for spot FX traders

Diversification is particularly difficult for spot FX traders, as they can only trade a single asset class: FX.

TABLE 42: INDICATIVE COSTS AND MINIMUM CAPITAL FOR SPOT FX TRADERS

	Product	Asset class	Minimum capital £	Minimum capital $	Risk-adjusted trading cost
AUDUSD	Spot FX	FX	£550	$800	0.045
EURGBP	Spot FX	FX	£800	$1,100	0.048
JPYUSD	Spot FX	FX	£450	$550	0.048
GBPUSD	Spot FX	FX	£450	$600	0.054
EURUSD	Spot FX	FX	£450	$550	0.058

Minimum capital has been rounded up. Cost calculations using appendix B, and minimum capital calculations using formula 21 (page 103). Only instruments with trading cost less than 0.08 are shown.

Assuming you begin with a developed market pairing like AUDUSD, the most diversifying instrument to add would be an emerging market currency, like MXPUSD. However, wide trading spreads mean that these instruments are often too expensive to trade; MXPUSD has a risk-adjusted trading cost of 0.15. This is well above my speed limit of 0.08.

You will have to settle for adding other developed market pairs; a selection is shown in table 42. For obvious reasons EURGBP is highly correlated with GBPUSD and EURUSD. Because of their close economic ties, AUDUSD and JPYUSD are also fairly correlated. Bear these results in mind when choosing your currencies. For example, if you begin with AUDUSD then you should avoid adding JPYUSD next.

If your instruments come from a single asset class, the instrument diversification multiplier (IDM) will be lower. I will explain how you can adjust the IDM appropriately later in the chapter.

Mix and match

There is no reason why you can't trade different instruments with different leveraged products, assuming there are no regulatory barriers. So, for example, a UK-based spot FX trader trading AUDUSD could add a gold spread bet to their account, getting access to commodities.

Further diversification

Once you have one instrument in each asset class then you can continue to diversify *within* asset classes; as long as you have sufficient funds, and don't run into issues with the speed limit of risk-adjusted costs below 0.08. Here are the priorities for further diversification. First of all, for commodities:

- Instruments from a different grouping:
  - The commodities groups are: Agricultural, Metals and Energies
- Next: instruments from different subgroups:
  - Agricultural subgroups: Grains, Softs, Meats
  - Metal subgroups: Precious, Base
  - Energy subgroups: Crude oil and products, Natural Gas
- Finally: instruments within different subgroups:
  - Grains: Wheat, Corn, Soybean (also Meal and Oils), Oats, Rough rice
  - Softs: Cotton, Orange Juice, Cocoa, Lumber, Sugar, Coffee
  - Meats: Live Cattle, Feeder Cattle, Lean Hogs
  - Precious: Gold, Silver, Platinum, Palladium
  - Base metals: Copper
  - Oil and products: WTI Crude, Brent Crude, Gasoline, Ethanol, Heating oil
  - Natural Gas: US Natural Gas (Henry Hub), UK Natural Gas

Now for the other asset classes: FX, equities, volatility, bonds, and STIR; your priorities should be as follows:

- Firstly, add instruments from countries at different stages of economic development:
  - Emerging markets
  - Developed markets
- Next, add instruments from different geographical regions:
  - Emerging markets: Central and South America, EMEA (Europe, Middle East and Africa), Asia
  - Developed markets: North America, Europe, Asia (including Oceania)
- Instruments from different countries

Finally, for individual equities only:

- Equities from different industry sectors

Also, for bonds (or bond indices) only:

- Bonds with different credit ratings
- Bonds with different maturity profiles

Which instruments should you remove if you lose money?

Earlier I noted that if you lose money, you should remove instruments from your trading account. But which instrument should you remove first?

Use this simple method: **remove the last instrument you added** when you were building your initial trading strategy. For traders who started with three or more instruments, if you have already removed one instrument and things continue to go badly, then remove the penultimate instrument you initially added, and so on. This is a 'last in, first out' policy.

What if you become profitable, and your account value reaches the point where an instrument was previously removed? Then you can start adding instruments again, beginning with the last instrument you removed: 'last out, first back in'.

Sharing out capital between markets

If you trade S&P 500 futures, which require capital of $178,000, then there is no benefit in adding US 10-year bond CFDs with capital of $6,000. Around 97% of your returns will still be coming from the S&P 500, with just 3% from US 10-year bonds. This is diversification in name only. You are effectively trading a single instrument.

For maximum diversification **each instrument in your trading account should have exactly the same capital allocation**. This isn't always possible, but you should try and pick instruments to get as close as possible to equally weighted capital. Then, if you have the extra funds, you can get to an equal split by adding just a little more cash to the account.

For the example I've used throughout this chapter, we trade both Euro Stoxx and US 10-year bonds using CFDs. The minimum capital for each is $6,500 and $6,000 respectively. This is a split[102] of 52% and 48%, very close to even. But, if you can manage to add another $500 in your trading account for US 10-year bond trading, then you will have exactly $6,500 in each instrument.

With more than one instrument in each asset class, you should first share out the capital between asset classes, and then split it between the instruments in each asset class.[103]

Calculating the IDM

The *instrument diversification multiplier* (IDM) is the factor we use to calculate the target risk on individual instruments: we multiply the account level risk by the IDM. It exactly compensates for the reduction in account level expected risk which we see

---

[102] Total capital 6,500 + 6,000 = $12,500. Share of Euro Stoxx 6,500 ÷ 12,500 = 52%, share of US 10-year bonds 6,000 ÷ 12,500 = 48%.

[103] There is more detail in my first book, *Systematic Trading*. (If your account value is large enough to be in this position you can probably afford to buy another trading book.)

when we trade several instruments. This ensures we hit our risk target, and it converts higher Sharpe ratios into higher returns.

Calculating the theoretically correct instrument diversification multiplier (IDM) is a relatively complex task,[104] so I've used my back-testing software to do it for you. Table 43 shows the multiplier you should use for different numbers of instruments. The values in the first column assume that you're adding instruments to your portfolio from different asset classes to provide the maximum diversification.[105] The second column shows the IDM to use if you are limited to a single asset class, for example, if you are a spot FX trader who can only trade FX.

TABLE 43: INSTRUMENT DIVERSIFICATION MULTIPLIER (IDM) TO USE FOR A GIVEN NUMBER OF INSTRUMENTS

	IDM (multiple asset classes)	IDM (single asset class)
1 instrument	1.0	1.0
2 instruments	1.20	1.15
3 instruments	1.48	1.22
4 instruments	1.56	1.27
5 instruments	1.70	1.29
6 instruments	1.90	1.31
7 instruments	2.10	1.32
8 to 14 instruments	2.20	1.34
15 to 24 instruments	2.30	1.36
25 to 29 instruments	2.40	1.38
30+ instruments	2.50	1.40

[104] Technical note: Given N trading subsystems with a correlation matrix of returns H and instrument weights W summing to one, the diversification multiplier will be $1 \div [(W \times H \times W^T)^{0.5}]$.

[105] The IDM for two instruments with multiple asset classes (1.2), is a little lower than the value I calculated for the earlier example of Euro Stoxx equity and US 10-year bonds (1.3). My recommended IDM is based on taking an average across many instruments. It is better to use this, rather than a value calculated for just one specific pair of products.

Values calculated from back-tests using 37 futures instruments

Higher values for IDM increase your leverage, so I have put a maximum ceiling on the IDM. It should never be larger than 2.5, regardless of how many instruments you're trading.

The diversification multiplier and risk targeting

Back in chapter five,[106] I calculated the optimal risk target of the Starter System and came up with a figure of 12%. This was determined by the performance of the system. The higher the expected Sharpe ratio (SR) of a trading strategy, the higher the risk target can be.[107] The Starter System has a relatively modest 12% risk target because it has a relatively modest expected pre-cost SR of 0.24.

But with more instruments you can expect to get better performance. Earlier in this chapter, for the example of two instruments, the expected pre-cost return was increased from 4.88% to 5.74%. In general, the expected Sharpe ratio increases proportionally with the instrument diversification multiplier (IDM). I can prove this by taking formula 3 (page 61), for the pre-cost SR of the Starter System:

$$SR^{old} = (r - b) \div s^{old}$$

Where **r** is the expected average return, **b** is the rate we can borrow at and s^{old} is the original risk target. If we diversify our system and do not apply an IDM, then the standard deviation will reduce proportionally with the IDM, whilst the expected returns remain unchanged:[108]

$$SR^{new} = (r - b) \div (s^{old} \div IDM) = SR^{old} \times IDM$$

Applying leverage doesn't affect the calculation of a Sharpe ratio. As the IDM is always greater than 1, applying the IDM will increase the Sharpe ratio, regardless of which risk target we decide to use.

For example, the Starter System with a single instrument has **r** = 4.9%, with a standard deviation s^{old} = 12%, and I assume a borrowing rate **b** = 2%.

$$SR^{old} = (r - b) \div s^{old} = (4.9\% - 2\%) \div 12\% = 0.24$$

---

[106] Page 99.

[107] As long as it is no higher than the risk target implied by broker leverage limits, prudent leverage limits, or your own personal tolerance for risk.

[108] This calculation also assumes that all instruments have the same costs. As you will see I am quite conservative with my Sharpe ratio expectations, partly to account for any higher costs when additional instruments are added.

With two instruments from different asset classes, the IDM from table 43 is 1.2:

$$SR^{new} = 0.24 \times 1.2 = 0.288$$

Table 44 shows how to use the IDM to calculate a new risk target if you are trading multiple asset classes.

TABLE 44: INSTRUMENT DIVERSIFICATION MULTIPLIER (IDM), THEORETICAL SHARPE RATIO (SR), THEORETICAL AND RECOMMENDED ACCOUNT LEVEL RISK TARGETS FOR MULTIPLE ASSET CLASSES

Number of instruments	IDM (A)	Theoretical SR (B) SR = 0.24 × A	Theoretical risk target (C = B × 0.5) DO NOT USE	Recommended risk target (account level) (D)	Recommended instrument level risk target E = A × D
1	1.00	0.240	12.0%	12%	12.0%
2	1.20	0.288	14.4%	13%	15.6%
3	1.48	0.355	17.8%	14%	20.7%
4	1.56	0.374	18.7%	17%	26.5%
5	1.70	0.408	20.4%	19%	32.3%
6	1.90	0.456	22.8%	20%	38.0%
7	2.10	0.504	25.2%	23%	48.3%
8 to 14	2.2	0.528	26.4%	24%	52.8%
15 to 24	2.3	0.552	27.6%	25%	57.5%
25 to 29	2.4	0.576	28.8%	25%	60.0%
30+	2.5	0.600	30.0%	25%	62.5%

IDM values from table 43 (first column, multiple asset classes). Recommended risk targets (D) are more conservative than the theoretical targets (C), as in back-tests the Sharpe ratio from higher diversification is lower than expected.

The column A of table 44 is just a copy of the IDM values in the first column of table 43. Multiplying these IDM by the Sharpe ratio for the Starter System (0.24) gives a theoretical SR, which can be found in column B. From this, I can work out the theoretical risk target (column C), assuming I use the 'half Kelly criterion rule' that the risk target should be half the expected Sharpe ratio.

In column D I've put the risk target that I'd actually recommend running your trading system at. These recommended risk targets don't quite rise as fast as the theoretical values, because I find in my back-tests that actual improvements in performance tend to lag the increase that the IDM hopes you will get.

No matter how many instruments there are in your portfolio, you shouldn't use a risk target of higher than 25%. This is the target I use myself – and I have nearly 40 instruments in my portfolio! I've also assumed here that the other determinants of risk target aren't a constraint: broker leverage limits, prudent leverage limits, and your personal risk appetite. You should revisit the section starting on page 94 to check this for yourself.

Don't forget, changing the risk target for your entire trading account will also affect the risk target you have for each instrument. You should multiply the account level risk target by the IDM to get the instrument level risk target. The recommended values for instrument level risk targets are shown in column E of table 43.

For the two instruments I've used as examples in this chapter, which are from different asset classes, the IDM from table 43 will be 1.2 (a little more conservative than the value we worked out earlier), and the recommended account level risk target from table 44 is 13%. That means the instrument level risk target will be 1.2 × 13% = 15.6%.

Table 45 calculates the recommended account level, and instrument level, risk target when your instruments come from a single asset class. There is less diversification, so the IDM and expected Sharpe ratios are lower.

TABLE 45: INSTRUMENT DIVERSIFICATION MULTIPLIER (IDM), THEORETICAL SHARPE RATIO (SR), THEORETICAL AND RECOMMENDED ACCOUNT LEVEL RISK TARGETS FOR A SINGLE ASSET CLASS

Number of instruments	IDM (A)	Theoretical SR (B) SR = 0.24 × A	Theoretical risk target (C = B × 0.5) DO NOT USE	Recommended account level risk target (D)	Recommended instrument level risk target A × D
1	1.00	0.240	12.0%	12.0%	12.0%
2	1.15	0.276	13.8%	12.5%	14.5%
3	1.22	0.293	14.6%	13.0%	15.9%
4	1.27	0.305	15.2%	13.5%	17.1%
5	1.29	0.310	15.5%	14.0%	18.1%
6	1.31	0.314	15.7%	14.0%	18.3%
7	1.32	0.317	15.8%	14.5%	19.1%
8 to 14	1.34	0.322	16.1%	14.5%	19.4%
15 to 24	1.36	0.326	16.3%	15.0%	20.4%
25 to 29	1.38	0.331	16.6%	15.0%	20.7%
30+	1.40	0.336	16.8%	15.0%	21.0%

IDM values from table 43 (second column, single asset class). Recommended risk targets (D) are more conservative than the theoretical targets (C), as in back-tests the Sharpe ratio from higher diversification is lower than expected.

The diversification multiplier and minimum capital requirements

To recap: if you have a diversified set of instruments then you will: (a) be running at a higher overall risk target for your account due to improved performance expectations, and (b) applying a diversification multiplier to the risk targets on each individual instrument. Together these imply that the risk targets on each instrument will be higher than the 12% we used in the Starter System. One useful side effect of this is to reduce the minimum capital required to trade each instrument: the higher your risk target, the lower the capital that is required.

To calculate minimum capital we use formula 21 (page 103):

Minimum capital = (Minimum exposure × instrument risk %) ÷ target risk %

To adjust minimum capital for a different risk target we multiply by the ratio of the original and the new instrument level risk target:

FORMULA 27: ADJUST MINIMUM CAPITAL FOR DIFFERENT RISK TARGET

New minimum capital = Minimum capital × (original target risk ÷ new target risk %)

For the two instruments I've used as an example in this chapter (Euro Stoxx and US 10-year bonds, both traded via CFDs), the correct risk target for each instrument is 15.6% (from table 44, as they are in different asset classes). The minimum account sizes are $6,500 (Euro Stoxx) and $6,000 (10-year bonds). To adjust for higher risk targets, I multiply the minima by the ratio of the original and new risk target. For Euro Stoxx:

New minimum capital = 6,500 × (12% ÷ 15.6%) = $5,000

For US 10-year bonds:

New minimum capital = 6,000 × (12% ÷ 15.6%) = $4,165

Remember, if you start with multiple instruments, you don't need to apply the rule of using twice the minimum capital. To start trading these two markets you need just $5,000 + $4,165 = $9,165. This is less than the $13,000 required to trade Euro Stoxx in the Starter System for a single instrument![109]

---

[109] Of course, ideally you should put $5,000 in each so they've got the same capital allocation.

Trading the Starter System adapted for multiple instruments

Before you start trading

There is a bit more work to do before you begin trading with multiple instruments.

Choose your first instrument	Use the guidance in chapter five. Remember that you don't need to multiply the minimum capital by two.
Add other instruments to your portfolio	Pick instruments which will add diversification, with low costs and affordable minimum capital requirements. Remember that you don't need to multiply the minimum capital by two.
Calculate the new account level risk target	From table 44 or 45.
Get the instrument diversification multiplier (IDM)	From table 43.
Work out the risk target for each instrument	Multiply the new account level risk target by the IDM or use the values from table 44 or 45.
Recalculate minimum capital allocations	Multiply the minimum capital by the ratio (original risk target of 12% ÷ new risk target for instrument).
Decide on risk allocation for each instrument	Ensuring that the new minimum capital requirements are met, try and get as close as possible to allocating your risk capital equally.

Running the system

Here are the changes required to the Starter System's trade plan for multiple instruments:

Instrument	Trade multiple instruments each allocated their own capital.
Position sizing rule	**Notional exposure = (instrument level target risk % × capital) ÷ instrument risk %** Use instrument level target risk to scale positions. Instrument level target risk equals account level risk target multiplied by instrument diversification multiplier (table 43). Use an account level risk target adjusted for diversification (tables 44 and 45).

Once you've done the initial setup, then running the Starter System for multiple instruments is just like running many individual systems, each with its own capital allocation and its own instrument level risk target (which is equal to the account level risk multiplied by the IDM).

Monitor minimum account size: removing and adding instruments

Trading with multiple instruments does involve one additional task: making sure that you can still meet the minimum instrument capital requirements for your current account size. If you cannot, then you need to remove instruments, starting with the last instrument you added in the setup stage, then the penultimate instrument you added, and so on (remember: 'last in, first out').

If you subsequently make your money back, then you can start adding back the instruments you've removed, starting with the most recently removed ('last out, first back in'). If you're lucky and get a rise in your account value above what you began with, then you can add additional instruments into your trading account, using the same logic that you used in the system design phase.

Let's look at an example. Suppose you are trading Euro Stoxx and decide to add US 10-year bonds as your second instrument. You begin with $12,000 in capital. A couple of pages ago I calculated that the minimum capital required to trade these two instruments was $9,165 ($5,000 + $4,165). If you start with $12,000 you could split that 50/50 and put $6,000 in each instrument.

Unfortunately, you now start to lose money. Initially you should reduce your capital equally in each instrument, until there is $5,000 in each. After further losses, since you have to leave the absolute minimum $5,000 in Euro Stoxx, you start reducing your allocation to US 10-year bonds, which have a lower minimum capital ($4,165). Then, once your total capital is under $9,165, you will have to drop US 10-year bonds entirely, since they were the last instrument you added ('last in first out') and their capital allocation would otherwise be under the minimum level of $4,165.

With a single instrument (Euro Stoxx), your account level and instrument level risk target will be back to the 12% used in the Starter System. The minimum capital required for Euro Stoxx is now the original $6,500 from chapter five. You do not apply the rule of requiring double the minimum capital, since that only applies when you *start* trading with a single instrument.

If your losses reach the point where you have less than $6,500, you will have to stop trading entirely or find a new instrument with an even lower minimum capital requirement. Naturally, once you get more than $9,165 in capital,[110] you can start trading US 10-year bonds again, assuming that the opening rule confirms you should do so.

This process is summarised in table 46.

TABLE 46: EXAMPLE OF A TRADING PLAN TO ADD OR REMOVE INSTRUMENTS AS PROFITS OR LOSSES ARE MADE

Capital range	Action
Greater than $10,000	Allocate capital 50% to Euro Stoxx and US 10-year bonds
$9,165 to $10,000	Allocate $5,000 to Euro Stoxx, remainder to US 10-year bonds
$6,500 to $9,165	Allocate 100% of capital to Euro Stoxx
Less than $6,500	Stop trading, or choose an instrument with a lower minimum capital

Plan assumes we are trading two CFDs. First CFD chosen: Euro Stoxx, with minimum capital of $5,000 when trading two instruments, or $6,500 when trading one instrument. Second CFD chosen: US 10-year bonds, with minimum capital of $4,165 when trading two instruments.

When removing instruments, **do not close existing trades**. Wait until a position has been closed naturally by hitting a stop loss before taking it out of your portfolio. Otherwise, if your account balance moves around near the $9,165 threshold, you will end up incurring additional trading costs from constantly closing and reopening trades.

Until you close your position, you will be temporarily taking on too much risk. To alleviate this, you should avoid opening new positions in other instruments if that means you are trading more markets than you'd ideally want to.

---

[110] These figures all assume that the minimum capital required will remain the same, but in practice this needs recalculating as instrument risk changes.

For example, suppose we were trading Euro Stoxx and US 10-year bond CFDs and our capital has just dropped below $9,165. We want to stop trading US 10-year bonds. What happens next depends on our current positioning:

- **No position in anything**: Don't open a new position in US 10-year bonds. When the opening rule dictates it, open a new position in Euro Stoxx.

- **Position in Euro Stoxx, not in US 10-year bonds**: Don't open a new position in US 10-year bonds: from now on only trade Euro Stoxx.

- **Position in US 10-year bonds, nothing in Euro Stoxx**: Wait until you have closed your US 10-year bond trade – do not open up a position in Euro Stoxx. When your US 10-year position is closed, stop trading US 10-year bonds and open up a new Euro Stoxx position when your opening rule dictates it.

- **Position in both US 10-year bonds and Euro Stoxx**: Wait until one of the positions is closed by a stop loss, then see the relevant procedure for a single position in one instrument.

Eventually you will only be trading Euro Stoxx.

CHAPTER EIGHT
Adding New Trading Rules

WHEN ASKED TO DESCRIBE MY last proper job working for a large systematic hedge fund, I'd usually waffle, saying something like, "Looking for patterns in data to predict the movements in financial markets." (That was before the 2008 financial crisis. After the crisis had struck, once hedge fund managers and bankers had become public enemies number one and two, I used to mumble that I did, "Something with computers", and then hurry away before I was unmasked as a capitalist scumbag.)

"Looking for patterns in data..." suggests that I spent my office hours carefully searching for one, amazing, new trading rule. Surely this is the path to riches, requiring great expertise and skill? Isn't this what every trader should be doing – combing through charts, trying to find the undiscovered opening rule which will earn massive profits?

Such a rule would no doubt have to very complicated, such as this horrendous example which was 'generously' shared by the author in an online trading forum:

> "S&P Overnight – If Top 3 30-Minute Candles the Same Colour Trades Inverse 3rd Tallest Volume Candle Colour – If Flat Subsequent (S&P & Nasdaq Rotate Between Excluding Open & Close & Including Open & Close Including 16:00 Candle) Overnight Sunday Trades 3rd Highest 30-Minute Candle Volume Including Opening & Close Including 16:00 Candle from 18:00–00:30 & 00:30–9:30 Trades 3rd Highest Volume Excluding Opening & Close but Including 16:00 Candle (Overnight Thanksgiving from Trades 3rd Highest Open Excluding Opening & Close from 16:00–3:00 am & Trades 3rd Highest Volume Including Opening & Close but Including 16:00 Candle from 3:00–9:30)" ... and so it continues for another 620 words.

> Trading rule posted on elitetrader.com

Traders love such complexity as it validates the time and effort they spend searching for patterns and increases the chance that they have found something unique. They think it gives them an edge. It does not.

Such insanely complicated rules are almost guaranteed to fail. They are more likely to be *over-fitted*; remember this means they are closely adapted to historical market movements, making them less robust if the future isn't exactly like the past. They are very unlikely to meet the key characteristics I look for in a trading rule, which I outlined in chapter five: **objective**, **simple**, **explicable**, and **intuitive**.

It is better to stick with simple intuitive rules, and to use several of these rules rather than a single, insanely complicated, rule. This chapter will explain how to use **multiple trading rules** to decide when to open positions, in addition to the single 16,64 moving average crossover rule used in the Starter System.

The case for diversification of trading rules

Why are multiple rules better than one

As with instrument choice there is no strong evidence that any particular trading rule is better than another. Figure 20 illustrates this. The six boxes on the left-hand side show the Sharpe ratio of the moving average cross over rule (MAC) introduced in chapter five for different crossover lengths, whilst the other seven boxes are for new rules which I will discuss later in this chapter. Remember the overlapping boxes and whiskers mean that we can't be confident that one rule is significantly better than another.

FIGURE 20: COMPARISON OF SHARPE RATIOS FOR VARIOUS TRADING RULES

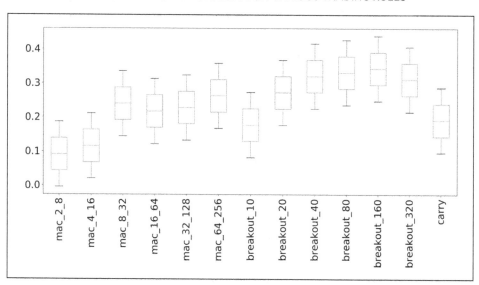

If additional rules don't provide higher returns, then why would we bother?

In fact, the logic for adding multiple trading rules is the same as for trading multiple instruments: they provide **diversification**. The Starter System's moving average crossover (MAC) 16,64 rule won't always work. Sometimes markets will show clear trends lasting several weeks that the MAC 16,64 rule is looking for, but most of the time they won't, and then other rules will come into play.

What is the value of adding new trading rules?

In chapter seven I showed you could significantly improve the Starter System by taking one simple trading rule and applying it to many different instruments. This is a purely mechanistic task which doesn't require much skill or intelligence. You would expect there to be much more value in the more creative and difficult task of finding new trading rules.

As figure 21 shows, there are indeed some benefits from adding trading rules. The first box on the left-hand side of this new figure 21 assumes we are trading the Starter System: a single instrument, with one trading rule. This has a Sharpe ratio (SR) of 0.24. Now suppose we pick a randomly selected trading rule[111] to add to the Starter System opening rule, and trade with both rules. Doing this improves our SR to 0.27. Adding a third rule improves it further,[112] and so it continues. It's clear that adding trading rules improves the expected performance of a trading system.

---

[111] This test was done using the trading rules in my own system, which comprise the 13 rules discussed in this book, plus some additional rules which I discuss on my blog: qoppac.blogspot.com.
[112] For reasons of space I can't show the improvement if you started with the Starter System and two (or three, or four...) instruments and then added further rules (without adding additional instruments), as these will be a little different depending on exactly which instruments you started with. But the overall pattern in expected improvement will be the same, regardless of how many instruments you're trading when you start to add rules.

FIGURE 21: SHARPE RATIO AS TRADING RULES ARE INCREMENTALLY ADDED

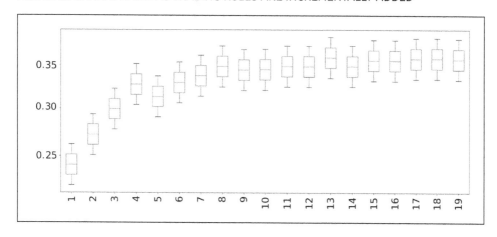

But let us look more closely and contrast the improvements in figure 21 with those in figure 19 (from chapter seven, which showed the effect of adding more instruments). In table 47, I compare the increases in average Sharpe ratios for the two figures.

TABLE 47: RELATIVE IMPROVEMENTS IN SHARPE RATIOS ARE HIGHER WHEN ADDING INSTRUMENTS THAN WHEN ADDING TRADING RULES

	Sharpe ratio [A]		**Sharpe ratio [B]**
One instrument	0.24	One trading rule	0.24
Two instruments	0.30	Two rules	0.27
Five instruments	0.35	Five rules	0.32
Ten instruments	0.45	Ten rules	0.34
19 instruments	0.55	19 rules	0.36

Column A Sharpe ratios from figure 19, and column B from figure 21.

There is clearly more diversification from adding just a few instruments compared to the same number of rules. Going from one to two instruments improves the SR to 0.30, whilst moving from one to two trading rules results in a more modest rise in SR, to 0.27. The relative improvement from adding rules also tails off more quickly than the benefits from adding instruments. With 19 instruments we have a SR of 0.55, more than twice the performance of a single rule. But with 19 trading rules the Sharpe ratio is just 0.36.

So, **adding instruments is better than adding opening rules**.

However, adding rules doesn't require more money, whilst adding multiple instruments to the Starter System usually bumps up your minimum capital requirement. My advice is: **first add as many instruments as you can afford to, given the capital you have available, and then consider adding trading rules**.

My suite of trading rules

There are thousands of ideas for trading rules out there in books, and on the internet. But it's difficult to sort the usable wheat from the vast quantity of chaff. To get you started I've included some more trading rules in this section. Like the moving average crossover, these are trading rules I use myself.

Although I won't show you the data (to avoid making this book even longer), I've already checked that there is no evidence that any of these rules should be used on one instrument rather than on another.[113] At this stage I won't be offering any advice as to *which* rules you should include in your system. That will come later in the chapter.

More moving average crossovers

In chapter five I introduced the general form of the moving average crossover rule, and then explained why I chose one specific variation for the Starter System: the 16-day moving average minus 64-day moving average. Depending on which instruments you are trading, some of the faster variations might be too expensive to trade (2 & 8 days, 4 & 16 days, 8 & 32 days). I also said that the slower moving average pairs probably trade too infrequently (32 & 128 days, and 64 & 256 days).

However, it still makes a lot of sense to combine *several* moving average crossovers. By adding both faster and slower variations you can keep your expected number of annual trades – and also costs – at about the same level, whilst benefiting from the diversifying power of multiple rules. I'll discuss how this is done later in the chapter.

Breakout

Consider the chart in figure 22, which shows crude oil from 2010 to 2016.

---

[113] At least for pre-cost returns. As I'll discuss later in the chapter some rules trade too quickly to make them viable for certain instruments.

FIGURE 22: CRUDE OIL (2010–2016)

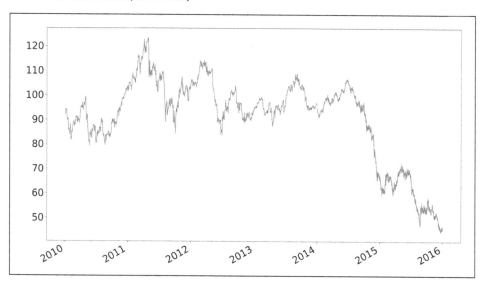

Until late 2014 crude seemed to stay within a tight *range*, between $80 and $120. I started trading crude, amongst other instruments, with my own money in April 2014. Great timing because the price *broke out* of its range and then collapsed. My short position in crude was nicely profitable.

This idea of a *breakout from a range* is a classic trading strategy. There are numerous ways to define a range, and to determine when a price has broken out of a range. I use the following definition, where P_t is the price at time **t**:

FORMULA 28: BREAKOUT CALCULATIONS

Rolling maximum over last N days, $R^{MAX}_N = Max(P_t, P_{t-1}, P_{t-2}, ... P_{t-N+1})$

Rolling minimum over last N days $R^{MIN}_N = Min(P_t, P_{t-1}, P_{t-2}, ... P_{t-N+1})$

Rolling average over last N days $R^{AVG}_N = (R^{MAX}_N + R^{MIN}_N) \div 2$

Scaled price in range $= (P_t - R^{AVG}_N) \div (R^{MAX}_N - R^{MIN}_N)$

The *scaled price* will vary between +0.5 (if the current price is at the top of its range) and −0.5 (if the price is at the bottom of the range). Because I like to catch breakouts early, I will open trades if the scaled price is greater than zero (i.e., the price is greater than the average, which would be a long), or lower than zero (the price is lower than average: a short).

This makes the rule work a little differently from breakout trading strategies you might have seen elsewhere. In particular there is nothing special about the price reaching the edge of its previous range. Arguably 'breakout' is the wrong name for this rule, but I couldn't think of a better one.

The breakout rule has a single parameter, *N*. If *N* is small then we look at the price range just for the last few days. We will identify lots of breakouts, but the large number of resulting trades could be expensive. Conversely if *N* is large the rule will look further back into the history of the price, and there will be fewer trades. We'll have fewer opportunities, but it will be cheaper to trade.

FIGURE 23: CRUDE OIL WITH ROLLING MINIMUM, MAXIMUM AND AVERAGE VALUES

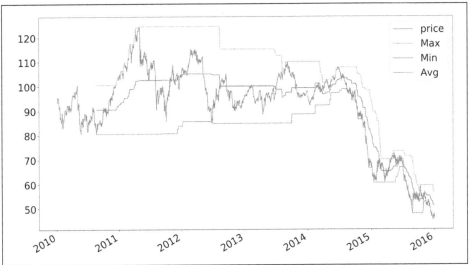

I've added the rolling minimum, maximum and average values to the price of crude oil in figure 23, using N=320 (since the N in my trading software is measured in business days, this is about 15 months).[114] The wiggly line is the original price, and the two ranges are in grey; halfway between them is the average. Remember the rule will go short if the price is below the average line and go long when it is above the line.

The price is mostly near the bottom of the range from mid-2014 to the end of the year: a clear signal to go short. Here is my calculation for the breakout signal on 13 August 2014:

Rolling maximum R^{MAX}_{320} = 107.78

Rolling minimum R^{MIN}_{320} = 98.76

Rolling average R^{AVG}_{320} = (R^{MAX}_{320} + R^{MIN}_{320}) ÷ 2 = (107.78 – 98.76) ÷ 2 = 103.3

Scaled price in range = (P_t – R^{AVG}_N) ÷ (R^{MAX}_N – R^{MIN}_N)

= (100.3 – 103.3) ÷ (107.78 – 98.76) = –0.33 [Short Position]

As we saw in chapter five, when considering the choice of moving average lengths, selecting the right N involves considering both expected pre-cost returns, and costs. Figure 20 at the start of this chapter showed there is no evidence that any single value of N is significantly better than another on a pre-cost basis. That leaves us with just costs to consider. Table 48 has all the relevant numbers.

---

[114] My back-testing results confirm that N=10 (about two weeks) is about as fast as we can successfully trade the breakout. I also found that repeatedly doubling the value of N gives a set of breakouts that aren't too similar. Beyond N=320 the rule starts to trade too slowly; its profitability falls and it becomes too much like a constant long position in many instruments.

TABLE 48: INDICATIVE TRADING COSTS FOR DIFFERENT LENGTH BREAKOUTS, IN RISK-ADJUSTED UNITS

			Trading costs			
	Average Trades per year	1/3 of Pre-cost Sharpe ratio	Corn Future	Euro Stoxx CFD on future	Gold Quarterly spread-bet	S&P 500 Margin trade	AUDUSD spot fx
Breakout 10	43.9	0.059	0.023	0.153*	0.110*	0.113*	0.072*
Breakout 20	30.5	0.091	0.017	0.114*	0.081	0.081	0.063
Breakout 40	21.4	0.107	0.012	0.087	0.062	0.059	0.056
Breakout 80	14.8	0.110	0.009	0.067	0.048	0.043	0.052
Breakout 160	10.3	0.114	0.006	0.054	0.039	0.032	0.049
Breakout 320	7.3	0.103	0.005	0.045	0.032	0.025	0.047

* An instrument / rule combination is too expensive to trade: the cost is higher than the speed limit of one-third of pre-cost Sharpe ratio shown in the second column.

Total cost is $H + (TC \times T)$ where T is the number of trades per year (first column), TC transaction cost per trade, and H annual holding cost. All costs are calculated in appendix B.

I'll explain exactly which value(s) of N you should use later in the chapter. Spreadsheets which help you to implement this, and all the rules in this book, are available from the book's website: systematicmoney.org/leveraged-trading.

Carry

The moving average crossover and breakout rules work best when prices trend strongly in one direction or another. *Carry* is a trading rule which makes a profit when nothing happens. Carry is defined as **the return that you expect if asset prices remain stable**. We have already learned about carry in chapter one. You may want to re-read that section before continuing.

For physical products like margin trades and spot FX the carry is equal to any interest or dividends we receive, less financing and borrowing costs. For derivatives like futures, CFDs and spread bets, the carry is received through the price of the derivative changing even when the spot price remains fixed.

For the carry rule we define the carry return as the **expected annualised percentage return on a long position if the underlying price remains unchanged**. The underlying price is the actual price for physical products, and for derivatives the price of the product they are based on. If we expect **a positive carry return then we would go long** (to capture the positive carry). If the **carry return is negative then we would go short** (which should be profitable if carry is negative for a long position).

The exact calculation of carry is different depending on which leveraged product you are trading.

Equities bought with margin

The trading rule expects the carry return to be identical in magnitude for both long and short positions. This is fine for derivatives, but for physical products it will not be the case because of the financing spread we learned about in chapter one. To get around this we calculate carry for physical products by taking an average of (i) the carry for long positions, and (ii) the carry for short positions with a minus sign. Hence, the carry calculation excludes the funding spread, as this is already accounted for in our holding cost calculations.

Dividend yield, %	The expected dividend yield per year during the holding period, or for simplicity the historic dividend divided by current price.
Net return when long	To calculate this you need the dividend yield (**D**) and the funding charge on a long position (**F$_{long}$**). The net return equals: $$(D - F_{long})$$
Net return when short	You need the dividend yield (**D**), the cost of borrowing stock (**B**), and the interest you receive on cash when you've sold short (**i**). The net return equals: $$(i - B - D)$$
Expected annualised return, %	Average of net return when long (**r$_L$**) and the negative of net return when short (**r$_s$**): $$(r_L - r_s) \div 2$$

EXAMPLE: S&P 500 SPY ETF, BOUGHT WITH MARGIN

Dividend yield, %	Dividend yield for this ETF is currently: **D** = 1.77%.
Net return when long	I pay **F$_{long}$** = 3.7% a year to borrow when buying stocks. Net return: $$(D - F_{long}) = 1.77\% - 3.7\% = -1.93\%$$
Net return when short	I pay **B** = 0.25% as a borrowing charge when shorting. Sadly, I receive no interest on credit positions (**i** = 0%). Net return: $$(i - B - D) = (0\% - 0.25\% - 1.77\%) = -2.02\%$$
Expected annualised return, %	Average of net return when long (**r$_L$**) and the negative of net return when short (**r$_s$**): $$(r_L - r_s) \div 2 = (-1.93\% - [-2.02\%]) \div 2 = 0.045\%$$

We would go **long S&P 500** because the carry return is (just) positive.

Equities: undated contracts for difference (CFDs) or spread bets

Dividend yield, %	The expected dividend yield per year during the holding period, or for simplicity just the historic dividend divided by current price.
Funding cost, %	The average of the interest rate you pay to fund a long position, and what you receive on short positions.
Expected annualised return, %	Dividend yield minus funding cost.

Spot FX

Deposit interest, %	The interest you expect to receive in a particular currency, excluding any lending margin spread. You can calculate this by taking an average of the rates you pay to borrow and earn on deposit for a given currency.
Funding cost, %	The rate you pay to borrow a currency, excluding any lending margin spread. You can calculate this by taking an average of the rates you pay to borrow and earn on deposit for a given currency.
Expected annualised return, %	Deposit interest minus funding cost.

Here is an example, for AUDUSD. With a long position in AUDUSD we make money if the USD depreciates and AUD gets stronger. Therefore, we are effectively borrowing in USD, to deposit in AUD.

Deposit interest, %	I pay 2% to borrow AUD and earn 1.05% as a deposit rate for AUD. The average of these is 1.53%.
Funding cost, %	I pay 2.75% to borrow USD and earn 2.25% as a deposit rate. The average of these is 2.5%.
Expected annualised return, %	Deposit interest minus funding cost: 1.53% – 2.5% = **–0.98%**

This is negative, so we'd have a **short position in AUDUSD**.

Derivatives: Futures, and CFD or spread bet based on futures

To calculate the carry for derivatives we compare the price of the derivative with the price of something else that we expect the derivative price to converge on. There are three different methods, depending on what other prices are available.

Method one: Relative to nearer contract price

To calculate the carry for a future, or another derivative product based on a future, we compare the price of the contract we are trading with a nearer contract:

Current contract price	The price of the contract you are trading.
Nearer contract price	The price of the next closest contract. So, if you are trading June 2020 Eurodollar it would be March 2020.
Price differential	Nearer contract price minus current contract price.
Distance between contracts	The time in years between the two contracts (current and nearer). For adjacent quarterly expiries it is 0.25 and for monthly 0.083.
Net expected return in price units	We need to annualise the price differential by dividing by the distance between contracts.
Expected annualised return, %	Net expected return in price units, divided by current contract price.

Sharper eyed readers may realise that we know whether to go long or short by step three of these calculations (spot level minus spread bet level). Nevertheless, it's important to know how to work out the expected annualised return, since we'll need to use that in part four of this book.

EXAMPLE: CORN FUTURE

Current contract price	When I was demonstrating the Starter System (in chapter six), I decided to trade December 2018 corn. The price of December 2018 corn: $379.
Nearer contract price	The price of the next closest contract: September 2018: $372.
Price differential	Nearer contract price minus current contract price: **$372 – $379 = –$7**
Distance between contracts	The time in years between the two contracts (current and nearer). For adjacent quarterly expiries it is 0.25.
Net expected return in price units	We annualise the price differential by dividing by the distance between contracts: **–$7 ÷ 0.25 = –$28**
Expected annualised return, %	Net expected return in price units, divided by current contract price: **–$28 ÷ $379 = –7.4%**

Negative carry return, so we go **short corn**.

To calculate carry using method one we need to ensure that we aren't holding the nearest contract, since this method only works if there is a nearer contract relative to the contract we are trading. This is why back in chapter six I rolled corn from December 2018 to December 2019, in late September before the September 2018 contract expired.

Method two: Relative to spot price

If you can only trade the nearest contract you obviously can't use method one. If a spot price is available for your instrument, then you can compare the dated price to the spot price.

Current contract price	The price of the contract you are trading.
Spot level	The level of the spot price of the relevant instrument at the same time.
Net expected return over bet period	Spot level minus current contract price.
Time to maturity	Time to expiry, in years. So, a quarterly 3-month bet would be 0.25.
Net expected annual return in price units	Net expected return over bet period divided by time to maturity.
Expected annualised return, %	Net expected annual return in price units, divided by current contract price level.

EXAMPLE: DATED GOLD SPREAD BET BASED ON FUTURE

Spread bet level	**$1,268**
Spot level	**$1,262**
Net expected return over bet period	Spot level minus Spread bet level: **$1,262 – $1,268 = –$6**
Time to maturity	Time to expiry of the bet, in years. When I put this bet on there were two weeks remaining before the expiry. On average there are 365.25 days in a year: **14 ÷ 365.25 = 0.03833**
Net expected annual return in price units	Net expected return over bet period divided by time to maturity: **–$6 ÷ 0.03833 = –$156.54**
Expected annualised return, %	Net expected annual return in price units, divided by spread bet level: **–$156.54 ÷ $1262 = –12.4%**

Carry return is negative so we'd go **short gold.**

Method three: Relative to spot price

Sometimes no spot price is available. In that case you can use the following method, which assumes you can get the same amount of carry on the first two available contracts:

Current contract price	The price of the contract you are trading.
Next contract price	The price of the contract with the next expiry. So if you had June 2020 US Treasury bonds it would be September 2020.
Price differential	Current contract price minus next contract price.
Distance between contracts	The time in years between the two contracts (current and next). For adjacent quarterly expiries it would be 0.25, for monthly 0.083 and so on.
Net expected return in price units	We need to annualise the price differential by dividing by the distance between contracts.
Expected annualised return, %	Net expected return in price units, divided by current contract price.

EXAMPLE: EURO STOXX 50 BASED ON FUTURE[115]

We are trading the nearest Euro Stoxx (September 2018). The next contract was December 2018.

Current contract price	The price of September 2018: $3,391.
Next contract price	The price of December 2018: $3,373.
Price differential	Current contract price minus next contract price: **$3,391 – $3,373 = $18**
Distance between contracts	The time in years between the two contracts (current and next). For adjacent quarterly expiries it would be 0.25.

---

[115] We could use the spot price here, but this example is included for completeness as there are many futures with no spot price, such as government bonds.

Net expected return in price units	We need to annualise the price differential by dividing by the distance between contracts: **$18 ÷ 0.25 = $72**
Expected annualised return, %	Net expected return in price units, divided by current contract price: **$72 ÷ $3391 = 2.1%**

We'd go **long Euro Stoxx** when using the carry rule.

Trading costs

The trading costs of the carry rule are similar to those of the 16,64 moving average crossover used in the Starter System. As table 49 shows, that means we can trade it with all the instruments I used in chapter six.

TABLE 49: ESTIMATED RISK-ADJUSTED TRADING COSTS FOR CARRY STRATEGY

			Trading costs				
	Average trades per year	1/3 of pre-cost Sharpe ratio	Corn future	Euro Stoxx CFD on future	Gold quarterly spread bet	AUDUSD spot FX	S&P 500 margin trade
Carry	5.4	0.080	0.004	0.04	0.028	0.054	0.021

Values shown in body of table are total cost calculated as H + (TC × T) where T is the number of trades per year (first column), TC is the transaction cost per trade and H is the annual holding costs; all costs are risk-adjusted. T has been estimated as an average over back-tests for all the instruments in my own data set. Costs calculated using the formulas in appendix B.

How do we use multiple trading rules?

There can only be one opening rule...

How can we use multiple opening rules in the Starter System? For example, suppose that we are trading gold using three rules: the moving average 16,64 rule from the Starter System, the carry rule I introduced in this chapter, plus one of the new breakout rules.

If all three rules think we should go long, then it's a slam dunk: we should buy the market. But what if two rules think we should go short, and the other rule wants to go long? With more rules the number of permutations gets increasingly mind boggling.

There are a few possible solutions here, but only one which I recommend:

Trade separately **AVOID THIS**	One of the most famous trading systems was used by the Turtle Traders[116] in the 1980s. In that system there were two methods for deciding opening positions, and traders were encouraged to trade using both criteria. Effectively that means putting on two sets of trades; more if you have three or more trading rules.
	The downside of this approach is that it requires more capital, and if you have spare cash you are better off using it to trade more instruments. It's also a lot of work.
Weird interactions **AVOID THIS**	Consider the absurdly complex S&P 500 trading rule I quoted at the start of this chapter. With some thought we could come up with something almost as complicated. How about this: if carry is long and the breakout rule is short, but moving average crossover is long, then go short. If carry is short, and the breakout rule is long, but moving average is long, then go long. And so on.
	I'm not a fan of weird rules like this. When I've tested them in the past they have not added significant value to my back-tests, as they tend to be *over-fitted*. There are too many complex permutations to evaluate once you have more than two or three rules. They're also hard to implement in a spreadsheet.
Unanimous voting **AVOID THIS**	This is the same system used by juries in most criminal trials: all rules have to agree on the same trade before we open a new position.
	The problem here is that with large numbers of rules you will be waiting for ages for them all to align. You'd spend most of your life twiddling your thumbs and waiting to trade.

---

[116] The "Turtle Traders" were a group of trading novices who were taught how to use a simple trading system and given capital to trade it. Many then went on to become professional traders. See *The Complete Turtle Trader* by Michael Covel.

Majority voting NOT RECOMMENDED	Effectively we create an electorate out of our trading rules and take the majority opinion. For three rules that would be two out of three. Majority opinion isn't a bad way to trade, but there are times when I want to give some rules a bigger say than others. For example, it makes sense to give the carry rule more weight than moving average crossover and breakout rules. The latter two rules are similar, as both are looking for trends, whereas carry is a bit different and deserves a bigger vote. Hence, I prefer using a *weighted average*.
Weighted average RECOMMENDED	A weighted average is similar to majority voting, but we have the option of giving some rules a bigger say than others. Each opening trading rule has its opinion converted into a number: +10 if it wants to be long, -10 if it wants to be short.[117] We then take a weighted average of those values, and round the result to the nearest ten: –10 or +10. The rounded value tells us what trade to open up: short (–10), or long (+10). For example, suppose your weights are 40% for the moving average 16,64 rule, 10% for a breakout rule, and 50% for the carry rule. If their respective positions are long, short, and long; then the weighted average will be: $$0.4 \times (+10) + 0.1 \times (-10) + 0.5 \times (+10) = +8$$ $$= +10 \text{ (rounded to nearest 10)}$$ In this simple example we'd go long the instrument. Note: if all the weights are equal then this method is equivalent to majority voting.

I discuss how we calculate weights for trading rules later in the chapter.

---

[117] I use ten here to be consistent with a concept I introduce in part four. In practice you can use any number you like here.

Improvement in Sharpe ratio

Back in chapter four I explained that the more optimistic your expectation of Sharpe ratio, the higher your account level risk target could be. In chapter seven I used this result to increase the risk target on trading systems which had more than one instrument. Similarly, adding more trading rules also improves our expected Sharpe ratio. With more trading rules we can use a higher risk target.

Table 50 shows the recommended account level risk target as more trading rules are added to the Starter System. As I did for instruments, I started with the improvement in Sharpe ratio as trading rules are added, from figure 21. Then I halved the Sharpe ratio to get a theoretical risk target. Finally, I came up with some recommended risk targets, which are a little more conservative than the theoretical values.

TABLE 50: ACCOUNT LEVEL RISK TARGET WHEN TRADING RULES ARE ADDED TO THE SIMPLE SYSTEM

	Expected Sharpe ratio (A)	Theoretical risk target DO NOT USE (B = A ÷ 2)	Recommended account level risk target
1 trading rule	0.24	12.0%	12%
2 rules	0.27	13.5%	13%
3 rules	0.30	15.0%	14%
4 to 9 rules	0.34	17.0%	15%
10+ rules	0.35	17.5%	16%

Expected Sharpe ratios (A) from figure 21. Theoretical risk target (B) is half expected Sharpe ratio. Recommended risk target is a conservative target derived from the theoretical value.

What if you are fortunate enough to have both multiple instruments *and* multiple rules in your trading system? You need to multiply the proportionate increase in Sharpe ratio for instruments (from table 44 or 45 in chapter seven) by the relevant ratio for trading rules (above in table 50). I'd also recommend that you never use an account level risk target higher than 30%, to avoid your leverage getting too high.

So, for example, suppose you are trading three instruments which are drawn from multiple asset classes, using five different trading rules. From table 44, which is relevant for multiple asset classes, the recommended account level risk target (column

D) for three instruments is 14%. This is a proportionate increase on the Starter System of 14% ÷ 12% = 1.1667.

From table 50 the recommended account level risk target for five trading rules is 15%. Proportionally the increase is 15% ÷ 12% = 1.25. If I multiply the two proportionate increases together, I get 1.1667 × 1.25 = 1.458. To find the recommended risk target I multiply this by the Starter System target: 1.458 × 12% = 17.5%, or 18% rounded.

Table 51 does this calculation for you, if your instruments come from multiple asset classes. The relevant values for instruments drawn from a single asset class are in table 52.

TABLE 51: MAXIMUM ACCOUNT LEVEL RISK TARGET WHEN BOTH INSTRUMENTS AND TRADING RULES ARE ADDED TO THE SIMPLE SYSTEM, WHERE INSTRUMENTS COME FROM MULTIPLE ASSET CLASSES

	1 rule	2 rules	3 rules	4 – 9 rules	10+ rules
1 instrument	12%	13%	14%	15%	16%
2 instruments	13%	14%	15%	16%	17%
3 instruments	14%	15%	16%	18%	19%
4 instruments	17%	18%	20%	21%	23%
5 instruments	19%	21%	22%	24%	25%
6 instruments	20%	22%	23%	25%	27%
7 instruments	23%	25%	27%	29%	30%
8 to 14 instruments	24%	26%	28%	30%	30%
15 – 25 instruments	25%	27%	29%	31%	30%
25+ instruments	25%	27%	29%	31%	30%

Multiply the proportionate increase in Sharpe ratio for instruments (from table 44 in chapter seven) by the relevant ratio for rules (table 50). Values are then rounded to nearest %, and limited to 30%.

TABLE 52: MAXIMUM ACCOUNT LEVEL RISK TARGET WHEN BOTH INSTRUMENTS AND TRADING RULES ARE ADDED TO THE SIMPLE SYSTEM, WHERE INSTRUMENTS COME FROM THE SAME ASSET CLASS

	1 rule	2 rules	3 rules	4 – 9 rules	10+ rules
1 instrument	12%	13%	14%	15%	16%
2 instruments	13%	14%	15%	16%	17%
3 instruments	13%	14%	15%	16%	17%
4 instruments	14%	15%	16%	17%	18%
5 instruments	14%	15%	16%	18%	19%
6 instruments	14%	15%	16%	18%	19%
7 instruments	15%	16%	17%	18%	19%
8 to 14 instruments	15%	16%	17%	18%	19%
15+ instruments	15%	16%	18%	19%	20%

Multiply the proportionate increase in Sharpe ratio for instruments (from table 45 in chapter seven) by the relevant ratio for rules (table 50). Values are then rounded to nearest %.

Remember, from part two, page 99, that your risk target should be the minimum of calculated values related to: (i) allowable leverage, (ii) prudent leverage, (iii) your appetite for risk, and (iv) the expected Sharpe ratio of your system. Adding more rules or instruments only affects the expected Sharpe ratio. You should check that the other calculated values don't give you a lower risk target.

Also bear in mind that the figures in table 51 are *account level risk targets*; with more than one instrument in your account you need to multiply these by the instrument diversification multiplier (IDM) to get the risk target for individual instruments, as I explained in the previous chapter.

For example, suppose you are trading three instruments which are drawn from multiple asset classes, with five trading rules. I already calculated the account level risk target: 18%. The IDM for three instruments across multiple asset classes is 1.22 (from table 43 in chapter seven). So, the correct instrument level risk target is 1.22 × 18% = 22%.

What criteria do we use for selecting and weighting trading rules?

Which rules and which weights?

How should you choose your opening rules, and which weights should you use when averaging them to work out your opening position? Potentially important criteria are: (a) pre-cost performance, (b) capital required, (c) time constraints, (d) different cost levels, and (e) how much diversification they provide.

In fact, we can safely ignore both (a) pre-cost performance and (b) capital requirements. Figure 20 near the start of this chapter suggests that we can't distinguish the pre-cost performance of different trading rules. The number of *instruments* you can trade simultaneously is limited mainly by your **capital**; each additional instrument needs its own capital allocation. But no such constraint exists for multiple trading rules, as they share the same pool of capital. The same minimum capital is required regardless of whether you are using one opening rule or a hundred.

A more serious problem is the extra *time* needed to run additional calculations. Some of the trading rules in this chapter don't need much additional effort: moving averages, and breakouts. If you use spreadsheets to calculate the value of your moving averages, then you can set up multiple sheets, each linking to your price data. You can then add extra sheets for different breakout rule variations. If you are using an internet data provider to calculate your moving averages or breakout signals, then you can bookmark multiple web pages.

Carry is more work as you need to gather extra data. For spot FX you'll need interest rates; whilst for CFD, spread bets and futures you require a spot price, or the price of another traded contract. Margin traders will need interest rates, borrowing fees, and dividend yields.

How do costs and diversification affect the choice of rules and weights to use when averaging? Let's assume for the moment that you have sufficient time to handle numerous trading rules. You decide to include six moving average crossovers (from 2,8 to 64,256), six breakouts (from N=10 to N=320), and the carry rule. How would you set your weights?

Firstly, you should **exclude any trading rules that are too expensive**. Discard any rule with risk-adjusted costs that are greater than one-third of their expected pre-cost Sharpe ratio.[118] For the six instruments I used in part two to illustrate the Starter System, here is a list of trading rules that are too expensive to trade:

---

[118] See page 78.

Moving average crossovers	From table 8, page 91: • Euro Stoxx CFD: MAC 2,8. MAC 4,16 • Gold spread bet: MAC 2,8. MAC 4,16 • AUDUSD spot FX: MAC 2,8. MAC 4,16 • S&P 500 margin trade: MAC 2,8. MAC 4,16
Breakout	From table 48, page 200: • Euro Stoxx CFD: Breakout 10. Breakout 20. • Gold spread bet: Breakout 10. • AUDUSD spot FX: Breakout 10. • S&P 500 margin trade: Breakout 10.
Carry	From table 49, page 208: All instruments can be traded.

Here are the rules that I would keep:

- Corn future: Moving averages 2&8, 4&16, 8&32, 16&64, 32&128, 64&256. Breakouts N=10,20,40,80,160,320. Carry.

- Euro Stoxx CFD on future: Moving averages 8&32, 16&64, 32&128, 64&256. Breakouts N=40,80,160,320. Carry.

- Gold spread bet on future: Moving averages 8&32, 16&64, 32&128, 64&256. Breakouts N=20,40,80,160,320. Carry.

- S&P 500 margin account: Moving averages 8&32, 16&64, 32&128, 64&256. Breakouts N=20,40,80,160,320. Carry.

- AUDUSD: Moving averages 8&32, 16&64, 32&128, 64&256. Breakouts N=20,40,80,160,320. Carry.

If you are trading multiple instruments you could end up with a different set of trading rules for each instrument. This might sound too complicated. If you prefer using the same rules for all your instruments, then implement those that are viable for the most expensive instrument you are trading. For example, if you are trading corn futures and Euro Stoxx CFD, then you would use the set of rules which worked for Euro Stoxx CFD.

Now we have chosen which rules to use, what weight should we use? You should give more **weight to the most diversifying trading rules**. I recommend doing this with a *top down* allocation method.[119] First, we allocate our weights equally across different **styles** of trading. Trend following is one style (which includes both moving average crossovers, and breakout); whilst carry is another style. I'd allocate half my weighting to trend following, and then another half to carry.

---

[119] There is much more on this technique in my first book, *Systematic Trading*.

Since there is only one carry trading rule that will get the entire 50% weight. The other 50% I'd split equally between the two **types** of trend following rule: moving average crossovers (25%), and breakout (25%). Finally, I'd split rule allocations equally across **variations** of each rule (different length crossovers, and different values of N for breakout).[120]

For example, consider the weights for gold spread bets. We put half into carry (50%) and split the other 50%: 25% into moving average crossovers (MAC), and 25% into breakout. The 25% for MAC is divided four ways, as there are four MAC rules which are cheap enough to trade. Each gets 25% ÷ 4 = 6.25%. In the breakout allocation there are five rules we can allocate to, since breakout 10 is too expensive, so each gets a weight of 25% ÷ 5 = 5%.

Table 53 shows the calculation of weights for the six example instruments.

TABLE 53: WEIGHTINGS TO USE WHEN AVERAGING TRADING RULES FOR DIFFERENT INSTRUMENTS

	Corn future	Euro Stoxx CFD on future	Gold quarterly spread bet	S&P 500 margin account	AUDUSD spot FX
Moving average 2,8	4.17%	0%	0%	0%	0%
Moving average 4,16	4.17%	0%	0%	0%	0%
Moving average 8,32	4.17%	6.25%	6.25%	6.25%	6.25%
Moving average 16,64	4.17%	6.25%	6.25%	6.25%	6.25%
Moving average 32,128	4.17%	6.25%	6.25%	6.25%	6.25%
Moving average 64,256	4.17%	6.25%	6.25%	6.25%	6.25%
Breakout 10	4.17%	0%	0%	0%	0%
Breakout 20	4.17%	0%	5%	5%	5%
Breakout 40	4.17%	6.25%	5%	5%	5%
Breakout 80	4.17%	6.25%	5%	5%	5%
Breakout 160	4.17%	6.25%	5%	5%	5%
Breakout 320	4.17%	6.25%	5%	5%	5%
Carry	50%	50%	50%	50%	50%

[120] Because we drop variations that are too expensive (and exceed the 'speed limit' of one-third of expected pre-cost Sharpe ratios spent in costs) this will always lead to allocations that trade slower than the 'speed limit'. This is conservative, but sensible given the uncertainty in pre-cost Sharpe ratios.

For each instrument allocate half to carry, and half to trend following. Then split the trend following allocation: half to moving average crosssover (MAC), half to breakouts. Then divide the MAC and breakouts between the variations of these rules that are cheap enough to trade.

If you are short of time then you can drop the Carry rule, which is very time consuming to calculate. You should double all the remaining values shown in this table for moving averages and breakout rules to get the appropriate weighting.

Should you change your closing rule?

If you use different opening rules, do you also need to modify your closing rule? The closing rule is a stop loss level calculated as a fraction of instrument risk, and this fraction is calibrated to match the typical holding period of the opening rule. In the Starter System I set this fraction at 0.5, which corresponds to the expected trading frequency of the 16,64 moving average crossover rule. If you start using opening rules with a shorter or longer trade horizon, then you need to recalibrate your closing rule.

Firstly, calculate your **expected number of trades**, as a weighted average of the trading frequency of your opening rules and the weights you have on those rules. For example, suppose you are running a system with 25% in the 16,64 moving average crossover (5.4 trades per year, from table 8 on page 91), 25% in breakout with N=80 (14.8 trades per year, from table 48, page 200), and 50% in Carry (5.4 trades per year, from table 49, page 208). The weighted average number of trades per year is:

$$(0.25 \times 5.4) + (0.25 \times 14.8) + (0.5 \times 5.4) = 7.75$$

This is a little quicker than the Starter System, which with just the 16,64 moving average rule is expected to place 5.4 trades each year.

Now consult table 54 to find **the most appropriate volatility fraction given your trading speed.**

TABLE 54: FASTER TRADING NEEDS TIGHTER STOP LOSSES

Average trades per year	Fraction of volatility
97.5	0.025
76.5	0.05
46.9	0.1
21.4	0.2
11.9	0.3
7.8	0.4
5.4	**0.5**
4.0	0.6
3.1	0.7
2.4	0.8
2.1	0.9
1.7	1.0
1.3	1.2
1.1	1.4
1.0	1.5

All values calculated from back-testing different MAV opening rules and stop loss fractions over the instruments in my data set. Row in bold is Starter System. Figures are copied from table 12, page 110.

For an opening rule with 7.5 trades annually the closest matching fraction would be 0.4. If you are using the recommended rules and weights from the last section (set out in table 53), then you can use table 55 to find the appropriate volatility fraction for your closing rule.

TABLE 55: TRADING SPEED AND RECOMMENDED STOP LOSS VOLATILITY FRACTION IF USING SUGGESTED TRADING RULES AND WEIGHTS FROM TABLE 53

	Corn future	Euro Stoxx CFD on future	Gold quarterly spread bet	S&P 500 margin account	AUDUSD spot FX
Number of trades per year	9.91	7.20	8.05	8.05	8.05
Suggested volatility fraction	0.35	0.43	0.39	0.39	0.39

Number of trades per year calculated as a weighted average of trades for each rule (from tables 8, 48 and table 49) using weights from table 53. Suggested volatility fraction from table 54, with interpolated values.

Does it ever make sense to add or remove trading rules?

It is absolutely fine to add new trading rules to your system at any time. Just use the new set of opening rules when you are ready to open a new position, and don't forget to update your weighting scheme. What about removing a trading rule?

In theory, if you find that a trading rule is losing money, and those losses are statistically significant, then you should remove it from your trading system. In practice it is extremely unlikely that your losses will ever be large enough, or that you will trade for long enough, to reach that point. Tracking the performance of every individual opening rule is also extremely difficult and time consuming, unless your system is automated.

I recommend: **do not remove trading rules from your system**.

Using multiple trading rules in practice

Before you start trading

There is a bit more work to do before you begin trading with multiple trading rules.

Select your extra trading rules	See page 214.
Choose weights for averaging rules	See page 215.
Calculate the appropriate volatility fraction for the closing rule	See page 217.
Calculate the new account level risk target	See page 211. Trading a single instrument: from table 50 Multiple instruments, different asset classes: Use table 51 Multiple instruments, same asset class: Use table 52

Here is the updated trade plan for multiple rules:

Opening rule	Multiple opening rules. Use a weighted average of your rules to work out what position should be opened (page 210).
Closing rule	If necessary, use a recalibrated volatility fraction on the stop loss rule (See page 217).
Position sizing rule	Use an account level risk target which reflects the diversification benefit of multiple rules (and possibly multiple instruments). See page 211. If trading multiple instruments: Don't forget to apply an instrument diversification multiplier to calculate the instrument level risk target.

Running the system with multiple opening rules

The only change when operating the Starter System is to the opening rule: when considering whether to open a trade you need to check each trading rule. Once you have the buy or sell decisions from each rule then you need to come up with a single buy or sell decision, using the weighted average as I discussed back on page 210.

PART FOUR

Advanced

— *Trading* —

CHAPTER NINE
From Discrete to Continuous Trading

"You've got to know when to hold 'em. Know when to fold 'em. Know when to walk away. And know when to run."

Lyrics from the Kenny Rogers song '*The Gambler*' written by Don Schiltz in 1976

Kenny Rogers was singing about playing poker, but these lyrics apply equally well to trading. Knowing when to fold – when to close an unsuccessful trade – is a vital part of any trading strategy. The Starter System introduced in part two, and developed in part three, does this with a stop loss.

The Starter System has a pretty simple structure. We use one or more trading rules to decide whether we should be long or short the market. Then after a position has been opened, we wait for our stop loss to be triggered.

Pretty simple, but we can make it even simpler: **by dropping the stop loss**. This may sound like dangerous lunacy, and no doubt Kenny would be very sceptical. But the Starter System doesn't really need a stop loss.

Why it can be safe to trade without a stop loss

Why do we have stop losses?

- They control your risk, by limiting how much money you can lose in any individual trade.

- They get you out of losing trades before they get any worse.

They seem like pretty important jobs, but they can be covered by other parts of the Starter System. Stop losses are effectively redundant.

Firstly: **risk control**. Stop losses provide *trade level risk control*. The stop loss used in the basic Starter System works out to a maximum capital loss of 6%, on any given trade. We can work this out using formula 25 (page 113):

Capital at risk per trade % = Annualised risk target % × stop loss fraction

= 12% × 0.5 = 6%

But the maximum loss depends on how long we are expecting to hold positions for, since this in turn determines the stop loss fraction. The capital at risk on each trade isn't consciously set in the Starter System. It is just a value implied by the stop loss fraction and our risk target.

In the Starter System the annualised risk target is the primary method of risk control. We design our system so we know how much we expect to make or lose on any given day, and that determines how large our positions should be. This is *time-based* rather than *trade-based* risk control. Without stop losses we would still be controlling our risk, but it is the risk of how much we might lose over a given time period, not on any given trade.

Now let us turn to the other function of stop losses: **getting you out of losing trades**. How can we do this without stop losses?

We use the opening rule to close trades.

The rule used in the Starter System is a *trend following* rule; we buy when the market has rallied, and sell when it has fallen. If a trend reverses then we would start losing money and would close our positions. But we don't need the stop loss rule for this. Instead we can track the opening rule throughout the life of the trade and close our position when it reverses in direction.

Stop losses aren't perfect

Trade-based stop loss risk control feels safer to most traders, which is why I specified them in the Starter System. There is something comforting about knowing there is a maximum amount you can lose on each trade. But it is cold comfort, as you can easily lose more.

Here is a stop loss horror story. I bought shares in the UK postal service, Royal Mail Group, in January 2017 for £4.47. After some sideways movement they rallied in early 2018 reaching a high of £6.31 in May 2018, at which point my trailing stop[121] was at £4.42. Over the next few months the price drifted downwards, reaching £4.77 on 28 September. Although this was disappointing, I consoled myself that if they hit my stop at least I'd get away with a modest £0.05 loss (£4.47 versus £4.42). Including dividends received I would even have a small profit.

Then late on the afternoon of Monday 1 October 2018 Royal Mail put out a profit warning, and the share price plummeted below £4. By the time I managed to sell, the price was down to £3.60, crystallizing a loss of several thousand pounds. So much for the safety of stop losses.[122]

Of course, *time-based* risk control is not perfect. It assumes we can predict the volatility of prices with unnatural foresight. Actually, standard deviation is the one of the most predictable values in financial markets, although of course it can never be perfectly forecasted.

But time-based risk control only tells you what your *average* loss will be. It does not promise to limit your daily losses to some maximum level, like a stop loss does. Unlike stop losses time-based risk control doesn't make promises it can't deliver.

Continuous trading

With no stop loss rule the trading process looks like this:

1. Day one: starting with no position, we check our opening rule.

2. We enter into a position in the direction of the trend found by the opening rule.

---

[121] If you have been paying attention you may be thinking that is quite a wide stop: it equates to 30% of the price. The volatility of Royal Mail shares was about 25% a year at this point, implying a stop loss of 12.5% of the price using the normal volatility fraction of 0.5. In this particular trading account, I have opted for wider stops to increase my expected holding period, partly because I am trading the actual shares in this account rather than CFDs or spread bets, and actual UK shares are quite expensive to trade because of the 0.5% stamp duty tax. This is an example of adapting a system to your own requirements.

[122] As I've mentioned before you can avoid this scenario by using a guaranteed stop loss. But these are too expensive.

3. We continue to hold the position whilst the opening rule is in the same direction.

4. When the opening rule switches to the opposite direction, we close our position.

5. We then immediately open a new position in the new trend direction.

This type of trading is sometimes called *stop and reverse*. However, I prefer the term *continuous trading*, because we always have a trade in place.

What if you have added multiple opening rules, as I advised in chapter eight? The procedure for continuous trading with multiple rules is equally simple. Take a weighted average of your rules, using the method described in chapter eight, to determine which direction your initial position should be. You then continue to monitor all of your rules and close the trade when the average has changed its mind. Then it's time to open a new trade in the opposite direction.

Advantages of continuous trading

FIGURE 24: EFFECT OF DROPPING THE STOP LOSS FROM THE STARTER SYSTEM

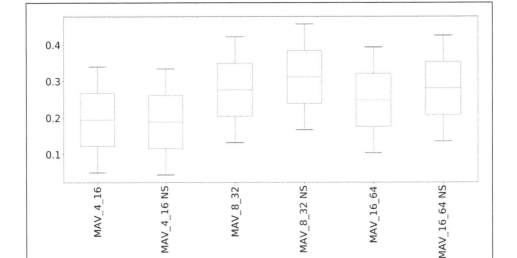

I tested the effect of dropping the stop loss from the Starter System trading rule, plus two other moving average crossovers that I use in my own system. The results are shown in figure 24, using the usual box and whiskers plots that show how statistically significant the results are. There are three pairs of boxes, each covering a particular trading rule. The first box in each pair shows the Sharpe ratio (SR), with error bars, for a particular trading rule using the stop loss. The second box (suffixed *NS* – no stop) shows the same data with the stop loss dropped.

You can see that in all cases the second box is at least as good as, or better than, the first. Admittedly, none of the differences are statistically significant, as the boxes all overlap. But taken together there is good evidence that **dropping the stop loss improves the performance of the Starter System** by around 13% (from a SR of 0.24 to SR 0.27).

This is a nice improvement, although it is not as high as the gains we saw from diversifying across instruments and opening rules in part three. But there is another advantage of dropping the stop loss. It makes designing your trading system easier. If you want to change to a different set of trading rules, you do not need to worry about recalibrating your stop loss so that it matches up.

Finally, do not use these higher SR expectations to increase your risk target as you would do if you were adding instruments or trading rules. The improvement is not statistically significant, so it is better to be conservative and not increase your leverage to match a higher risk target.

When you should keep a stop loss

There are three reasons why dropping the stop loss from the Starter System might not make sense. Firstly, the **stop loss is a comfort blanket**, which makes you feel like you are more in control. If getting rid of stop losses worries you, then you should keep them. The slim benefits of removing the stop losses are not worth the loss in sleep.[123] Secondly, **continuous trading might involve more work**, especially if you have multiple trading rules. However, if you have set up your trading system on a spreadsheet this should not be a serious issue.

Finally, **for some styles of trading, dropping the stop loss would be dangerous**. Suppose you're not using a trend following rule, but instead using a trading rule which doesn't get out of positions when the price reverses. Then you'd be stuck in a loss-making position as it got worse and worse. Here it would be better to use a stop loss. I would advise keeping the stop loss if significantly more than 50% of your opening rule weighting is in non-trend following rules (like the carry rule).

In my own trading I take a mix-and-match approach to stop losses. There are three components to my portfolio. Firstly, I have a fully automated futures trading system with no stop loss. This is mostly a trend following system, although it does include a 40% weighting to carry. So, the actual trading rules do the duty of closing loss-making positions. Additionally, as it is automated there is no extra work involved in recalculating the forecasts for each rule.

---

[123] Traders who are **really** nervous should consider leaving stop loss orders with their broker, or even using guaranteed stop losses, though I'm not keen on either of these options: if you leave a stop loss order with your broker then they can deliberately push the price or widen the spread to trigger the stop, and guaranteed stop losses cost more.

The second part of my portfolio trades UK equities, picking cheap shares based on valuation metrics like dividend yields. Here I use an explicit stop loss (this sub-portfolio is where I bought those Royal Mail shares). Because I'm buying cheap shares my trading rule won't close positions when prices fall: it will usually want to buy more. Removing the stop loss would be dangerous. Also, I am running this portfolio manually, and I don't have the time to do the extra calculations required for continuously trading without a stop loss.

Finally, I have a buy and hold sub-portfolio of exchange traded funds. Because I'm investing, and not trading, these instruments don't need a stop loss rule.

Practical trading without a stop loss

Here is the updated trading plan for trading without a stop loss:

Closing rule	Close a trade when the opening rule(s) have reversed from their original direction.
Opening rule	Immediately open a new trade in the opposite direction once the previous trade is closed.

How would I have traded differently with the examples from chapter six, if I hadn't been using a stop loss?

Let's begin with corn.

Corn

You might remember that I originally opened a short, and I closed this trade on 10 October. A new long trade was then opened on 26 October. Now look at figure 25. I would have kept the original trade open longer, until 26 October when the opening rule changed its mind (though it comes close to being closed in mid-August).

FIGURE 25: CORN TRADE WOULD HAVE BEEN CLOSED SLIGHTLY LATER WITH NO STOP LOSS

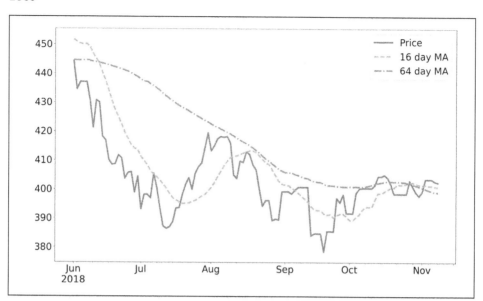

Comparing the original trade log (table 56) to the new one (table 57), you can see there is an additional 2.2 point loss when the trade is closed on 26 October. We are trading two contracts at $50 a point, so this costs:

2.2 × $50 × 2 = $220

The original profit was $1,165; using a stop loss would reduce it slightly to $945.

TABLE 56: CORN FUTURE TRADE LOG WITH STOP LOSS

	Date in 2018	Dated expiry	Trade	Size	Price	P&L	Comm.
	19 June	Dec 2018	Short	2 contracts	379		$2
	26 Sep	Dec 2018	Close	2 contracts	362.75	16.25	$2
Corn	26 Sep	Dec 2019	Short	2 contracts	397		$2
future	10 Oct	Dec 2019	Close	2 contracts	401	−4	$2
	26 Oct	Dec 2019	Long	1 contract	403		$2
	8 Nov	Dec 2019	Close	1 contract	402	−1	$2

'Comm': commissions. Excludes spread cost, since the price shown reflects the effect of paying the spread. P&L is profit or loss in price points for closing trades only.

TABLE 57: CORN FUTURE TRADE LOG WITHOUT STOP LOSS

	Date in 2018	Dated expiry	Trade	Size	Price	P&L	Comm.
	19 June	Dec 2018	Short	2 contracts	379		$2
	26 Sep	Dec 2018	Close	2 contracts	362.75	16.25	$2
Corn	26 Sep	Dec 2019	Short	2 contracts	397		$2
future	26 Oct	Dec 2019	Close	2 contracts	403.2	−6.2	$2
	26 Oct	Dec 2019	Long	1 contract	403		$2
	8 Nov	Dec 2019	Close	1 contract	402	−1	$2

'Comm': commissions. Excludes spread cost, since the price shown reflects the effect of paying the spread. P&L is profit or loss in price points for closing trades only.

Now for gold.

Gold

In chapter six this particular trade was kept open until I'd finished in early November, for a 53.1 point profit. Figure 26 shows that using the opening rule rather than a stop loss would have closed the position in October, and I would then have gone long. Because volatility has risen the second trade is smaller: a buy at £1 a point.

FIGURE 26: GOLD TRADE WOULD HAVE BEEN CLOSED IN MID-OCTOBER

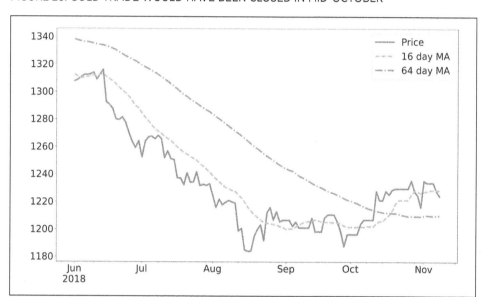

TABLE 58: GOLD TRADE LOG WITH STOP LOSS

	Date in 2018	Dated expiry	Trade	Size	Price	P&L
	19 June	Aug 2018	Short	£1.03 per point	1,268.0	
Gold spread bet	26 July	Aug 2018	Close	£1.03 per point	1,228.1	39.9
	26 July	Dec 2018	Short	£1.03 per point	1,237.4	
	8 Nov	Dec 2018	Close	£1.03 per point	1,224.2	13.2

There are no commissions. Excludes spread cost, since the price shown reflects the effect of paying the spread. P&L is profit or loss in price points for closing trades only.

TABLE 59: GOLD TRADE LOG WITHOUT STOP LOSS

	Date in 2018	Dated expiry	Trade	Size	Price	P&L
	19 June	Aug 2018	Short	£1.03 per point	1,268	
	26 July	Aug 2018	Close	£1.03 per point	1,228.1	39.9
Gold	26 July	Dec 2018	Short	£1.03 per point	1,237.4	
spread bet	10 Oct	Dec 2018	Close	£1.03 per point	1,227.6	9.8
	10 Oct	Dec 2018	Long	£1 per point	1,227	
	8 Nov	Dec 2018	Close	£1 per point	1,224.2	−2.8

There are no commissions. Excludes spread cost, since the price shown reflects the effect of paying the spread. P&L is profit or loss in price points for closing trades only.

I made a total of 39.9 + 9.8 = 49.7 points at £1.03 a point, and then lost a further 2.8 points at £1 point. With no commissions or holding costs the profit is:

(£1.03 × 49.7) + (£1 × − 2.8) = £48.39

For comparison, in chapter six the original profit using a stop loss was £54.69.

The next trade we'll consider is AUDUSD.

AUDUSD

In chapter six the initial short trade was kept open for the entire period. Figure 27 shows that without a stop loss the opening rule does exactly the same thing as before.

FIGURE 27: AUDUSD STAYS SHORT

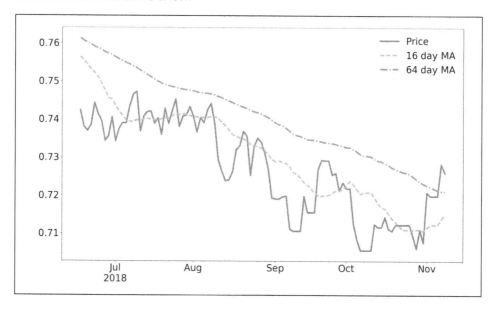

Now let's look at Euro Stoxx.

Euro Stoxx 50

This was a pretty disastrous trade in chapter six; I went long and was then stopped out at a loss on 10 October. My short then lost money when the market rebounded in early November. Figure 28 shows a completely different story.

FIGURE 28: EURO STOXX LONG IS SHORT LIVED, AND EVENTUALLY GOES SHORT QUITE EARLY

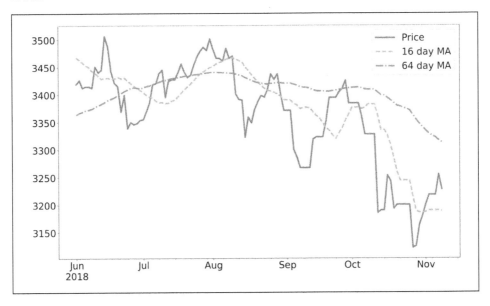

The initial long is short lived and gets closed after only a few weeks. Then I go short for a month or so, again on the wrong side of the market and this trade is closed in mid-July. A short-lived, unprofitable long follows. Finally, I go short, and this time it pays off. By 8 November this final short has made me nearly 200 points.

The original and new trade logs are in tables 60 and 61.

TABLE 60: FINAL TRADE LOG FOR EURO STOXX CFD, WITH STOP LOSS

	Date in 2018	Dated expiry	Trade	Size	Price	P&L
	19 June	Sep 2018	Long	2 contracts at €2 each	3,391	
	19 Sep	Sep 2018	Close	2 contracts	3,365	−26
Euro Stoxx 50 CFD (per contract)	19 Sep	Dec 2018	Long	2 contracts	3,346	
	10 Oct	Dec 2018	Close	2 contracts	3,330	−16
	10 Oct	Dec 2018	Short	1 contract at €2	3,329	
	8 Nov	Dec 2018	Close	1 contract at €2	3,202.5	26.5

There are no commissions. Excludes spread cost, since the price shown reflects the effect of paying the spread. P&L is profit or loss in price points for closing trades only.

TABLE 61: FINAL TRADE LOG FOR EURO STOXX CFD, WITHOUT STOP LOSS

	Date in 2018	Dated expiry	Trade	Size	Price	P&L
	19 June	Sep 2018	Long	2 contracts at €2 each	3,391	
	22 June	Sep 2018	Close	2 contracts	3,360	−31
	22 June	Sep 2018	Short	2 contracts	3,358	
	19 July	Sep 2018	Close	2 contracts	3,491	−133
Euro Stoxx 50 CFD (per contract)	19 July	Sep 2018	Long	2 contracts	3,493	
	16 Aug	Sep 2018	Close	2 contracts	3,421	−72
	16 Aug	Sep 2018	Short	2 contracts	3,419	
	19 Sep	Sep 2018	Close	2 contracts	3,365	54
	19 Sep	Dec 2018	Long	2 contracts	3,346	
	8 Nov	Dec 2018	Close	2 contracts	3,202.5	143.5

There are no commissions. Excludes spread cost, since the price shown reflects the effect of paying the spread. P&L is profit or loss in price points for closing trades only.

I'm using the bet per contract CFD here, and the position size is always two contracts at €2 per contract, so the total loss is:

$$(-31-133-72-54+143.5) \times 2 \times €2 = -€154 = -\$174$$

This is a slightly larger loss than before – when using a stop loss, I lost $131. The numbers would be very similar for the bet per point CFD.

S&P 500

Finally, have a look at figure 29 which shows the S&P 500. Originally the stop loss got out of this trade on 24 October. I then opened a short, but this was at the worst possible level as the market then rebounded to $280. Using the opening rule instead this trade is closed a few days earlier on 16 October at a much better level. The short that follows is kept open until 8 November and ekes out a small profit. This is a much better outcome than in chapter six.

FIGURE 29: S&P 500 GETS TAKEN OUT EARLIER

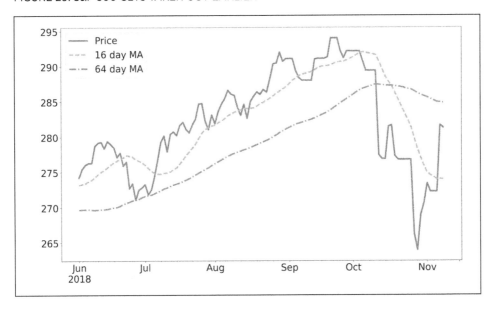

The original and new trade logs are shown in tables 62 and 63.

TABLE 62: TRADE LOG FOR S&P 500 MARGIN TRADING, WITH STOP LOSS

	Date in 2018	Dated expiry	Trade	Size	Price	P&L	Comm.
	19 June	N/A	Long	19 shares	276		$1
S&P 500 ETF margin trade	24 Oct	N/A	Close	19 shares	265	−11	$1
	24 Oct	N/A	Short	17 shares	265		$1
	8 Nov	N/A	Close	17 shares	280	−15	$1

'Comm': commissions. Excludes spread cost, since the price shown reflects the effect of paying the spread. P&L is profit or loss in price points for closing trades only.

TABLE 63: TRADE LOG FOR S&P 500 MARGIN TRADING, WITHOUT STOP LOSS

	Date in 2018	Dated expiry	Trade	Size	Price	P&L	Comm.
	19 June	N/A	Long	19 shares	276.0		$1
S&P 500 ETF margin trade	16 Oct	N/A	Close	19 shares	282.2	12.2	$1
	16 Oct	N/A	Short	17 shares	282.19		$1
	8 Nov	N/A	Close	17 shares	280.0	2.19	$1

'Comm': commissions. Excludes spread cost, since the price shown reflects the effect of paying the spread. P&L is profit or loss in price points for closing trades only.

The first trade made $12.20 per share:

$$12.20 \times 19 = \$231.80$$

Commissions cost me another $2, but there was no funding cost as my leverage factor was less than 1. The net profit was $231.80 − $2 = $229.80.

The second trade was also closed at a profit of $2.19 per share:

2.19 × 17 = $37.23

Commissions cost me another $2, but as I was short I also had to pay a borrowing fee of 0.25% a year; this came to $0.49. Sadly, my broker didn't pay me any interest on the cash I realised from selling short. The profit on the second trade works out to:

$37.23 – $2 – $0.49 = $34.74

The total profit was 229.80 + 34.74 = $264.54.

TABLE 64: SUMMARY OF TRADING PROFIT AND LOSS, WITH AND WITHOUT STOP LOSS

		With stop loss		Without stop loss	
	Capital	P&L	% P&L	P&L	% P&L
Gold spread bet	£1,200	£54.69	4.60%	£48.39	+4.0%
Corn future	$40,000	+$1,165	+2.9%	+$945	+2.4%
Euro Stoxx 50 CFD (per contract)	$13,000	−$131	−1.0%	−$174	−1.3%
AUDUSD spot FX	£1,100	£39.93	+3.6%	£39.93	+3.6%
S&P 500 ETF margin trade	$7,100	−$468.47	−6.6%	$264.54	+3.7%

In three of the five examples profits are slightly lower with a stop loss (gold, corn, and Euro Stoxx), with no difference in AUDUSD, and a substantial improvement in S&P 500.

Of course, a handful of trades don't by themselves establish a clear case for removing stop losses. Looking at a few isolated case studies like these is meaningless: the large improvement in S&P 500 in particular was pretty fluky. Decisions should be made on back-tests done with many years of history, and over large numbers of instruments. But they should reassure you that it's safe to trade without a stop loss.

CHAPTER TEN

Position Adjustment

I MAGINE YOU ARE PLAYING TEXAS hold 'em poker. Do not worry if you are not familiar with the rules. At the start of the game you are dealt two cards. You then decide whether to play, and how much to bet, based on how strong your hand is.[124] 'Pocket aces' – a pair of aces – is the best possible starting hand. Being dealt a pair of nines isn't nearly as good but is still a hand that's worth playing. An experienced poker player would bet heavily if they got pocket aces, but with a pair of nines they would place a more modest stake.

After the initial round of betting the dealer lays three further cards face up on the table. Players can then choose to bet more, match the bets made by other players, or leave the game (known as 'folding'). Two further rounds follow where more cards are dealt, and more betting or folding is possible.

A smart poker player will modify their betting strategy as the game goes on. As more cards are revealed, and other players make their bets, they will revise their opinion about the likely outcome of the game. They will change their opinion about how much risk they should take, given the information available.

But in the Starter System we always bet the same amount. The same amount of cash is at risk each time, regardless of how confident we are about our trade. Also, we keep the same position on, even if our confidence or the risk in the market changes. This makes no sense in a poker game and, in this chapter, I explain why it makes no sense when you are trading.

Specifically, I will discuss:

- adjusting position size according to how much confidence you have in your trading rule

- adjusting position size as risk changes.

---

[124] Footnote for poker experts: I realise this is a gross oversimplification that ignores the big and small blinds, and the possibility of bluffing.

Adjusting position size for confidence: non-binary trading

Consider figures 30 and 31 (these should look familiar: they are exact copies of figures 11 and 12 back in part two).

FIGURE 30: OPENING RULE GOES LONG EURO STOXX EQUITY INDEX WITHOUT MUCH CONVICTION

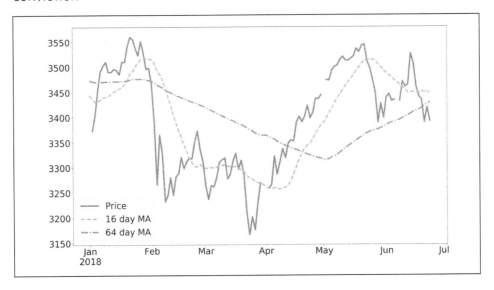

FIGURE 31: OPENING RULE GOES SHORT CORN WITH HUGE ENTHUSIASM

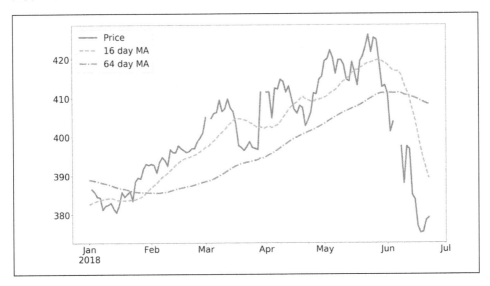

In one situation (Euro Stoxx) we go long two CFD contracts, and in the other (corn) we go short two futures contracts. By coincidence the size of our position is the same (two contracts), but more importantly the **risk of the positions we take in the Starter System will be identical** (and equal to whatever it takes to get 12% target risk on our trading capital). The rule in the Starter System is a *binary* trading strategy: there are only two options – long or short.

But on closer inspection the two scenarios are quite different.

In figure 30 (Euro Stoxx) the two moving averages are really close together on 18 June, and on the verge of re-crossing. Whereas in figure 31 (corn) on the same day there is a large, and growing, gap between the two moving averages. Euro Stoxx shows a relatively weak uptrend, corn a really strong downtrend. Yet we have the same sized risk for both positions.

Does that make sense?

It does not.

Ideally, **you should size your positions according to how confident your trading rule is**. If the basic Starter System wants to hold two contracts, then with a weak signal as in figure 30 you might only buy a single contract. If the signal is exceptionally strong as in figure 31 you might go short three, or even four, contracts. This is *non-binary* trading.

Why non-binary trading makes sense

Non-binary trading only makes sense when combined with the idea of continuous trading without a stop loss, which I introduced in the last chapter.[125] With these two methods together the trading process now looks like this:

1. Starting with no position, we check our opening rule.

2. We enter into a position in the direction indicated by the opening rule. The magnitude of that position depends on how confident the rule is.

---

[125] If we were using non–binary trading, and also retaining a stop loss, then we'd size our original position according to forecast strength, but then keep it constant. Except for our first trade, we'd likely have a very weak signal, since we open a new position when the trading rule has only just changed sign. We'd then keep this very small position until a stop loss was hit. That makes no sense.

3. We monitor the opening rule. If the rule gets more confident about the position, then we increase it.[126] If it gets less confident, then we reduce it.

4. When the rule has insufficient confidence, and is unsure whether to be long or short, then our position would be closed.

5. Once the rule has some confidence again, we'd open a small new position in the appropriate direction.

6. Our position would then get larger if the rule got more confident, and vice versa.

Why does it make sense to increase your position when you are more confident?

Consider the trend following rule used in the Starter System. On 18 June in figure 30 the trend is finely balanced, with the moving averages really close together. A relatively small movement in price either way will tip you from long to short. But small price movements are pretty random, and in this tight situation you can't be sure about the trend direction. Your position should be much smaller than in figure 31 where the trend is well established. I could make a similar argument for the breakout rule I introduced in chapter eight, and any other trend following rule.

What about the carry rule that I introduced in chapter eight?

Let's use an FX example, as that will be intuitively clearer. The carry rule for FX uses the difference between the interest rates of different countries. As I write this chapter, interest rates are at these levels: for USD 1.919%, for AUD 1.898%, and for GBP 0.569%.

The carry rule would want to go long USD vs GBP, as 1.919% is well above 0.569%. It would also go long USD vs AUD, since 1.919% is higher than 1.898%. But the difference in interest rates here is tiny: 0.021%. A tiny change in the USD rate would cause the rule to change its opinion about AUDUSD. This justifies a much smaller position in AUDUSD than the larger rate differential seen in GBPUSD. Similar arguments apply when trading carry in other leveraged products.

Intuitively it seems to make sense to alter position size depending on how confident the opening rule is. But we are systematic traders, so let us check the evidence. Have a look at figure 32, which is an updated version of figure 24 from the previous chapter. In this figure I've shown the result of back-testing different variations of the Starter System; with and without binary trading and stop losses.

---

[126] You will sometimes hear traders talk about *pyramiding* or, as one online pundit describes it, "adding to winning positions with new trades, when prices reach key technical levels". These levels, like the entry into the initial trade, are often determined subjectively. If the trading rule you are using is a trend following rule, like in the Starter System, then your non-binary trading will look a lot like pyramiding. But non-binary trading using trading rules is superior to pyramiding – it doesn't use subjective judgement and is simpler (as you don't need a separate stop loss rule for each new trade you put on).

FIGURE 32: REMOVING THE STOP LOSS IS GOOD. DROPPING BINARY TRADING IS BETTER. EFFECT OF REMOVING STOP LOSS (NS), AND ALSO MOVING TO NON-BINARY TRADING (NS NB)

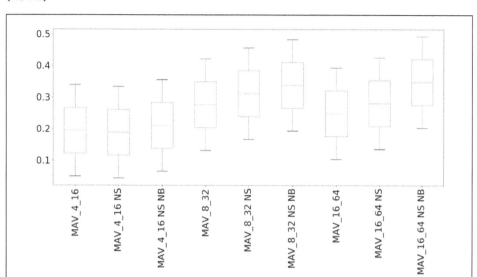

Figure 32 shows the average Sharpe ratio (SR) plus statistical uncertainty of three moving average rules, including the 16,64 pair used in the Starter System. The first box in each set of three shows the rule with a stop loss and binary trading, as used in the basic Starter System introduced in part two. The second box (suffix *NS*) shows the effect of removing the stop loss. We have seen these statistics before, in figure 24 from chapter nine. Finally, the third box in each triplet (suffix *NS NB*) shows the effect of removing the stop loss *and* moving to non-binary trading.[127]

You can see that moving to non-binary trading improves performance relative to the normal Starter System, and also compared to trading without a stop loss. Because the boxes and whiskers overlap the improvement isn't statistically significant on any individual rule. But the consistent pattern means there is good evidence that non-binary trading will lead to higher risk-adjusted returns. We boost the expected SR by 13% when dropping the stop loss on the Starter System MAV 16,64 rule (SR goes from 0.24 to 0.27), and subsequently add another 26% by moving to non-binary trading (SR goes from 0.27 to 0.34).

Because these results aren't statistically significant you should not use these higher SR expectations to increase your risk target, as you would do if you were adding instruments or trading rules. It's better to be conservative and limit your leverage.

---

[127] I haven't shown results for systems that have non-binary trading combined with a stop loss as this doesn't make any sense.

The forecast: A risk-adjusted prediction of the future

How do we actually adjust positions depending on how confident our trading rule is?

Here is formula 14, which I introduced back in part two, for calculating required notional exposure for the Starter System:

Notional exposure = (risk target × capital) ÷ instrument risk %

The risk target will normally be 12%, but if using multiple instruments or trading rules then it should be adjusted using the calculations in chapters seven and eight. Now I am going to modify the formula as follows:

FORMULA 29: NOTIONAL EXPOSURE INCORPORATING FORECAST STRENGTH

Notional exposure = [(forecast ÷ 10) × risk target × capital] ÷ instrument risk %

There is a new variable in the formula: the *forecast*. This is a prediction of what our risk-adjusted return is currently expected to be, compared to the long run average. **The forecast is a scaled measure of how confident our trading rule currently is**.

With a forecast of 10 the position will be the same as it is in the original formula. Hence **a forecast of 10 is average.**[128] Higher values for the forecast mean a larger position: a forecast of 20 is a position that's double the average. A lower forecast equates to a smaller position: a forecast of 5 would give a position that is half the average.

Forecasts can be positive or negative; **a positive forecast means we buy, and a negative implies we go short**. In principal forecasts could also be zero, which implies we do not know what the price will do next.

Importantly, I don't use forecasts outside of the range −20 to +20. If a forecast comes out larger than +20, I cap it at +20. Strongly negative forecasts below −20 are floored at −20.

---

[128] The choice of scaling factor is arbitrary, I prefer to use 10 but other values are equally valid.

What's wrong with large forecasts?

There are a couple of reasons[129] why I don't use forecasts that have absolute values larger than 20. Firstly, **a larger forecast means you're taking on more risk,** and using more leverage. This will increase your potential loss if things go wrong.

How bad can things get? Well, back in chapter six I showed you the likely losses from different risk targets. From table 10 (page 97) the chance of a 25% monthly loss with the 12% risk target in the Starter System is tiny. However, suppose you had a rule that produced a forecast of 40? Then your current expected risk would be four times greater than the average of 12%, equivalent to a risk target of 48%.

From table 10 the chance of losing 25%, with an elevated risk target of 48%, is substantial: 3.6%. You could expect to lose a quarter of your capital every couple of years. Ouch. If, however, you capped your forecast at 20, equivalent to a risk target of 24%, then theoretically a loss of this magnitude will still be *very* unlikely (0.02% to be precise – once every 400 years or so).

Secondly, **most trading rules don't seem to work so well at extremes.**

First, consider trend-following rules like the moving average crossover, and breakout rule. Very strong forecasts will appear when the market has been trending for some time. But after a prolonged bull market there is nobody left to buy, and a sell off becomes more likely. Sharp sell offs also produce strong negative forecasts for trend following rules, but markets tend to rally immediately after market crashes. (This is known as the 'dead cat bounce', since apparently dead cats bounce if you drop them off a building. I haven't personally checked the veracity of this fact.) So, when trend forecasts are too strong, reversals become more likely, and the forecast for a continuing trend will often be wrong.

There are similar effects in carry trading. This is especially true in FX markets, where substantial differences in interest rates usually arise in emerging markets that are on the brink of a crisis.

For example, in Thailand interest rates reached around 11% in early 1997 versus 6% in the US. This produced a strong carry forecast, buying Thai baht and selling US dollars. For several years this had worked well as the Thai baht to US dollar FX rate was fixed, or in economist jargon it was 'pegged'. Unfortunately, in July 1997 the Thai government was forced to drop the peg, and the Thai baht halved in value. There were catastrophic losses for carry traders.

Limiting your forecast to +20 or –20 reduces the harm you will do to your trading account when disaster strikes.

---

[129] Other more technical reasons are elucidated in *Systematic Trading*, page 113 (print edition).

Approximate position scaling for trading rules: eyeballing

How do we go from charts, like figure 30 and figure 31, to a numeric forecast between −20 and +20? The simplest option is to eyeball the chart. At the end of figure 31 it looks like a really strong short forecast is required: perhaps −15 or −20. In contrast the forecast on our long position in figure 30 should be quite small; perhaps +5. Just make sure you have enough history on your charts to judge how strong a forecast is compared to historical averages.

Precise position scaling for trading rules

I don't use the eyeballing method, since it is very subjective. Instead I calculate the correct forecast systematically. The method for doing this will vary depending on the trading rule you are using, but there are usually four steps involved:

1. Get the raw forecast from the trading rule.

2. Divide the raw forecast by instrument risk to get a risk-adjusted forecast (we adjust forecasts for risk, because a forecast is a prediction of risk-adjusted returns).

3. Rescale the risk-adjusted forecast so that the average value for a forecast is 10 (it is unlikely that the risk-adjusted forecast will have the right scaling, so a second adjustment is usually needed).

4. Cap any large forecasts at +20 or −20.

Moving average crossover

Let's see how to work out the forecast for the Starter System rule, a moving average crossover (MAC). The calculation for a moving average pair of f (fast) and s (slow) days is formula 13:

$$MAC^{f,s}_t = MA^f_t - MA^s_t$$

Moving averages are in the same units as prices, so *MAC* is in units of price difference. By coincidence in both figure 30 (Euro Stoxx) and figure 31 (corn) the difference between the two moving averages is 20 price units:

$$MAC^{corn} = -20$$

$$MAC^{Euro\ Stoxx} = +20$$

Now we need the instrument risk (step 2). To match the units of *MAC* this is measured in units of **annual standard deviation of price returns**. We derive this from the usual instrument risk, a standard deviation of returns in *percentage* terms, which I showed you how to estimate back in chapter six (page 129). To convert this into *price* units we use formula 22 (which was originally introduced for stop loss calculations in chapter five):

> Instrument risk in price units = Instrument risk as percentage volatility × current price

The percentage standard deviation of returns for corn that I used in chapter six was 11.9% a year, and 9.6% for Euro Stoxx. The price of corn was 379, and 3,391 for Euro Stoxx; again from chapter six. So, the instrument risk in price units comes in at:

> Instrument risk in price units = 379 × 11.9% = 45.10 for corn

> Instrument risk in price units = 3391 × 9.6% = 325.54 for Euro Stoxx

Now we need to divide the MAC value (−20 for corn and +20 for Euro Stoxx) by the instrument risk.

> Risk-adjusted MAC forecast = MAC ÷ instrument risk in price units

That gives us risk-adjusted forecasts of:

> Risk-adjusted MAC forecast = −20 ÷ 45.10= −0.443 for corn

> Risk-adjusted MAC forecast = +20 ÷ 325.54 = +0.061 for Euro Stoxx

As the charts suggest, once we have accounted for volatility **the forecast for corn is much stronger than that of Euro Stoxx.**

Next, we need to rescale the forecast (step 3). Scaling factors for the MAV pair used in the Starter System, plus several others,[130] are shown in table 65. Sometimes the magnitude of the scaled forecast will come out at more than 20; if this happens you should limit it to +20 (for a long) or −20 (for a short) (step 4).

---

[130] All the scaling factors in this chapter have been calculated using a back-test over my own set of 37 instruments, and verified using an even wider set of artificial data. However, they are valid regardless of what you are trading, as my estimates are very similar across different markets.

> Rescaled forecast if long = Min(+20, Risk-adjusted forecast × scaling factor)

> Rescaled forecast if short = Max(−20, Risk-adjusted forecast × scaling factor)

TABLE 65: SCALING FACTORS FOR DIFFERENT MAV PAIRS

MAV pair	Scaling factor
2,8	180.8
4,16	124.32
8,32	83.84
16,64	57.12
32,128	38.24
64,256	25.28

Scaling factors calculated by averaging across back-tests of 37 instruments.

Let's return to the two instruments I've been using as an example. For the 16,64 moving average crossover used in the Starter System, the scaling factor is 57.12. We multiply the risk-adjusted forecasts by this number, and apply a limit −20 or +20:

> Rescaled forecast = Max(−20, −0.443 × 57.12) = Max(−20, −25.3) = **−20** for corn

> Rescaled forecast = Min(+20, +0.061 × 57.12) = Min(+20, +3.5) = **+3.5** for Euro Stoxx

As expected, the forecast for corn, which we'd cap at −20, is much stronger than the forecast for Euro Stoxx at just +3.5.

Breakout

Here is a reminder of the final step in the calculation of the breakout rule I introduced in chapter eight, formula 28:

$$\text{Scaled price in range} = (P_t - R^{AVG}_N) \div (R^{MAX}_N - R^{MIN}_N)$$

This will vary between +0.5 (if the current price is at the top of its range) and −0.5 (if the price is at the bottom of the range). This calculation is already risk-adjusted,[131] so all we need to do is multiply the scaled price by a scaling factor.[132] These can be found in table 66. Notice that these are quite different from those in table 65. This is quite normal, different rules can legitimately have completely different scaling factors. Remember to cap any forecasts lower than −20 or higher than +20.

TABLE 66: SCALING FACTORS FOR DIFFERENT BREAKOUT LOOK BACKS

Breakout N	Scaling factor
10	28.6
20	31.6
40	32.7
80	33.5
160	33.5
320	33.5

Scaling factors calculated by averaging across back-tests of 37 instruments.

---

[131] We don't use instrument risk explicitly in the breakout calculation. However, we do divide by the price range, and instruments with larger price ranges also have greater volatility, so it has roughly the same effect as dividing by instrument risk.

[132] Technical note: You might expect that the scaling factor would be around 40, since an average value for breakout rules is probably about 0.25 (in the middle of the range from 0 to 0.5), and we require a scaled forecast of around 10: 10 ÷ 0.25 = 40. In fact, as table 66 shows, (a) the correct scaling factors are all under 40, and (b) come in slightly differently depending on the value of N. This is because (a) the raw breakout signal is not uniformly distributed, and (b) square root time scaling effects.

As an example, here's the raw and scaled forecast calculation using N=320 for crude oil, with the values I used as an example in chapter eight, and with the appropriate scaling factor of 33.5 (final row of table 66):

Scaled price in range = $(P_t - R^{AVG}{}_N) \div (R^{MAX}{}_N - R^{MIN}{}_N)$

= (100.3 − 103.3) ÷ (107.78 − 98.76) = −0.33

Scaled forecast = Max(−20, risk-adjusted forecast × scaling factor)

= Max(−20, −0.33 × 33.5) = −11.1

We'd be short crude oil in this situation, with a forecast a little stronger than the average of 10.

Carry

Back in chapter eight I defined the carry rule as the *expected annual percentage return*. This means that volatility scaling is simple; we just need to divide by the *instrument risk*, which I explained how to estimate back in chapter six. We also need the scaling factor. After back-testing I would recommend using a scaling factor of 30 for carry.

TABLE 67: EXAMPLE OF CARRY FORECAST CALCULATION AS OF JUNE 2018

	Expected annual percentage return (A)	Instrument risk (B)	Risk-adjusted forecast C = A ÷ B	Scaling factor (D)	Scaled carry forecast E = C×D	Capped forecast Min(E,+20) Max(E,−20)
Gold	−12.40%	11.00%	−1.13	30	−33.8	−20.0
Corn	−7.40%	11.90%	−0.62	30	−18.7	−18.7
Euro Stoxx 50	2.10%	9.60%	+0.22	30	+6.6	+6.6
AUDUSD	−0.98%	8.70%	−0.11	30	−3.4	−3.4
S&P 500	0.05%	16.00%	+0.03	30	+0.09	+0.09

Expected percentage return (A) calculated in chapter seven, page 201 onwards. Instrument risk (B) from table 16. Scaling factor (D) calculated using a back-test averaging across 37 instruments.

Table 67 shows how I'd calculate current values of the carry forecast for the example instruments in chapter six, using the expected annual percentage carry returns I worked out in chapter eight, and annual standard deviation figures from chapter six. Notice the *capped* forecasts in the final column. It's possible for scaled carry forecasts to come out with an absolute value greater than 20, so you should cap forecasts as I've done here for gold.

Non-binary trading with multiple trading rules

With multiple rules you should use the same weighting scheme I suggested in chapter eight. However instead of weighting values of +10 and –10 you should weight the *forecasts* from each rule.[133] There is also no need to round the value of the weighted forecast.

For example, suppose your weights are 40% for the moving average 16,64 rule, 10% for a breakout rule, and 50% for the carry rule. If their respective forecasts are +6, –12, and +10; then the weighted average will be:

$$[0.4 \times (+6)] + [0.1 \times (-12)] + [0.5 \times (+10)] = +6.2$$

In this simple example we'd use a forecast of +6.2 to calculate our position using formula 29.

Do we need more capital for non-binary trading?

Non-binary trading makes a lot of sense, but it also has a big disadvantage: **it requires more capital** – at least in theory.

Imagine that you are trading the Euro Stoxx, which is the instrument I recommended in chapter six for CFD traders. This requires a minimum of $6,500 to trade a single contract,[134] and ideally twice that: $13,000. With $13,000 you can trade the binary Starter System using two CFD contracts, and should you lose some money you would revert to trading a single contract.

Now suppose you decide to change the size of your position according to forecast strength, again with initial capital of $13,000 for an average position of two contracts. On average (forecast of +10 or –10) the trading rule will tell you to buy, or sell, two contracts. With a weak forecast (+5 or –5) you would trade one contract, and if

---

[133] Technical note: In theory we should compensate for the diversification benefit across forecasts by applying a second diversification multiplier; in *Systematic Trading* this factor is the 'forecast diversification multiplier' (FDM). Without the FDM the mean absolute value of our combined forecasts will not be equal to the desired value of 10, but will be slightly lower. Omitting the FDM makes the system simpler and safer, and hence I have not included it in this book.
[134] From table 5, page 82.

the forecast is exceptionally strong (+20 or −20) you would hold four contracts. So far, so good.

Your problems begin if you lose some money and end up with less than $13,000. Now, instead of an average of two contracts, you can only hold one. With a very strong forecast you'd buy or sell twice the average: two contracts. But if your forecast is weaker than average you can't buy or sell half a contract, so you would end up with no position at all. This somewhat reduces the benefit of non-binary trading.

One solution is to begin with even more capital: four times the absolute minimum. So, for Euro Stoxx CFD trading, you would have 4 × $6,500 = $26,000. This means you could take an average position of four contracts; owning up to eight contracts if the forecast was strong, and less than four for weaker forecasts. If you lost half your money, you would be down to an average of two contracts, but you could still reduce your position to a single contract if the forecast was weak.

But I do not advise this. Instead, if you have extra capital you're almost certainly better off using it to diversify your trading strategy across multiple instruments.[135]

Let me explain. From chapter seven,[136] going from one to two instruments improves the expected Sharpe ratio (SR) of the Starter System from 0.24 to 0.30, an increase of 0.06 SR units. From earlier in this chapter, the benefit of non-binary trading, assuming you've already dropped the stop loss, is the same: 0.06 SR units. This looks like a dead heat, but although similar in magnitude, the improvement from adding extra instruments has greater statistical significance than the benefits of non-binary trading.

Additionally, you would still keep some of the benefit of non-binary trading, even if you end up trading with reduced capital.[137] Only traders who have lost money, and who subsequently have weak forecasts, are affected. We expect smaller profits when forecasts are weak, so we are not giving up much return. In my own back-testing, I have found that the average degradation in performance from having insufficient capital with non-binary trading was minuscule: less than 0.02 SR units. The gains from diversifying across two instruments (0.06 SR units) exceed the small cost of occasionally not being able to hold a position.

In summary, you should not use extra capital to ensure you can continue non-binary trading when losses occur; instead use it to add more instruments to your system. **You can ignore the theoretical requirement for higher minimum account size when conducting non-binary trading.**

---

[135] In fact the capital required with multiple instruments may be even lower than for a single instrument, because (i) we drop the requirement for double the absolute minimum capital, (ii) the effect of the instrument diversification multiplier, and (iii) higher account level risk targets, due to the expected benefits of diversifying.

[136] Page 183.

[137] I discuss this in a blog post: **qoppac.blogspot.com/2016/03/diversification-and-small-account-size.html**

Adjusting position size for risk

If our forecast changes, then our position should also be adjusted. However, there is another important factor that affects position sizing: the **current risk of an instrument**.

When instrument risk changes you should, in theory, change the size of your position. To understand why, consider the following example:

- US 10-year bond CFD on future, $ bet per point

- Capital $45,000. FX rate is 1.0.

- Risk target 12%

- Forecast +10 (long)

- Instrument risk 3% a year

- Price $119

- Value of a point 0.01

- Minimum and incremental trade size $1 per point

Our notional exposure target, using formula 29, would start out at:

Notional exposure = [(forecast ÷ 10) × risk target % × capital] ÷ instrument risk %

= [(10 ÷ 10) × 12% × $45,000] ÷ 3% = $180,000

To work out the CFD bet per point we use the appropriate version of formula 20 introduced earlier in the book:

CFD bet per point = (notional exposure × FX Rate × point size) ÷ price

= ($180,000 × 1 × 0.01) ÷ 119 = $15.13 per point = $15 per point (rounded)

Now, imagine that there was a market panic of a similar scale to 2008, where equities were brutally crushed and bonds rallied. This would be great for our long bond position. But in those circumstances the risk of the US 10-year bond would also skyrocket. If the instrument risk rose to 9%, trading capital rose to $50,000, and the forecast remained at 10, and we recalculate what our notional exposure target should be:

> Notional exposure = [(forecast ÷ 10) × risk target % × capital] ÷ instrument risk %
>
> = [(10 ÷ 10) × 12% × $50,000] ÷ 9% = $66,666.67

So, our current position (with a notional value of around $180,000) is nearly three times larger than it should be, and hence nearly three times riskier! This has been caused by the threefold increase in risk, slightly offset by the rise in capital. We need to reduce our position significantly.

Adjusting position size without incurring heavy trading costs

Your estimate of instrument risk and your trading rule forecast will change daily. Does this mean you should make small adjustment trades to our position every day? It's a nice idea in theory, but every time you trade you lose money: the execution spread, and possibly commissions.

To avoid this, it's necessary to avoid making frequent small adjustments, and only trade when your position is way off target. To do this you need to compare your *ideal notional exposure* to the *current exposure* implied by your position. If these differ by more than 10% of the *average exposure*, then a trade is required.

Let's look at the calculations in more detail.

First you need to calculate your ideal notional exposure using formula 29, on a daily basis:

> Ideal notional exposure = [(forecast ÷ 10) × target risk % × capital] ÷ instrument risk %

Next, work out the *current exposure* in home currency that is implied by the current position. If I rearrange the various versions of formula 20 I used to work out how much to bet, then I get these formulas for current exposure:

FORMULA 30: CALCULATING EXPOSURE, GIVEN CURRENT POSITION

> Spot FX exposure = Value of FX position in home currency
>
> Spread bet exposure = (bet per point × price) ÷ (FX Rate × point size)

CFD (per contract) exposure = (CFD contracts × price × contract size) ÷ FX Rate

CFD (per point) exposure = (bet per point × price) ÷ (FX Rate × point size)

Futures exposure = (futures contracts × price × multiplier) ÷ FX Rate

Margin trade exposure = (number of shares × share price) ÷ FX Rate

We will also need to work out the *average exposure*. This is the size of position for a forecast of 10:

FORMULA 31: AVERAGE EXPOSURE

Average exposure = [target risk % × capital] ÷ instrument risk %

Now, **if the current exposure deviates from your actual notional exposure by 10%[138] or more of the average exposure**, then you need an adjusting trade:[139]

FORMULA 32: DEVIATION FROM IDEAL EXPOSURE

Deviation % = (Ideal exposure – current exposure) ÷ average exposure

Let us return to the US 10-year bond example above:

- US 10-year bond CFD on future, $ bet per point.

- Capital $45,000. FX rate is 1.0.

- Risk target 12%.

- Forecast +10 (long).

- Instrument risk 3% a year.

- Price $119.

---

[138] Technical note: The optimal size of the non trade region depends on the trading costs, and a few other factors. 10% is a sufficiently conservative value given the costs paid by smaller traders using the leveraged products in this book.

[139] We use the average exposure as the denominator in this formula, not the current exposure. Otherwise when current exposure is low this percentage will be meaninglessly large.

- Value of a point 0.01.

- Notional exposure: $180,000 which works out to $15 per point (calculated earlier).

Suppose that the capital and forecast are unchanged, but the instrument risk now rises to 3.1% annually and the price has also changed, to $118. The ideal notional exposure is now:

> Ideal notional exposure = [(forecast ÷ 10) × risk target % × capital] ÷ instrument risk %

> = [(10 ÷ 10) × 12% × $45,000] ÷ 3.1% = $174,194

Now for our current exposure. We use the current price of $118, and a new exchange rate if that was relevant (it isn't in this case). The point size is still 0.01, and the current position is $15 per point:

> Current exposure, CFD (per point) = (bet per point × price) ÷ (FX Rate × point size)

> = ($15 × 118) ÷ (1 × 0.01) = $177,000

We also need the average exposure (which on this occasion is identical to the ideal exposure, since the forecast is 10):

> Average exposure = [target risk % × capital] ÷ instrument risk %

> = 12% × $45,000 ÷ 3.1% = $174,194

The ideal exposure is different from the current exposure by:

> Deviation % = (Ideal exposure – current exposure) ÷ average exposure

> = (174,194 – 177,000) ÷ 17,4194 = –1.6%

Since this is less than 10% we would not do any adjusting trade. Now, imagine things get a little more exciting:

- Price rallies to $120.

- Capital rises to $48,000.

- Forecast changes to +12.

- Instrument risk goes up to 4.3%.

The ideal notional exposure has fallen further to:

Ideal notional exposure = [(forecast ÷ 10) × risk target % × capital] ÷ instrument risk %

= [(12 ÷ 10) × 12% × $48,000] ÷ 4.3% = $160,744

The current exposure is at $15 per point is:

Current exposure = (bet per point × price) ÷ (FX Rate × point size)

= ($15 × 120) ÷ (1 × 0.01) = $180,000

Average exposure is now:

Average exposure = [target risk % × capital] ÷ instrument risk %

= (12% × $48,000) ÷ 4.3% = $133,953

The deviation from the ideal exposure is:

Deviation % = (Ideal exposure – current exposure) ÷ average exposure

= (160,744 – 180,000) ÷ 133,953 = –14.4%

This is larger than 10%, so at this point we do a trade necessary to reduce our exposure. The bet per point required by the ideal exposure of $160,744 is:

$ bet per point = (Ideal exposure home currency × FX Rate × point size) ÷ price

= ($160,744 × 1 × 0.01) ÷ 120 = $13.4 = $13 rounded

As we are long $15 per point, we need to close $2 per point of our position. Any adjusting trades also have to be larger than any minimum specified by the broker for the product and instrument you're using. If your account value is modest it's quite likely that many of your adjusting trades won't meet the minimum trade size. You will have to keep your position at the same size.

These calculations have been pretty gruesome but remember in practice that you would be using a spreadsheet to automate them.

Practical non-binary trading

Updated trade plan

Here are the required updates to our trade plan for non-binary trading:

Opening rule	One or more rules that calculate a *scaled forecast* between –20 and +20. A negative forecast is a short position, and a positive forecast is a long position.
Weighting multiple rules	If you are using multiple rules, then you should use the same weights as in chapter eight to weight the *forecasts* from each rule. You do not need to round the weighted forecast.
Initial position sizing rule	**Notional exposure = (forecast ÷ 10) × (target risk % × capital) ÷ instrument risk %** Where target risk is normally 12% and instrument risk is measured as annual standard deviation of returns.
Position management (new rule)	**Ideal exposure = (forecast ÷ 10) × (target risk % × capital) ÷ instrument risk %** **Average exposure = [target risk % × capital] ÷ instrument risk %** **Deviation % = (Ideal exposure – current exposure) ÷ Average exposure** Adjusting trade if (i) Deviation is 10% or more, and (ii) adjusting trade is above broker's minimum size.
Closing rule	No explicit closing rule. Trades will be closed when an adjusting trade requires it.

Example of position management

Let's see how the initial trades from chapter six would have been different if I take forecast values into account.

Step one

Work out the required notional exposure (formula 29):

Notional exposure = [(forecast ÷ 10) × target risk × capital] ÷ instrument risk %

TABLE 68: NOTIONAL EXPOSURE FOR INITIAL TRADES IN JUNE 2018, INCLUDING FORECASTS

Instrument	Instrument risk (A)	Capital (B)	Forecast (C)	Notional exposure [(C ÷ 10) × B × 12%] ÷ A
Gold	11.0%	£1,200	−18.2	Short £2,383
Corn	11.9%	$40,000	−20.0	Short $80,672
Euro Stoxx 50	9.6%	$13,000	+3.4	Long $5,525
AUDUSD	8.7%	£1,100	−14.9	Short £2,261
S&P 500	16.0%	$7,100	+1.42	Long $765

Instrument risk (A) from table 16. Capital (B) from chapter six, page 121. Forecasts (C) calculated using MAC 16, 64 trading rule and formulas on page 246 onwards. Notional exposure (D) calculated with 12% target risk using formula 29.

Table 68 shows the notional exposure calculations for the initial example trades, using the appropriate capital.

Step two

Calculate how large the position should be in the appropriate units for each product (formula 20). All the values are from chapter six and are correct as of 18 June 2018. Instrument parameters are from table 14, prices from table 15, and the FX rates are the same I used to calculate the original notional exposures in chapter six, on page 135.

	Spread bet per point = (Exposure home currency × FX Rate × point size) ÷ price
Gold: spread bet on future	For gold the FX rate is 1 (since you can bet in pounds per point and your capital is in £), the point size is 1, and the price is 1,268.
	(£2,383 × 1 × 1) ÷ (1,268) = £1.88 per point
	The minimum bet per point is £0.50 and I can bet in one penny increments beyond this: the bet is **short gold at £1.88 per point**.
	Futures contracts = (Exposure home currency × FX Rate) ÷ (price × contract multiplier)
Corn: futures	For corn, the FX rate is 1 (since the example capital is in dollars), the price is 379, and the multiplier is $50.
	($80,672 × 1) ÷ (379 × $50) = 4.26
	This needs to be rounded: **go short four contracts of corn futures**.
	CFD contracts to bet = (Exposure home currency × FX Rate) ÷ (price × contract size)
Euro Stoxx: CFD per contract	For Euro Stoxx the FX rate to convert dollars into euros is currently 0.86, the contract size is €2, and the price is 3,391.
	($5,525 × 0.86) ÷ (3,391 × 2) = 0.7 contracts
	I round this to **long one contract of Euro Stoxx**.
	CFD bet per point = (Exposure home currency × FX Rate × point size) ÷ price
Euro Stoxx: CFD per point	For Euro Stoxx the FX rate to convert dollars into euros is currently 0.86, the point size is 1, and the price is 3,391.
	($5,525 × 0.86 × 1) ÷ 3,391 = €1.40 per point
	The minimum bet is €2 per point, so if I round I get a required position which is **long €2 per point of Euro Stoxx**.
	FX exposure = Exposure home currency × FX Rate
AUDUSD: Spot FX	The AUDGBP rate on 18 June was 1.781 (note, we're using this not the AUDUSD rate as our home currency is GBP).
	For AUDUSD with an FX rate of 1.781 I'd go short (buy USD, sell AUD) £2,261 × 1.781 = A$4,026
	My broker requires this to be rounded to **A$4,000**.

Number of shares = Exposure home currency × FX Rate ÷ price

S&P 500: Margin account

For the S&P 500 SPY ETF the share price is $276, the FX rate is 1, so the number of shares is:

765 × 1 ÷ 276 = 2.74

This would be rounded to **three shares**. However, the minimum viable position you can hold in this instrument is ten shares (see appendix B for an explanation), so our position would be **zero shares**.

Example of position management

You should check daily that the exposure implied by your open positions hasn't deviated too much from the ideal exposure. The ideal exposure is calculated using the latest forecast, current instrument risk, and the level of capital in your brokerage account.

Let's see how this could be done with the example trades from chapter six, and the prices and risk that were prevailing in the market on 4 July 2018, a few weeks after the original trades were put on.

The first step is to work out my *ideal notional exposure*, as shown in table 69. I have also calculated the average exposure, as that will be needed shortly.

TABLE 69: IDEAL NOTIONAL AND AVERAGE EXPOSURE ON 4 JULY 2018

Instrument	Instrument risk (A)	Capital (B)	Forecast (C)	Notional exposure [(C ÷ 10) × B × 12%] ÷ A	Average exposure (B × 12%) ÷ A
Gold	9.3%	£1,070	-17.9	Short £2,471	£1,380
Corn	23.9%	$40,300	-13.8	Short $27,923	$20,234
Euro Stoxx 50	12.7%	$12,940	-3.4	Short $4,157	$12,227
AUDUSD	8.6%	£1,007	-4.7	Short £722	£1,535
S&P 500	16.0%	$7,002	-2.4	Short $745	$5,252

Instrument risk (A) estimated on 4 July 2018. Capital (B) includes profits or losses made since initial trade. Forecasts (C) calculated using MAC 16, 64 trading rule and formulas on page 246 onwards. Notional exposure calculated with 12% target risk using formula 29. Average exposure calculated using formula 31.

Step two is to work out my *current exposure* using the various flavours of formula 30. I'm using up-to-date prices[140] from 4 July 2018 and, when required, updated FX rates from the same day.

Gold: Spread bet on future	**Exposure = (bet per point × price) ÷ (FX Rate × point size) = (£1.88 × 1,267) ÷ (1 × 1) = £2,382 (short)**
Corn: Future	**Exposure = (futures contracts × price × multiplier) ÷ FX Rate = (4 × 398 × 50) ÷ 1 = $79,600 (short)**
Euro Stoxx 50: CFD on future (bet per contract)	**Exposure = (CFD contracts × price × contract size) ÷ FX Rate = (1 × 3,385 × €2) ÷ 0.87 = $7,782 (long)**
Euro Stoxx 50: CFD on future (bet per point)	**Exposure = (bet per point × price) ÷ (FX Rate × point size) = (€2 × 3,385) ÷ (0.87 × 1) = $7,782 (long)**
AUDUSD: Spot FX	**Exposure = AUD exposure × FX Rate (GBP/ AUD) = A$4,000 ÷ 1.791 = £2,233 (short)**
S&P 500: Margin account	**Exposure = Number of shares × price ÷ FX Rate = 0 × 271 × 1 = $0 (flat)**

Notice that the current exposure is long for Euro Stoxx, but the ideal exposure is short: the sign of the forecast has changed since the original trade was put on.

Step three is to check the deviation (formula 32):

> **Deviation % = (Ideal exposure – current exposure) ÷ average exposure**

If this deviates from my actual notional exposure by **10% of the average exposure**, then I need to make an adjusting trade. Table 70 checks this for each position.

---

[140] Of course, 4 July is a US holiday, so there was no price for corn futures or the S&P 500 that day. I've used the price from the previous day.

TABLE 70: COMPARING IDEAL AND CURRENT EXPOSURE ON 4 JULY 2018

	Ideal exposure (A)	Current exposure (B)	Average exposure (C)	Deviation, D = (A – B) ÷ C	Adjusting trade? ABS(D)>10%
Gold	–£2,471	–£2,382	£1,381	–6.5%	No
Corn	–$27,923	$79,600	$20,234	–255.4%	Yes
Euro Stoxx 50 (per point)	–$4,157	+$7,782	$12,227	–97.6%	Yes
Euro Stoxx 50 (per contract)	–$4,157	+$7,782	$12,227	–97.6%	Yes
AUDUSD	–£722	–£2,233	£1,535	+98.4%	Yes
S&P 500	–$745	+$0	$5,252	–14.2%	Yes

Ideal exposure (A) and average exposure (C) from table 69. Current exposure (B) as calculated above. Deviation (D) calculated using formula 32.

Apart from the gold spread bet I will need adjusting trades all of my positions. Finally, I recalculate what my positions would be with the ideal exposure (using the various versions of formula 20, with prices and FX rates for 4 July 2018), and check to see if the resulting trade is feasible:

Gold: Spread bet (No trade required, included as an example)

Spread bet per point = (Exposure home currency × FX Rate × point size) ÷ price = (2,471 × 1 × 1) ÷ 1,267 = short £1.95 per point

My current bet is short £1.88 per point. As the minimum bet is £0.50 I wouldn't be able to short an additional £0.07 per point of gold, unless my broker made an exception for existing positions. This is academic anyway, since the deviation in table 70 is less than 10%.

No adjusting trade is necessary.

Corn Futures

Futures contracts = (Exposure home currency × FX Rate) ÷ (price × contract multiplier) = (27,923 × 1) ÷ (398 × 50) = short 1.4 contracts

After rounding into whole contracts I'd want to hold one contract – I currently hold four.

Buy three contracts to partially close short position.

Euro Stoxx: CFD per contract	**CFD contracts to bet = (Exposure home currency × FX Rate) ÷ (price × contract size) = (4,157 × 0.87) ÷ (3,385 × 2) = short 0.53 contracts** I'm currently long one contract of Euro Stoxx, and the forecast wants to be short one contract. Adjusting trade: **Sell one contract Euro Stoxx to close.** **Open new trade in Euro Stoxx, short one contract.**
Euro Stoxx: CFD per point	**CFD bet per point = (Exposure home currency × FX Rate × point size) ÷ price = (4,157 × 0.87 × 1) ÷ 3,385 = short €1.07 per point** My current position is long €2 per point. The minimum bet is €2 per point with one cent increments beyond this. Adjusting trade: **Sell €2 per point of Euro Stoxx to close.** **Open new trade in Euro Stoxx, short €2 per point.**
AUDUSD: FX	**FX exposure = Exposure home currency × FX Rate = £722 × 1.791 = A\$1,293** My broker requires me to round this to: short A\$1,300 (smallest increment \$100). My current position is A\$4,000, implying I need to reduce my position by A\$2,700. Adjusting trade: **Buy \$2,700 AUDUSD, to partially close.**
S&P 500: Margin account	**Number of shares = Exposure home currency × FX Rate ÷ price** For the S&P 500 SPY ETF the share price is \$271, the FX rate is 1, so the number of shares required: **745 × 1 ÷ 271 = 2.75** This would be rounded to **three shares**. As we are flat the appropriate adjusting trade would be to sell three shares short. Again, however, this isn't large enough to meet the ten shares minimum trade I calculate in appendix B.

TABLE 71: SUMMARY OF ADJUSTING TRADES REQUIRED

	Ideal position (A)	Current exposure (B)	Adjusting trade?
Gold	−£1.95 / point	−£1.88 / point	No: Deviation<10%
Corn	−1.4 contracts	−4 contracts	+3 contracts (part close)
Euro Stoxx 50 (per point)	−€1.07 per point	+€2 per point	−€2 per point (close) −€2 per point (new)
Euro Stoxx 50 (per contract)	−0.53 contracts	+1 contract	−1 contract (close) −1 contract (new)
AUDUSD	−$1,300	−$4,000	+$2,700 (part close)
S&P 500	−3 shares	0 shares	No: Trade<minimum size

Table 71 summarises the adjusting trades. In practice, some of these trades would have happened earlier, had I checked them every day rather than waiting a few weeks. However, this book would have been even longer and extremely dull had it included several months of daily exposure calculations!

CHAPTER ELEVEN
What Next?

THE STARTER SYSTEM IS DESIGNED to help you learn how to trade safely. However, it's unlikely that anyone will want to use it for the rest of their trading career. I'm sure you will want to use your new found knowledge of the markets to develop your trading and increase your expected profitability.

What comes next for someone who is confidently trading the Starter System?

There are three possible routes you can take:

1. Improve upon the Starter System, using the ideas in part three and part four of this book.

2. Learn how to design and back-test your own systematic trading rules.

3. Move into Semi-Automatic Trading where you use your own experience and judgment to decide when to open positions, but use the system for risk control and position management.

Let's look at each of these in turn.

1. Improvements to the Starter System

The basic Starter System, introduced in chapters five and six, delivers a back-tested Sharpe ratio (SR) before costs of around 0.24, equating to pre-cost returns of around 4.9% per year.[141]

The improvements you can make will depend on your available capital, time, and expertise. Here is a recap of the upgrades you could make to the Starter System, listed in order of potential improvement, with the best first:

---

[141] If you want to know where these figures come from: Starter System (page 92), instruments (page 170), trading rules (page 195), stop loss (page 227), and non-binary trading (page 243).

- Adding **multiple instruments**, as in chapter seven, will improve your SR by a factor of around 1.25x (for two instruments) and 2.3x (for 20 or more). So, with two instruments your expected SR would rise to 0.24 × 1.25 = 0.30. This option is only available if you have sufficient capital to share between multiple instruments.

- Introducing **new trading rules**, like those in chapter eight, will increase your back-tested SR by a factor of between 1.13x (for two trading rules) and 1.48x (for 20 or more). However, using multiple trading rules can be time consuming.

- **Dropping the stop loss**, as in chapter nine, improves the expected SR by a factor of around 1.13x. This can also result in more work, since trading rule forecasts need to be monitored daily.

- If you have already dropped the stop loss then moving to **non-binary continuous trading**, which I discussed in chapter ten, increases the SR by a factor of about 1.25x.

2. Back-testing and designing your own system

If you are hooked on systematic trading you might want to continue developing the Starter System, beyond what is covered in this book. I recommend that you continue using the Starter System, and then add your own novel opening rules (if you aren't using a stop loss then these rules would also be used for closing positions). I strongly advise keeping all the other parts of the Starter System intact.

Here are the steps I take when I'm implementing a new trading rule:

1. Design the trading rule.

2. If you're using continuous trading, modify the rule so it's risk-adjusted, and estimate the required scaling factor (see chapter ten).

3. Estimate the typical number of annual trades, and hence likely costs.

4. Check that it is profitable (or at least not significantly loss making).

5. Decide on the weights to use when averaging it's forecast with other trading rules.

Ideally you would perform steps 2, 3 and 4 by *back-testing* across a large number of instruments (including ones you may not yet be trading). Whilst it is possible to perform all of these steps in a spreadsheet, it's much easier to use specialised software. Unfortunately, this software makes it all too easy to commit the sins I highlighted in chapter three: taking excessive risks, trading too quickly, and assuming the past will repeat itself (*over-fitting*). Careful handling of the software is required to avoid making serious mistakes.

There is much more I could say about the design and testing of trading rules. Naturally, I would recommend reading my first book, *Systematic Trading*, which covers all of these subjects in greater detail.

3. Semi-Automatic Trading

Perhaps you have concluded that systematic trading is not for you. It is way too boring mechanically following rules. You think you have some experience or insight into the market which cannot be implemented using a simple trading rule. You want to use your own subjective judgment to trade: *discretionary* trading.

Way back in chapter three I wrote this:

"Trading systems have two jobs:

1. Deciding when to open a new position, and whether to buy or sell.

2. Deciding the size of position you should have, and how long to hold it for.

I believe that everyone should use a system for the latter, and almost everyone should use a system for the former."

Let me repeat that: **even discretionary traders should use a system to decide on the size of their position and how long to hold it for.** So, if you want to move away from pure systematic trading, I strongly recommend that you do the following:

- Use your own judgment, analysis, subjective process, or examination of chicken entrails to decide whether to buy or sell a particular instrument. This step replaces the opening trading rule in the Starter System.

- Size your positions according to the rules of the Starter System.

- Use the stop loss from the Starter System to close your positions.

In my first book *Systematic Trading*, I named this hybrid of person and machine, a *semi-automatic trader*. There is slightly more to Semi-Automatic Trading than blithely replacing your opening rule with a well-informed guess. Questions we need to address include:

Which instruments and products to trade	If you are making discretionary judgements you may feel you can only trade certain instruments – ones you have a gut feel for. But the same criteria still apply as we used in the Starter System: make sure the costs of the instrument are reasonable (less than the speed limit of 0.08 SR), and that you have the correct level of minimum capital.
What risk target should we use?	Initially you should use the same risk target for the Starter System (12%), or even lower. Risk targets are mainly driven by performance expectations. You cannot back-test discretionary trading decisions, so it's better to be conservative.
	Later in this chapter I discuss how you can use your live trading record to revise your performance expectations, and potentially adjust your risk target.
What stop loss volatility fraction should we use to calculate the stop loss gap?	To begin with you should use the same fraction as the Starter System, 0.5 of instrument risk. This will keep your trading costs under control. It also means you should be predicting price movements over a horizon of about 2 months, to match the trading frequency of the Starter System (5.4 trades per year).
	Later in this chapter I discuss how you could use your live trading record to revise your performance and cost expectations, and potentially adjust your stop loss fraction.
Can we trade multiple instruments? (chapter seven)	Yes, absolutely. This is the best way to enhance your trading performance, especially if you choose instruments that are more diversifying. Of course, it may be difficult to apply your subjective method to totally unrelated instruments, but the gains from doing so are likely to be significant.
	Semi-automatic traders may use instrument diversification multipliers to calculate their instrument level risk targets. They may also choose to increase their account level risk target to reflect the diversification in their portfolio.
Can we use multiple methods to decide when to open positions? (chapter eight)	Most discretionary traders look at a number of different things before deciding what position to take. To take a trivial example, it's often said that it's a bad sign when a corporation opens a new office. Another sell signal is the ownership of one or more private jets.
	You could treat these as two separate trading rules, and then weight them as we did for systematic opening rules in chapter eight.
	Warning: Semi-automatic traders should *not* increase their account level risk target if they are using multiple rules to open positions, as it is impossible to back-test the possible benefits of doing so.

Can we mix subjective judgement and systematic trading rules in the same system?

If you have the capital to trade multiple instruments, then it can make sense to trade some instruments purely systematically, and use a semi-automatic strategy on others. Perhaps there are a few instruments that you can trade with your gut feel. Then to get adequate diversification you can add other instruments from different asset classes, and trade these with a systematic opening rule.

You may also want to use both subjective and systematic opening rules for the same instrument. You could use one or more subjective methods, plus one or more systematic trading rules, and then weight them together as we did for systematic opening rules in chapter eight.

Don't switch between different methods for a given instrument: once you have decided how to trade something, stick to the plan.

Can semi-automatic traders drop the stop loss? (chapter nine)

No, I don't recommend this. **Semi-automatic traders must use a stop loss**.

Without a stop loss you'd be opening *and closing* positions at your own discretion. It would be all too easy to fall into the trap of trading too quickly, or making trading decisions based on emotion ("This has gone up a bit, I'm going to bank this profit quickly." or "Wow this has dropped a lot! But I'm going to hang on – I'm right, and it will come back.").

Is there an equivalent of non-binary trading for semi-automatic traders? (chapter ten)

Yes. Instead of producing a subjective buy or sell decision, you can come up with a finely graduated subjective forecast; from –20 for an instrument you think will plummet in value, up to +20 for something that is going to the moon.

You can also weight multiple non-binary subjective forecasts together, or weight subjective forecasts with non-binary systematic trading rules.

Very important: **You must not change the size of a forecast once a position is established**, and **you must not close a position until a stop loss is triggered**. This is to protect you from the dangers of overtrading.

So, make sure the size of your initial forecast reflects the fact you won't be changing it during the life of the trade.

Performance monitoring

Initially semi-automatic traders should use the same stop loss fraction as in the Starter System, and a risk target no greater than the 12% in the Starter System.[142]

This might seem overcautious. These values are set using the performance expectations we had for the Starter System. But you are a brilliant human trader, much better than a dumb system! Surely you will generate a much higher Sharpe ratio than the measly 0.24 expected for the Starter System, or the slightly higher performance you could expect to get from making the improvements in parts three and four of this book?

If you are on course to make a seriously high Sharpe ratio then you can set a higher risk target. You could also trade faster, since the speed limit I set for costs is based on spending one-third of your expected returns. This would translate to a lower stop loss fraction, a shorter holding period, and more trades per year.

Wait! Don't get carried away. You don't know how good you will be at discretionary trading until you've actually done it. It is better to start trading with the recommended values for risk target and stop loss, then monitor your live trading performance, and if it is respectable enough you could consider changing your system parameters.

In this section I'll explain how you can check to see if your trading is sufficiently profitable to justify an upwards revision of your performance expectations. In the next section I'll discuss how you can use these expectations to adjust your risk target and stop loss horizon.

You will not be recalibrating your system based on your average realised trading profits. Instead you will be using a *conservative* estimate of what your likely profitability will be. If you perform significantly better than the Sharpe ratio expected for the Starter System, then your expected Sharpe ratio will be higher. But your expected future Sharpe ratio will always be set at a lower, more conservative, level than what you have actually achieved.

There are two ways to check performance; using daily returns, or the returns from each trade. Given you will be trading quite slowly it is more appropriate to use the returns from each trade. Otherwise you can get several months of superficially attractive daily returns if you just happen to be the right way round on your first trade. Also, it is less work to use the returns from each trade, and if you are trading multiple instruments, you can gather evidence faster.

First you need to calculate the *performance ratio*[143] of your trading:

---

[142] If they are trading one instrument. For multiple instruments, it is okay to use a higher account level risk target to reflect the diversification in their portfolio, and to apply an instrument diversification multiplier to instrument level risk targets. See chapter seven.
[143] This is a bit like a Sharpe ratio (an average return over a standard deviation), except there is no borrowing rate and it is calculated per trade, rather than per year.

FORMULA 33: PERFORMANCE RATIO

Performance ratio = r ÷ s

Where **r** is the average profit from each trade after all costs have been paid, and **s** is the standard deviation of your trade by trade profits.[144] Once you have the performance ratio, plus the number of trades you have done so far, you can look them up in table 72. This will give you a *conservative expected Sharpe ratio after costs:*[145] the Sharpe ratio (SR) you can be reasonably confident of achieving given what you've done so far.

TABLE 72: CONSERVATIVE EXPECTED SHARPE RATIO FOR A GIVEN PERFORMANCE RATIO

	Number of trades												
Performance ratio	5	10	15	20	25	50	100	150	250	500	1K	2K	10K
0.18 or less	0.24	0.24	0.24	0.24	0.24	0.24	0.24	0.24	0.24	0.24	0.24	0.24	0.24
0.20	0.24	0.24	0.24	0.24	0.24	0.24	0.24	0.24	0.24	0.24	0.25	0.26	0.28
0.22	0.24	0.24	0.24	0.24	0.24	0.24	0.24	0.24	0.24	0.27	0.29	0.31	0.33
0.24	0.24	0.24	0.24	0.24	0.24	0.24	0.24	0.26	0.29	0.31	0.34	0.35	0.37
0.26	0.24	0.24	0.24	0.24	0.24	0.24	0.27	0.30	0.33	0.36	0.39	0.40	0.42
0.28	0.24	0.24	0.24	0.24	0.24	0.25	0.32	0.35	0.38	0.41	0.43	0.45	0.47
0.30	0.24	0.24	0.24	0.24	0.24	0.29	0.36	0.39	0.42	0.46	0.48	0.49	0.51
0.35	0.24	0.24	0.24	0.26	0.30	0.40	0.47	0.51	0.54	0.57	0.59	0.61	0.62
0.40	0.24	0.24	0.30	0.36	0.41	0.51	0.58	0.62	0.65	0.68	0.71	0.72	0.75
0.50	0.24	0.39	0.50	0.57	0.61	0.72	0.80	0.84	0.87	0.91	0.93	0.95	0.98
0.60	0.30	0.57	0.69	0.76	0.81	0.93	1.00	1.00	1.00	1.00	1.00	1.00	1.00
0.70	0.45	0.74	0.87	0.96	1.00	1.00	1.00	1.00	1.00	1.00	1.00	1.00	1.00
0.80 +	0.60	0.91	1.00	1.00	1.00	1.00	1.00	1.00	1.00	1.00	1.00	1.00	1.00

---

[144] I explain how to calculate these figures in appendix C, page 315.
[145] Very technical note: We can be 75% confident that the Sharpe ratio is equal to or higher than the values shown in the table, given the performance ratio. Assuming 5.4 trades per year as in the Starter System and a borrowing rate of 2% I can imply the annualised Sharpe ratio from the performance ratio. This in turn gives the mean estimate for the Sharpe ratio distribution. For Gaussian returns the variance of the sampling estimate for a Sharpe ratio is given by $(1+0.5SR^2)/N$, where N is the number of periods. I then take the 25% percentile point from the resulting implied distribution of the Sharpe ratio estimate.

We can be 75% confident that the Sharpe ratio is equal to or higher than the value shown, given the performance ratio. Where there are insufficient trades, I assume the expected Sharpe ratio is 0.24.

Where the performance ratio is too low, or there is not enough history, then we are unable to say what the expected SR is with much confidence, and you should stick with the expected SR from the Starter System, 0.24. Notice also that I have capped the expected Sharpe ratio at 1.0, even when theoretically it could be higher. This is to stop you using an excessively high-risk target.

Let's take an example. Suppose you do 12 trades, and the average return on each trade after costs is 2% of your capital, with a standard deviation of 3.9% of your capital. The performance ratio will be:

$$0.02 \div 0.039 = 0.513$$

To be conservative we round this value down and look at the row in table 72 relating to a performance ratio of 0.5. We also round down 12 trades to ten. In the row for a ratio of 0.5, and the column for ten trades the conservative expected Sharpe ratio is 0.39.

Using the original stop loss fraction and opening rule, it would take about two years to do 12 trades. A performance ratio of 0.513 is extremely good: it is more than four times better than what I expect the Starter System to achieve.[146] So you can see that fairly strong evidence is needed to justify a higher expected Sharpe ratio, either in the form of a high performance ratio, or a very long track record of actual trading, or both.

System calibration for semi-automatic traders

From the last section you should have estimated your *conservative expected Sharpe ratio after costs*. Assuming this is higher than the 0.24 for the Starter System, you can now revisit chapter five (page 94) to see if you can increase your risk target. Assuming that your own personal risk tolerance is high enough, and that you wouldn't run into any problems with broker leverage limits,[147] this suggests you *could* increase your risk target to half the conservative expected Sharpe ratio.

FORMULA 34: RISK TARGET GIVEN CONSERVATIVE SHARPE RATIO

Risk target = Conservative SR ÷ 2

---

[146] The expected performance ratio of the Starter System is about 0.18. In reality we have to pay costs that would reduce that.

[147] See page 94.

In the example above, given 12 trades with a performance ratio of 0.513, the conservative Sharpe ratio from table 72 was 0.39. The new risk target could be 0.39 ÷ 2 = **19.5%**. This is an absolute maximum – you do not have to use that figure, but you must not have a higher risk target.[148]

With a higher Sharpe ratio you can also afford to spend more on costs. Remember from chapter five that using my speed limit, the maximum risk-adjusted cost is equal to the pre-cost Sharpe ratio divided by 3. This is equivalent to setting your cost budget at half your post-cost Sharpe ratio.[149]

Divide the expected conservative Sharpe ratio by 2. This gives you your risk-adjusted budget for total costs. Subtract holding costs for the relevant instrument, which you have to pay no matter how often you trade, and you have your budget for transaction costs. Then divide what is left by the expected cost per trade for each instrument you are trading. This will give you the maximum number of trades you can afford to do per year, for a given instrument.

FORMULA 35: MAXIMUM TRADES PER YEAR GIVEN A CONSERVATIVE ESTIMATE OF SHARPE RATIO

Maximum trades per year = [(Conservative SR ÷ 2) – holding costs] ÷ cost per trade

Now consult table 73 to see how you could change the volatility fraction and forecast horizon, for a given number of trades per year.

---

[148] For traders with multiple instruments: This calculation is the same, even if you started with a higher account level risk target to reflect the diversification in your account. You will need better performance history to justify raising your expected Sharpe ratio even further, compared to a trader with only one instrument. Also, this is the **account level risk target**. If you are using multiple instruments you should still use an instrument diversification multiplier (IDM) to work out your instrument level risk target. The value of the IDM will remain unchanged, regardless of any increase you make to your account level risk target.

[149] Let SR^{pre} be the pre-cost Sharpe ratio (SR), SR^{post} be the after cost SR, and c the risk adjusted cost. $SR^{post} = SR^{pre} - c$. Then if $c = SR^{pre} \div 3 \rightarrow c = SR^{post} + c \rightarrow 2c = SR^{post} \rightarrow c = SR^{post} \div 2$.

TABLE 73: STOP LOSS FRACTION AND FORECAST HORIZON TO USE FOR A GIVEN NUMBER
OF ANNUAL TRADES

Average trades per year	Fraction of volatility used for stop loss	Approximate forecast horizon (calendar days)
97.5	0.025	4 days
76.5	0.05	5 days
46.9	0.1	8 days
21.4	0.2	18 days
11.9	0.3	1 month
7.8	0.4	7 weeks
5.4	**0.5**	**10 weeks**

Values calculated from back-testing different stop loss fractions over the instruments in my data set. Row in bold is Starter System. Figures are copied from table 12.

For example, suppose you're trading the Euro Stoxx CFD. This has risk-adjusted holding costs of 0.0246 per year, and transaction costs per trade of 0.00307 (figures calculated in appendix B). Suppose you estimate your conservative SR at 0.39:

Maximum trades per year = [(Conservative SR ÷ 2) – holding costs] ÷ cost per trade

= [(0.39 ÷ 2) – 0.0246] ÷ 0.00307 = 55.5

You can afford to trade no more than 55 times a year. Looking at table 73 you could get away with using a stop loss fraction of **0.1**, which is expected to trade 46.9 times per year. You don't have to lower the fraction that much, but you must not use an even lower fraction.

If you do change your stop loss fraction then you must also change your forecast horizon, which for a fraction of 0.1 will be eight days. You will be now be making predictions at a shorter time scale, with a horizon of around a week. Are you confident that your subjective method for picking trades will work with a one-week horizon? If you aren't comfortable predicting market movements with a shorter horizon then use a larger stop loss fraction.

Incidentally, it isn't compulsory to adjust your risk target or stop loss – it's completely okay to ignore these recommendations and stick with the levels used in the Starter System, or to make a partial adjustment towards the new levels. It's also fine to adjust the risk target, and leave the stop loss fraction alone, or vice versa.

What if your performance gets better or worse?

You should monitor your performance ratio regularly. If it improves then you can raise your conservative expectation of Sharpe ratio; and also consider making upward adjustments to the risk target and stop loss fraction.

If you hit a losing streak, and your performance ratio begins to degrade, then you **must** recalibrate your trading system to reflect a lower expectation for Sharpe ratio. If you find that your volatility target and stop loss fraction are too high, then they **must** be reduced.

Let us return to the example of a Euro Stoxx CFD trader who had a run of good performance. They had an expected Sharpe ratio of 0.39, after costs. Based on that the trader decided to change their stop loss fraction to 0.1, and their risk target to 19.5%.

Now suppose they hit a rocky patch, and after a total of 20 trades their performance ratio has fallen to 0.38. Rounding down to a ratio of 0.35 we can see that the expected Sharpe ratio in table 74 has fallen to **0.26**. That equates to a maximum account level risk target of 0.26 ÷ 2 = **13%**. Their current risk target of 19.5% is too high, and they need to cut it.

What about the volatility fraction? Euro Stoxx CFD has risk-adjusted holding costs of 0.0246 per year and transaction costs per trade of 0.00307 (figures calculated in appendix B). Using formula 35:

Maximum trades per year = [(Conservative SR ÷ 2) – Holding costs] ÷ cost per trade = [(0.26 ÷ 2) – 0.0246] ÷ 0.00307 = 34.3

From table 73 the maximum volatility fraction they could use is 0.20. Their current fraction of 0.1 is too high, and this parameter also needs to be changed.

Epilogue

"A little learning is a dangerous thing"

Alexander Pope, *'Essay on Criticism'* 1709

"The tyro knows nothing, and everybody, including himself, knows it. But the next, or second grade thinks he knows a great deal … It is this semi-sucker rather than the 100% article who is the real all-year-round support of the commission houses."

Edwin Lefevre, *'Reminiscences of a Stock Operator'* 1923

Newcomers to trading don't (usually) do anything too crazy. They are naturally sceptical of the whole business; and their instinct tells them to behave cautiously and keep their bets small. Many new traders speak of feeling frozen, like rabbits in the headlights of a car, when they try and make their first trade. Trading too often is unlikely to be a problem for novices.

The danger comes when you acquire a little learning and some experience. You graduate from being a 'tyro' (a beginner) and achieve the grade of 'semi-sucker'. You have some good luck – several trades in a row without any losses. You begin to think that nothing can possibly go wrong. You start to think you're a trading genius. You get greedy. You ignore your trading plan. You start to take unnecessary risks, use too much leverage, and increase the frequency of your trading.

Do not get carried away. A few good trades do not mean you've found the holy grail. Be careful – things can still go badly wrong.

Remember:

- **Stick to your system**
- **Don't use excessive leverage – keep your risk targets modest**
- **Don't trade too often – keep your trading costs low**
- **Stay sceptical**

Glossary

Words **in bold** refer to other entries in the glossary.

Asset class	A group of **instruments that have similar characteristics, and correlated returns**. Asset classes include **equities, bonds, FX** and so on. See page 37.
Auto-liquidation	What happens if you get a **margin call** and you cannot meet it: your positions are automatically closed. See page 12.
Average True Range (ATR)	A measure of risk commonly used by many traders. I prefer the **standard deviation** measure. See page 129.
Back-adjustment	Joining together the prices of **dated** products with different expiry dates to make a single price series. See pages 124 and 307.
Back-testing	Simulating the performance of a trading strategy using historic data to check its performance, and other characteristics.
Bid	How much the market, or your broker, is prepared to pay when you are selling to them. See pages 18 and 301.
Binary trading	A style of trading where you put on the same sized position regardless of how convinced (or not) you are about the trade, as used in the **Starter System**. Opposite of **non-binary trading**.
Bitcoin	The original, and still the most popular, **cryptocurrency**.
Bonds	An **asset class**, a type of **instrument** where you receive regular interest payments.

Box and whiskers plot	Statistical plot that shows how estimates of a particular value are distributed – in this book I use them to show **Sharpe ratio** estimates. In the middle of each vertical *box* is a horizontal line showing the average Sharpe ratio (SR).
	The other components of the plot show how confident we can be about these estimates. There is a 68% chance that the estimates of SR lie within the box. The statistical jargon for a range of uncertainty like this is a **confidence interval**. Furthermore, there is a 95% chance that the estimates of SR fall between the top and bottom ends of the lines extending from the box (the *whiskers*). See page 76.
Breakout	A type of **opening rule** which looks for prices that break out of a range. See page 196.
Buying on margin	Using **leverage** to trade an asset; you put up **margin** and borrow the rest. See page 18.
Capital	The amount of money that is at risk when you are trading. See page 56.
Carry, cost of carry	The return we get from a position even if prices remain unchanged. See page 10.
Carry (trading rule)	A type of **opening rule** which calculates the likely return if market conditions remain stable; for example, in FX we measure carry by looking at the difference between two interest rates. See page 201.
Cash price	The price of an **undated product**. Also called the **spot price**.
Clearing house	When you trade on an **exchange** the clearing house is responsible for making sure that the trade is successfully completed. This is why trading on exchanges is relatively safe. See page 41.
Closing rule	A rule used to close an open **position**. The basic Starter System uses **trailing stop losses** to close positions. In part four, chapter eight, I explain how to use the **opening rule** to close positions.
Commission	A fee paid to a broker for the privilege of trading. Commissions are usually paid on **futures** and stock **margin trading**, but **spread betting, CFDs**, and **FX** are normally traded without commission. See page 18.
Commodities	A type of **asset class**. Commodities include agricultural products (like corn), energy instruments (such as oil) and metals (e.g., gold).
Confidence interval	See **box and whiskers plot**.
Continuous trading	A style of trading where stop losses aren't used. See chapter nine.

Contract for difference (CFD)	A type of leveraged **product**. You make a contract with a broker that the price of a given **instrument** will go up or down. When the trade is closed you receive the difference between the entry and exit prices. See page 25.
Correlation	A figure which measures the linear relationship between the return of two instruments, or trading strategies. A correlation of zero means there is no relationship, and a correlation of one means the two instruments or strategies always move exactly together.
Cryptocurrency	Relatively new type of **asset class** that uses cryptography to secure financial transactions. The oldest and most famous example is **bitcoin**.
Curve-fitting	An informal name for **over-fitting**.
Daily funded bet	A type of **undated product**; a **spread bet** which doesn't expire on a specific date, but which is automatically rolled over to the next day.
Dated product	A variation of a leveraged **product** which expires on a specific date. Dated products include **futures, forward FX, quarterly spread bets**; as well as **spread bets** and **CFDs** based on futures. Opposite of **undated** products. See page 16.
Day trading	A style of trading where positions are always closed before the end of the day. Not recommended – see page 116 to understand why.
Discretionary trader	A trader who relies on gut feel rather than a system to decide when to trade. I'd strongly advise discretionary traders to become **semi-automatic traders**. See page 269.
Dividends	Payments made by companies to traders who have bought **equities**.
Equities	A type of **asset class**, which involves buying a share in a company's profits. Also called stocks and shares. You can buy collections of equities in indices like the FTSE 100 or S&P 500.
Exchange	A formal venue for trading, such as the New York Stock Exchange, London Stock Market or Chicago Mercantile Exchange. Specific physical or virtual venue where trading happens. As opposed to **Over the Counter**. See page 17.
Financing cost	The **holding cost** of **undated products**. You pay, or sometimes receive, interest to finance your long or short positions. The financing cost is calculated as the **reference rate** plus a **funding spread** if you have a long position, or the **reference rate** minus the **funding spread** if you are short. See page 14.
Fitting	Calibrating the parameters of a trading strategy depending on past data. See also **over-fitting** and page 268.

Forecast	A measure of how confident an **opening rule** is in the trade it wants to do. See page 244.
Foreign Exchange (FX, Forex)	A type of **product** and **asset class** which involves speculating on the change in exchange rates. See also **forward FX** and **spot FX**. See page 23.
Forward FX	A **dated product**; an **FX** trade which expires on a specific date.
Funding spread	Additional interest charged by brokers when calculating your **financing costs**. See page 18.
Futures	A type of **dated product** which trades on an **exchange**. See page 31.
Guaranteed stop loss	Variant of a **stop loss** which limits your maximum possible loss. Not recommended. See page 115.
Hedge fund	An investment fund that can use **leverage** and go both **long** and **short**.
High watermark	The price which gives you the most profit since a **position** was opened. If you're **long** it will be the highest price, if **short** the lowest price. Used to calculate the **stop loss** level. See page 111.
Holding costs	Costs you have to pay when you hold a position regardless of any trading you do. See page 69.
Home currency	The currency your trading **capital** is denominated in. See page 56.
Incremental trade size	See **minimum trade size**.
Instrument	The underlying asset whose price you are trying to predict when you trade a **product**. See page 55.
Instrument currency	The currency that the price of a particular **instrument** is denominated in. See page 56.
Instrument risk	How risky an instrument is before any **leverage** is applied. I measure instrument risk as an annual **standard deviation** of returns. See page 58.
Interest rate spread	A premium charged by brokers for borrowing or lending money for trading purposes. Forms part of your **holding costs**. See page 14.
Kelly criterion	A formula which calculates your **risk target** based on your expected **Sharpe ratio**. See page 66.

Leverage factor **Leverage ratio**	Two different measures of **leverage**: how much you are risking relative to the value of your account. The **leverage factor** is equal to the **notional exposure** of a trade divided by your **capital**. The **leverage ratio** is equal to the leverage factor, minus one. See page 11.
Leveraged product	See **product**.
Leverage	Borrowing money for trading purposes, either directly or indirectly via a leveraged **product** like a **future, CFD** or **spread bet**.
Long	Trader slang for betting on a price going up.
Margin	The minimum cash down payment you have to make to your broker when making a **leveraged** trade. See page 18.
Margin account	The account you need for **margin trading**.
Margin call	What happens when a **leveraged** trade goes wrong; the broker will ask you for more **margin** to keep the **leverage ratio** below their limits. If you don't meet a margin call you will face **auto-liquidation**. See page 12.
Margin trading	A type of **leveraged product** that allows you to borrow money to trade shares by buying or **short selling**. See page 18.
Mark to market	Brokers monitor open **positions** by revaluing them regularly at current market prices. If there is an adverse price move, then you may face a **margin call**. See page 12.
Mean reversion trading	A style of trading where you expect prices to return to some fair or equilibrium value. Opposite of **trend following**.
Minimum capital	The smallest possible amount of **capital** you need to trade a particular **instrument** with a specific **product**. See pages 66 and 103.
Minimum trade size	The smallest trade you're allowed to do in a given **instrument** using a specific product. See page 66.
Momentum	Another name for **trend following**.
Moving average crossover	A **trend following** rule which is used to determine when you should open a new **position** in the **Starter System**. See page 87.
Non-binary trading	Style of trading where you vary the size of your **positions** depending on how confident you are about your **forecast** and the current level of **instrument risk**. See chapter ten.
Notional exposure	The cash value of a **position**. See page 93.

Offer	How much the market, or your broker, will charge you when you are buying from them. See pages 18 and 301.
Opening rule	A rule to decide if **positions** should be opened. In the **Starter System** we use a **moving average crossover** as an opening rule. See page 86.
Over-fitting	A trading strategy is over-fitted if it has been tweaked to perform incredibly well when **back-tested** with historic data; sadly, such strategies won't do so well when traded with real money in the future.
Over the counter (OTC)	Trading outside of formal **exchanges**. See page 17.
Performance ratio	Measure of risk-adjusted trading profits, used to recalibrate your expectations of **Sharpe ratio**. See page 272.
Pips	Smallest amount that an **FX** price can change.
Point	The increment of a price unit that you bet on when placing **spread bets** or certain types of **CFD**. See page 29.
Position	When you place an opening trade you create an open position; you are then exposed to changes in the price of an **instrument**. A subsequent closing trade which reverses the original trade will close your position.
Price unit volatility	Calculation of **standard deviation** in units of price. Equal to the **instrument risk** multiplied by the current price. See page 111.
Product	One of several ways to trade a particular **instrument** using **leverage**. Products discussed in this book include **spot FX, margin trading, CFDs, spread bets** and **futures**. See page 17.
Quarterly spread bet	A type of **dated product**; a **spread bet** with expiry dates that occur every three months.
Reference rate	The interest rate used by brokers to calculate your **financing cost**. See page 18.
Rolling	For **dated products**, switching from holding a **position** in one expiry date to a later expiry date. See page 17.
Scaling factor (for forecasts)	Adjustment to a **forecast** to ensure that it has the right magnitude to size positions correctly. See page 246.
Semi-automatic trader	Trader who uses their own **discretion** to decide when to open new positions, but uses a trading system to size, manage, and close existing positions. See page 269.
Sharpe ratio	A method for measuring the risk-adjusted performance of a trader or trading system. See page 60.

Short	Fancy trader language for betting on the price going down.
Short selling	Trading to bet on the price of shares going down in price (i.e., going **short**). See page 14.
Speed limit	Recommended limit on trading speed given cost levels; equal to spending one-third of expected pre-costs **Sharpe ratio** on costs. See page 78.
Spot FX	A type of **undated product**, an **FX** trade without a specific expiry date.
Spot price	Synonym for **cash price**.
Spread cost	Part of the **transaction cost** that arises because you have to buy at the **offer** and sell at the **bid**. See pages 18 and 301.
Spread bet **Spread betting**	A type of leveraged **product** where you gamble on the price changes for a given **instrument**. See page 27.
Standard deviation	A measure of risk. The standard deviation is the typical variation in performance around the average for a given time period; usually one year. Used to calculate **instrument risk**. See page 56.
Starter System	The basic trading system introduced in part two of this book, which is designed for beginner traders with limited **capital**. See page 72.
Statistical uncertainty	We can quantify the uncertainty of an estimate, like the expected Sharpe ratio from a trading strategy, using statistical techniques to calculate the **confidence interval**. See page 75.
STIR	A type of **asset class** whose prices are linked to Short Term Interest Rates, such as Eurodollar, EURIBOR or Short Sterling.
Stop loss	A rule used to close open positions when the price has moved against you by a given amount. See **trailing stop loss**. See page 107.
Stop loss fraction	The fraction of **price unit volatility** that we use to determine the **stop loss gap**. A smaller fraction means we'd close positions more quickly, a larger fraction implies we trade more slowly. See page 109.
Stop loss gap	The amount a price can move from the **high watermark** before a **trailing stop loss** is triggered. Equal to the **stop loss fraction** multiplied by the **price unit volatility**. See page 109.
Target risk	The amount of risk you expect to see in when trading. I calculate target risk using the annual **standard deviation** of returns. See page 62.
Trade plan	A plan to follow when trading, covering the **instrument**(s), **opening rule**(s), **position** sizing, and **closing rule**. See page 119.

Trading spread	Brokers charge you more to buy than they pay you when you sell. The difference between these prices is the trading spread, and forms part of your **transaction costs**. See page 18.
Trailing stop loss	A type of **stop loss** which is adjusted when the price reaches a new high (if you're **long**) or new low (when **short**). This ensure the expected loss on an open position remains the same. If we are **long** we close trades when the price is below the **high watermark** minus the **stop loss gap**; if **short** when the price is above the **high watermark** plus the **stop loss gap**. See page 108.
Transaction costs	Costs of doing a trade. Consists of taxes, **commission** and **spread cost**. You need to add together transaction costs and **holding costs** to get the total cost of trading. See page 70.
Trend following	A style of trading which assumes that trends in prices will continue; can be implemented using trading rules like the **moving average crossover**. See page 87.
Undated product	A type of **product** which doesn't expire on a specific date, such as **spot FX** or a **daily funded** spread bet. Opposite of **dated product**.
Volatility	Another word for risk. I measure volatility using **standard deviation**.

APPENDICES

Appendix A: Useful Information

Further reading

Systematic Trading, Robert Carver, 2015, Harriman House

> My first book. Essential reading for traders who wish to develop their own trading systems (but then you would expect me to say that).

Following the Trend, Andreas F. Clenow, 2012, Wiley

> Great resource for developing a futures trading strategy if you have the capital to diversify across many different instruments.

The Complete Turtle Trader, Michael W. Covel, 2009, Harper Business

> True life story of a set of novice traders who learned to trade systematically.

Building Winning Algorithmic Trading Systems, Kevin J. Davey, 2014, Wiley

> Kevin is a 'celebrity trader', but unlike most he actually knows what he is doing.

Trading Systems and Methods, 5th Edition, Perry J. Kaufman, 2013, Wiley

> The bible of trading strategies. Great resource for trading rule ideas.

Fortunes Formula, William Poundstone, 2005, Hill & Wang

> Excellent and very readable book about the Kelly Criterion.

Technical Analysis, Jack Schwager, 1995, Wiley

> This is just one of many excellent books that Jack has written.

Fooled by Randomness, Nassim Taleb, 2007, Penguin

> Taleb has written a series of books on the nature of risk, especially in trading. This book, his first, is the best.

Useful websites

Links to external websites are accurate at the time of writing, but may break without warning. These links do not constitute recommendations or endorsements. Prices and charges may vary.

Brokers	fxcm.com
	interactivebrokers.com
	ig.com
	cmcmarkets.com
	tradestation.com
Free or cheap financial data	barchart.com
	quandl.com
	eoddata.com
	oanda.com/fx-for-business/historical-rates
	finance.yahoo.com
My websites	systematicmoney.org/leveraged-trading
	Website for this book; contains many useful resources including links to spreadsheets.
	qoppac.blogspot.com
	My blog, with many articles on trading systematically.

Appendix B: Costs

This appendix:

- explains in detail how to calculate costs, including calculations for the example instruments used in chapter six.

- explores the relationship between costs and minimum trade size.

- suggests some tactics you can use to reduce trading costs.

Spreadsheets that implement all the formulas in this appendix can be found on my website: systematicmoney.org/leveraged-trading

Transaction costs

There are two types of costs:

1. Transaction costs, that we pay every time we trade.

2. Holding costs, which we pay for holding positions regardless of how often we trade.

First let's calculate transaction costs. I will use the following symbols:

S = spread in price units, e.g., if the trading spread is 100.01 to 100.02, then S=0.01

C = Commission to trade the instrument minimum size, in units of instrument currency

P = Current price of instrument

TC_{ccy} = Transaction cost per trade in instrument currency

TC_{ratio} = Transaction cost per trade, as a proportion of the exposure value of the minimum size trade

TC_{risk} = Transaction cost per trade, risk-adjusted

Futures	$X_{futures}$ = Futures Multiplier $$TC_{ccy} = C + (S \times X_{futures}) \div 2$$ $$TC_{ratio} = TC_{ccy} \div (P \times X_{futures})$$ Example: Corn futures. Xfutures = $50, C = $1, S = 0.01, P = 379 $$TC_{ccy} = 1 + (0.01 \times 50) \div 2 = \$1.25$$ $$TC_{ratio} = \$1.25 \div (379 \times \$50) = 0.0060\%$$
FX	$X_{fx,value}$ = Value of a pip for minimum trade size (in same currency as commission) S_{pip} = Trading spread in pips $X_{fx,size}$ = Pip size $$TC_{ccy} = C + (S_{pip} \times X_{fx,value}) \div 2$$ $$TC_{ratio} = TC_{ccy} \div (X_{fx,value} \div X_{fx,size})$$ Example: AUDUSD. C = $0, $X_{fx,value}$ = $0.10, S_{pip} = 1.2 (average), $X_{fx,size}$ = 0.0001 $$TC_{ccy} = \$0 + (1.2 \times 0.1) \div 2 = \$0.06$$ $$TC_{ratio} = \$0.06 \div (0.10 \div 0.0001) = 0.006\%$$
Spread bet	B_{size} = Value of bet per point at minimum trade size, instrument currency X_{point} = Point size in price units S_{points} = Trading spread in points $$TC_{ccy} = C + (S_{points} \times B_{size}) \div 2$$ $$TC_{ratio} = TC_{ccy} \div ((B_{size} \times P) \div X_{point})$$ Example: Gold (based on future). X_{point} = 1, B_{size} = £0.50, S_{points} = 0.6, C = £0, P = 1,268 $$TC_{ccy} = £0 + (0.6 \times £0.5) \div 2 = £0.15$$ $$TC_{ratio} = £0.15 \div ((£0.50 \times 1,268) \div 1) = 0.023\%$$
CFD (priced per contract)	As for futures, but use the contract size instead of the futures multiplier. Example: Euro Stoxx (based on future). $X_{futures}$ = €2, C = 0, S = 2, P = 3,391 $$TC_{ccy} = 0 + (2 \times €2) \div 2 = €2$$ $$TC_{ratio} = €2 \div (3,391 \times €2) = 0.0295\%$$

CFD (priced per point)	As for spread bets. Example: Euro Stoxx. X_{point} = 1, B_{size} = €2, S_{points} = 2, C = €2, P = 3,391 $$TC_{ccy} = €0 + (2 × €2) ÷ 2 = €2$$ $$TC_{ratio} = €2 ÷ ((€2 × 3,391) ÷ 1) = 0.0295\%$$

N = Number of shares

D = Stamp duty (0.5% in the UK on ordinary shares, zero on UK traded ETFs, zero in the US)

Commission: Brokers charge commission on a per share, percentage, or fixed value basis; or using a mixture of these. For example, my broker charges $0.005 per share, with a minimum of $1 per order, and a maximum of 1% of trade value.

Per share basis:

$C_{perShare}$ = Commission per share

$$TC_{ccy} = (C_{pershare} × N) + [(S × N) ÷ 2] + (D × P × N)$$

$$TC_{ratio} = TC_{ccy} ÷ (P × N)$$

Example: 200 shares of SPY ETF. N = 100, $C_{perShare}$ = $0.005, S = $0.01, P = $274, D = 0

$$TC_{ccy} = (0.005 × 200) + [(0.01 × 200) ÷ 2] + 0 = $2$$

$$TC_{ratio} = 2 ÷ (274 × 200) = 0.00365\%$$

Margin trading

Minimum commission basis

C_{min} = Minimum commission

$$TC_{ccy} = Cmin + [(S × N) ÷ 2] + (D × P × N)$$

$$TC_{ratio} = TCccy ÷ (P × N)$$

Example: 10 shares of SPY ETF. N = 100, C_{min} = $1, S = $0.01, P = $274, D = 0

$$TC_{ccy} = 1 + [(0.01 × 10) ÷ 2] + 0 = 1.05$$

$$TC_{ratio} = 1.05 ÷ (274 × 10) = 0.0383\%$$

Percentage basis

C_{perc} = Percentage commission

$$TC_{ccy} = (C_{perc} × N × P) + [(S × N) ÷ 2] + D × (P × N)$$

$$TC_{ratio} = TC_{ccy} ÷ (P × N)$$

Example: 10 shares of SPY ETF. $N = 100$, $C_{perc} = 1\%$, $S = \$0.01$, $P = \$274$, $D = 0$

$$TC_{ccy} = (1\% \times 10 \times 274) + [(0.01 \times 10) \div 2] + 0 = 27.45$$

$$TC_{ratio} = 27.45 \div (274 \times 10) = 1.001825\%$$

Summary

Margin trading

For all but the largest trades the $1 minimum commission will usually apply. The ratio of transaction cost to trade size will depend on the size of the trade. For example, for SPY ETF at the current price level the transaction cost will vary from 0.367% (for one share, paying minimum commission) up to 0.00365% (for 200 shares upwards, on a per share basis).

As this is a book for smaller traders, I decided to perform my calculations assuming a trade of ten shares in the SPY ETF, which has a minimum account size in the Starter System of $3,700; this gives a transaction cost of 0.0383% (calculated above). Some brokers will not let you open an account with just $3,700. My own broker currently has a minimum of $10,000.

Now we have the transaction cost as a percentage, we need to calculate the risk-adjusted cost (remember from chapter four that it makes sense to express costs in risk-adjusted terms).

Total risk-adjusted transaction cost per trade:

$$TC_{risk} = TC_{ratio} \div V$$

Where V = Instrument risk of instrument, measured as an annual standard deviation.

For our example instruments:

- Corn futures, $V = 11.9\%$, $TC_{risk} = 0.0060\% \div 11.9\% = 0.000504$

- AUDUSD FX, $V = 6.84\%$, $TC_{risk} = 0.006\% \div 6.84\% = 0.000690$

- Gold spread bet, $V = 11.0\%$, $TC_{risk} = 0.023\% \div 11.0\% = 0.00209$

- Euro Stoxx 50 CFD, $V = 9.6\%$, $TC_{risk} = 0.0295\% \div 9.6\% = 0.00307$

- S&P 500 SPY ETF margin trade, $V = 16\%$, $TC_{risk} = 0.0383\% \div 16\% = 0.00239$

Holding costs

Now we can calculate holding costs: the costs paid to own a position regardless of how often it is traded. These are expressed as an annual figure.

Dated (Futures, quarterly spread bet, spread bet based on futures, CFD based on futures)	R = Number of rolls per year M = Multiplier to apply to roll trade costs. If you have to do two separate trades to roll, then M = 2. $$HC_{ratio} = TC_{ratio} \times R \times M$$ Example: Corn futures. $R = 1$, $M = 2$, $TC_{ratio} = 0.00602\%$ $$HC_{ratio} = 0.00602\% \times 1 \times 2 = 0.012\%$$ Example: Dated gold spread bet. $R = 4$, $M = 2$, $TC_{ratio} = 0.0243\%$ $$HC_{ratio} = 0.0232\% \times 4 \times 2 = 0.19\%$$ Example: Euro Stoxx CFD based on future. $R = 4$, $M = 2$, $TC_{ratio} = 0.0295\%$ $$HC_{ratio} = 0.0295\% \times 4 \times 2 = 0.236\%$$
Margin trading	We need to calculate the holding cost for long and short positions separately, and then take an average. $$HC_{ratio} = (HC_{long} + HC_{short}) \div 2$$ *For long positions*: The funding cost to borrow money (F_{long}) should be multiplied by the amount you are borrowing, which will be the maximum of 0 and $1 - L$, where L is the leverage factor. $$HC_{long} = \{F_{long} \times max\ (0,[1 - L])\} + m$$ *For short positions*: You will pay a stock borrowing charge on the entire position size (B). You may also receive cash interest on your account (i), which will contain the proceeds from short selling plus your original deposit. $$HC_{short} = B - (i \times [1 + L])$$ We ignore dividends for both long and short positions since these are paid to us if we buy, and deducted when we sell; so, on average they net to zero. We also ignore the ETF management fee as that will be paid by us if we buy (or paid out of dividends), or received by us if we sell (or it reduces the costs of the dividends we have to pay).

Example: SPY ETF

For long positions. Margin is charged by my broker at F_{long} = 3.7%. With the risk target in the Starter System (12%), and instrument risk of 16%, the leverage factor will be:

Margin trading

$$L = 12\% \div 16\% = 0.75$$

$$HC_{long} = 3.7\% \times max (0,[0.75 - 1]) = 3.7\% \times 0 = 0\%$$

Note – these costs will be higher if you invest in a less volatile stock or have a higher risk target than the Starter System.

For short positions: The borrowing fee charged by my broker for most stocks is currently B = 0.25%; they do not pay interest on balances less than $100,000 so i = 0%.

$$HC_{short} = 0.25\% - (0\% \times [1 + 0.75]) = 0.25\%$$

To find the average:

$$HC_{ratio} = (HC_{long} + HC_{short}) \div 2 = (0\% + 0.25\%) \div 2 = 0.125\%$$

Spot FX

F = Funding cost. Equal to the average of the interest rate funding spreads on long and short positions.

Example: AUDUSD FX. I can borrow USD at 2.75% and receive 2.25% when I lend:

$$F = (2.75\% - 2.25\%) \div 2 = 0.25\%$$

I can borrow AUD at 2% and receive 1.05% when I lend:

$$F = (2\% - 1.05\%) \div 2 = 0.475\%$$

$$HC_{ratio} = average (0.25\%, 0.475\%) = 0.3625\%$$

Other Undated (Daily funded spread bet, Undated CFD)

F = Funding cost. Half the spread between the funding cost for long positions, and the funding credit for short positions.

You will usually be charged the funding cost on the entire position.

$$HC_{ratio} = F$$

Now we need to risk adjust the holding cost. Total risk-adjusted holding cost per year:

$$HC_{risk} = HC_{ratio} \div V$$

Where V = instrument risk, measured as an annual standard deviation.

For the examples:

- Corn futures (dated), V = 11.9%, HC_{risk} = 0.012% ÷ 11.9% = 0.00101

- AUDUSD spot FX (undated), V = 8.7%, HC_{risk} = 0.3625% ÷ 6.84% = 0.0417

- Gold spread bet (dated), V = 11.0%, HC_{risk} = 0.19% ÷ 11.0% = 0.0173

- Euro Stoxx 50 CFD (dated), V = 9.6%, HC_{risk} = 0.236% ÷ 9.6% = 0.0246

- S&P 500 SPY ETF, margin trading (undated), V = 16%, HC_{risk} = 0.125% ÷ 16% = 0.00781

These calculations ignore any account management fees or custody charges. They also assume that we always have a position on. For the Starter System, this will not be true (however, it is more likely to be true if you use a continuous trading system with no stop loss, as outlined in chapter nine). There will be times when the stop loss has been triggered, but the opening rule has not yet reversed its position. However, it is better to be conservative and assume that we always hold a position.

Total costs

The total expected annual cost for a trading system will be the transaction cost, multiplied by the expected number of trades, plus the annual holding cost.

Total risk-adjusted cost, (i.e., in Sharpe ratio units):

$$Ctotal = (TC_{risk} \times N) + HC_{risk}$$

Where N = Expected number of trades per year.

For the example instruments, using N = 5.4 for the Starter System:

- Corn futures, C_{total} = (0.000504 × 5.4) + 0.00101 = 0.00373

- AUDUSD spot FX, C_{total} = (0.000690 × 5.4) + 0.0417 = 0.0454

- Gold dated spread bet, C_{total} = (0.00209 × 5.4) + 0.0173 = 0.0286

- Euro Stoxx CFD, C_{total} = (0.00307 × 5.4) + 0.0246 = 0.0412

- S&P 500 margin trading, C_{total} = (0.00239 × 5.4) + 0.00781 = 0.0207

For the Starter System we require C_{total} to be less than 0.08 to trade a given instrument and product.

Minimum capital and costs

Why is there an inverse relationship between the minimum amount of capital required to trade an instrument and product, and how costly they are to trade? Partly it's because cheaper products like futures have larger minimum trade sizes, and because of minimum commissions, but it's also related to instrument risk.

To see why, consider the definition of minimum capital. Remember from chapter four that we try to achieve a *risk target* for our trading, and that for most instruments there is a *minimum position size* (FX lot, one CFD, futures contract, or bet per point).

Suppose an imaginary instrument has a notional exposure at its minimum position size of $1,000 and we're trying to hit a risk target of 12% (annual standard deviation of returns).

If the returns of the instrument have a risk of 12%, then the risk of one minimum position unit is 12% × $1,000 = $120. We'd need at least $120 ÷ 12% = $1,000 of capital to trade this instrument. However, if the instrument has lower risk, say 6% per year, then we'd need just (6% × $1,000) ÷ 12% = $500 of capital instead. The converse is true: if the instrument risk was higher than 12% we'd need $2,000 in capital.

Now, how are costs and risk related? Let's assume that it costs $20 in costs for the minimum trade of $1,000, or: 20 ÷ 1,000 = 2%. But we're interested in risk-adjusted costs. So, with instrument risk of 12% the risk-adjusted costs work out at: 2% ÷ 12% = 0.1667. However, with 6% risk the costs would be doubled: 2% ÷ 6%=0.3333. As table 75 shows, in this simple example there is a clear inverse relationship between minimum capital and risk-adjusted transaction costs.

TABLE 75: HIGHER INSTRUMENT RISK MEANS HIGHER MINIMUM CAPITAL, BUT LOWER COSTS

Minimum capital and costs for a hypothetical instrument at different levels of instrument risk:

Instrument risk	Minimum capital $	Risk-adjusted transaction cost
6%	$500	0.3333
12%	$1,000	0.1667
24%	$2,000	0.0833

Of course, in real life it isn't quite that simple, but broadly speaking this relationship holds within product categories and across instruments. The cheapest future I trade (Nasdaq equity index) is also one of the riskiest (risk around 19% per year), and the most expensive future (German 2-year bonds) is one of the safest (around 0.3% per year).

Most instruments show a clear relationship: the lower the minimum capital required, the higher the costs you'll need to pay.

Smarter execution to avoid the spread

Parts three and four of this book are all about improving the pre-cost expected returns of the Starter System. However, it's also possible to increase your post-cost returns by reducing your costs. The *traded spread* that you pay when buying or selling is a significant part of the costs you have to pay when trading. The good news is that most traders can avoid paying the spread at least some of the time, resulting in lower costs, and better returns. This section explains how.

How important is the spread cost?

On my screen right now, the price of corn is quoted at $374.30 per futures contract. But I can't actually buy corn at that price, nor can I sell it. If I want to buy it will cost me $374.40, which is where the market is *offering* corn. Should I sell, I'd only receive $374.20, which is the market's *bid* for corn. Essentially, $374.30 is the *mid-market price*, but I can't actually trade at that level.

I define the *spread cost* as the difference between what I pay or receive, and the notional mid-market price. In both cases I'm paying a spread cost of $0.10 ($374.3 − $374.2, or $374.4 - $372.3). Alternatively, you can calculate this by taking the spread ($374.4 −$374.2 = $0.20) and halving it (half of $0.20 is $0.10).

Ten cents might not seem very much, but even with the limited amount of trading we do in the Starter System, it all adds up. Have a look at table 76. The top row shows the risk-adjusted trading cost for some of the products I analysed in chapter six, when I introduced the Starter System. These costs assume that I have to *pay the spread*: buying at $374.40 and selling at $374.20 and paying $0.10 each time.

But suppose I could somehow avoid paying the spread. I could pay $374.30 for corn or receive the same if I sold. If I can trade at *mid-market*, I'd pay the costs shown in the second row of the table. There are no spread costs here, just commissions and holding costs. Better still, suppose I could *capture the spread* – buying at the bid, and selling at the offer. If I can capture the spread I could buy corn cheaper than mid-market, at $374.20 (the market's bid); and sell it higher, at $374.40 (the best offer in the market). Then I'd actually earn $0.10 every time I traded. This would give me the risk-adjusted costs shown in the third row of the table.

TABLE 76: NOT PAYING THE SPREAD SAVES MONEY

Risk-adjusted trading costs with different execution assumptions

	Corn future	Euro Stoxx CFD on future	Gold quarterly spread bet	AUDUSD spot FX	S&P 500 ETF margin trade
Pay the spread	0.0037	0.040	0.028	0.045	0.0207
Mid-market	0.0030	0.024	0.017	0.042	0.0201
Capture the spread	0.0022	0.008	0.006	0.038	0.0195

'Pay the spread' is the normal situation where we buy at the offer and sell at the bid. 'Mid-market' is where we can trade at the average of the bid and ask. 'Capture the spread' is where we buy at the bid and sell at the offer. In all cases commissions and holding costs are still paid.

Not paying the spread is worth doing in corn futures, where I can save almost half my costs if I can capture the spread. However, these are already very cheap to trade, so the benefits are minimal. Similarly, in S&P 500 ETF trading, because we are trading ten shares at a time, the $1 minimum commission forms a large part of our costs and we still have to pay that even if we can avoid the spread. Avoiding the spread in spot FX markets is also of limited benefit. The holding costs, made up of the funding spread, make up the majority of total costs.

In CFDs and spread bets, the spread is far more important. Here there is no commission to pay and avoiding the spread by trading at mid-market will nearly halve the total costs. Earning the spread will reduce costs so that they are almost as low as in futures markets.

Limit and market orders

How can you hope to trade at mid-market, or even better capture the spread? The solution is to use a *limit order* rather than the standard *market order*. Unfortunately, not all brokers offer limit orders. If yours does not, then get yourself a new broker or skip this section.

A market order will be executed immediately at the best available price in the market at the time – the best bid if you're selling, or the best offer if you're buying. With market orders you always pay the spread.

In contrast, a limit order comes with a price tag attached and will only be executed if someone else in the market is willing to pay that price. Let us return to the example of corn futures, bid at $374.20 and offered at $374.40. To make the text readable I will now drop the $374 part of the price quote. Professional traders often do this when communicating with each other, and with their brokers. Using this method of quoting, a market buy order would cost 40, and I would get 20 if I was selling.

Suppose I want to buy. I could put in a buy limit order at the mid-market level of 30. Anyone putting in a market order to sell would trade with me, since my bid of 30 is higher than the current bid of 20. Similarly, if I was selling, I could enter a sell limit order at 30. The next buyer in the market would buy from me, since my offer is lower than the original offer of 40. In both cases I would trade at the mid-market price of 30.

Better still, I could put my buy limit order in at 20. Markets work using a queuing system, so these orders would be behind others at the same price which were submitted earlier.[150] However, once those orders were out of the way, the next market order to sell would be matched against my order. I'd *capture the spread*, by paying only 20 rather than the mid-market level of 30. The spread cost would actually be negative, as I earn $0.10 on each trade. This would also work if selling. I could put in a sell limit order at 40, and again end up earning $0.10 as a negative spread cost.

You might wonder why anyone would ever use a market order. Market orders have one huge advantage – they execute immediately. If you place a limit order there is a chance you will not trade at that level. For example, suppose you put in a buy limit order on corn at 20, hoping to capture the spread. Your order joins the queue of other orders at that price, but before it reaches the front of the queue some bullish news hits the market, and the price jumps to 60 bid and 80 offered.

Your order with a limit of 20 is now languishing behind all the better bids at 60, 50, 40 and 30. If you *really* need to trade then you have to cancel your bid and put in a new order. To reduce the risk of not trading this should be a *market order*. If you do it quickly enough, before the price rises further, you will end up paying the new offer price: 80. This is considerably higher than the original offer price of 40. You will pay $0.40 more than if you had submitted a market order in the first place. In an effort to save money, you end up paying out more.

---

[150] Some exchanges give priority to larger orders rather than those submitted earlier. Other more complicated queueing rules can also apply.

Who can execute smartly and how?

With market orders you have to pay higher costs, but with the certainty that they will execute quickly. That cost is pretty much fixed at half the size of the market spread. With limit orders you have the opportunity to pay lower or even negative costs, but with huge uncertainty about what those costs will be, and when your order will be filled. Neither order type is perfect. So, which should we use? It depends on what sort of trading you are doing.

Slow trend following (e.g., Starter System)

The Starter System looks for trends that last for several weeks. If you are holding a position for several weeks, it does not matter if it takes a few minutes or even hours to execute your trade. This style of trading is well suited to using limit orders. However, you need to have a plan B in case your initial limit order fails. Here is the tactical plan I use when submitting orders for my own trading system:

- I set an *execution window* during which I want my orders filled. For my system this is an entire trading day.

- At the start of the execution window I submit a limit order that would capture the spread if filled.

- If the order fills, relax and open the metaphorical champagne: I have captured the spread.

- If the order doesn't fill, and there is an adverse price change so that I am no longer the best bid or offer (i.e., the market price has moved higher if I am buying, lower if selling): cancel the limit order and submit a market order. I will end up paying significantly higher transaction costs, since the price has moved against me, and I'm also now paying the spread.

- If the order hasn't filled, and there is less than 10% of the execution window remaining (roughly 45 minutes if the window is a whole trading day):[151] cancel the limit order and submit a market order.

I have built my own software that executes this plan. However, there is nothing to stop you using this method when trading manually. If you are not willing to spend all day monitoring your orders, then use a shorter execution window: an hour or even ten minutes is fine. Just be aware that with shorter windows you will end up with slightly higher costs. It is more likely you will end up with an unfilled order near the end of a

---

[151] It might seem unlikely that an order won't be filled as this would require the price to remain unchanged for an entire day. But when writing any trading plan we need to be ready for any possibility, however improbable. This situation does regularly happen in certain illiquid markets with very low volatility – as I write this footnote the price of Swiss interest rate futures has been stuck at exactly 100.74 since 8:32am this morning – and it's now 3:05pm.

shorter execution window and have to submit a market order. Impatience comes with a price tag.

How successful are these tactics?

Table 77 shows the actual cost figures calculated from my own trading, since I started using this trading plan about four years ago. You can see that my actual costs were about halfway between what I would have paid if I had been paying the spread, and what I could have achieved if I was trading at the mid-market price.

TABLE 77: MY TRADING TACTICS MEAN I DON'T ALWAYS PAY THE SPREAD

Actual risk-adjusted trading costs from my own system

	Total cost
If I had always paid the spread	0.071
Actual, using trading tactics	**0.053**
If I could always trade at mid-market	0.030
If could always capture the spread	−0.011

Cost includes holding and transaction costs, as a proportion of annual risk target, using data from actual trading between October 2014 and May 2019. A negative cost means I would have been paid to trade.

Fast trend following

Suppose you are looking for trends that last a few hours, minutes or even seconds. You cannot spend an entire day patiently waiting for your orders to execute – you need to jump on the bandwagon *now*. In this situation, only market orders make sense. Traders looking for fast moving trends will *always* pay the execution spread. Combined with the high volume of trades this becomes a prohibitively expensive strategy, and hence not recommended.

Mean reversion trading

The opposite of trend following is *mean reversion* trading. Rather than expecting the market to move strongly in one direction or another, we hope that it will fluctuate around some equilibrium level. Mean reversion trading isn't easy, since it's hard to find assets that exhibit that kind of behavior. But the advantage they have is that they can use limit orders when opening new positions, and they will **always capture the spread when trading normally**.

Let's look at an example. In early October 2018, the price of gold was stuck in a range between about $1,180 and $1,210 per ounce. To exploit this with a mean reversion strategy, I put in orders just inside that range: a buy limit order at $1,185, and a sell limit order at $1,205. As it happens, the price rallied and very early on 11 October, the market reached a level of $1,204.8 bid versus $1,205.0 offer (gold futures normally trade with a $0.20 spread). Before the price could move higher, someone had to buy from me at my offer level of $1,205. I went short at $1,205, and captured the spread.

When doing this kind of trading it's vital to use stop losses, since the trading strategy doesn't automatically cut positions when the market moves against it.[152] I set a stop loss at $1,220. There were now two possible outcomes. Ideally, the price would begin to fall towards my bid of $1,185. I'd make a profit from this fall and, when the price reaches $1,185, I will capture the spread again when I close my trade.

But what if the price keeps rising? In fact, the price of gold did rise further, on the back of a minor panic in the US stock market. My stop loss level was reached just a few hours after my initial short was put in. I then submitted a *market order* to close the trade.

Why did I use a market order when I'd previously been using limit orders? **With stop loss trades you must always use market orders, never limit orders**. The extra spread cost of a market order is nothing compared to the risk you run if the market continues to move away from you.[153]

Nevertheless, assuming they have found an instrument which behaves as expected, mean reversion traders should end up with cheaper than average trading costs. Trend following day traders are unlikely to beat the drag of extremely high trading costs, but day traders running mean reversion strategies can be profitable.

---

[152] See discussion on page 227.

[153] Of course you could also use a guaranteed stop loss, although that is even more expensive than a market order, as discussed in chapter five, on page 114.

Appendix C: Calculations

This final appendix explains how to perform various kinds of key calculations used in the trading system. Spreadsheets that implement all the formulas in this book can be found on the website: systematicmoney.org/leveraged-trading

Back-adjusting prices

Historic prices

In this part of the appendix I explain how you could create a history of back-adjusted prices using a spreadsheet.

You begin with a series of end of day closing or settlement prices for different expiry dates. Let's keep things simple and just use three dated contracts (A, B and C), within a highly unrealistic example in which we only have a few days of prices for each contract. Here is the history of prices so far:

	A	B	C
2 January 2019	100		
3 January 2019	100.2		
6 January 2019	100.3		
7 January 2019	99.9	100.2	
8 January 2019		99.9	
9 January 2019		98.7	99.1
10 January 2019		99.0	99.5
13 January 2019			99.9
14 January 2019			100.1

Now to decide when we would have switched from one expiry to the next. For the switch from A to B we don't have any choice; there is only a single date when we have a price for both contracts (7 January). For the switch from B to C we have two options. Let's suppose we always pick the latest date (10 January).

We now need to create a new column for the back-adjusted price. This is populated in reverse, starting with the last day with data and going backwards. We begin by copying across the prices for the final contract, C, until we get to the first expiry date (expiry dates are shown in bold):

	A	B	C	Back-adjusted price
2 January 2019	100			
3 January 2019	100.2			
6 January 2019	100.3			
7 January 2019	99.9	100.2		
8 January 2019		99.9		
9 January 2019		98.7	99.1	
10 January 2019		99.0	99.5 ->	99.5
13 January 2019			99.9 ->	99.9
14 January 2019			100.1 ->	100.1

We now take the difference in closing price between the current contract C and the previous contract B on the roll date: 99.5 – 99.0 = 0.5. This difference has to be added to all the B prices to make them consistent with C on the roll date:

	A	B	B adjusted	C	Back-adjusted price
2 January 2019	100				
3 January 2019	100.2				
6 January 2019	100.3				
7 January 2019	99.9	100.2	100.2 + 0.5 = **100.7**		
8 January 2019		99.9	99.9 + 0.5 = **100.4**		
9 January 2019		98.7	98.7 + 0.5 = **99.2**	99.1	
10 January 2019		99.0	99.0 + 0.5 = **99.5**	99.5	99.5
13 January 2019				99.9	99.9
14 January 2019				100.1	100.1

The B adjusted prices are then copied across to become the final adjusted prices for the relevant dates:

	A	B	B adjusted	C	Back-adjusted price
2 January 2019	100				
3 January 2019	100.2				
6 January 2019	100.3				
7 January 2019	99.9	100.2	**100.7->**		**100.7**
8 January 2019		99.9	**100.4->**		**100.4**
9 January 2019		98.7	**99.2->**	99.1	**99.2**
10 January 2019		99.0	99.5	99.5	99.5
13 January 2019				99.9	99.9
14 January 2019				100.1	100.1

We now create adjusted prices for A: on the expiry date of the 7 January the difference between the back-adjusted price and the price of A is 100.7 – 99.9 = 0.8; this is added to the prices for A:

	A	A adjusted	B	B adjusted	Back-adjusted price
2 January 2019	100	100 + 0.8 = **100.8**			
3 January 2019	100.2	100.2 + 0.8 = **101.0**			
6 January 2019	100.3	100.3 + 0.8 = **101.1**			
7 January 2019	99.9	99.9 + 0.8 = **100.7**	100.2	100.7	100.7
8 January 2019			99.9	100.4	100.4
9 January 2019			98.7	99.2	99.2
10 January 2019			99.0	99.5	99.5
13 January 2019					99.9
14 January 2019					100.1

Finally, we copy across the adjusted prices for A to become the back-adjusted price:

	A	A adjusted	B	B adjusted	Back-adjusted price
2 January 2019	100	**100.8 ->**			**100.8**
3 January 2019	100.2	**101.0 ->**			**101.0**
6 January 2019	100.3	**101.1 ->**			**101.1**
7 January 2019	99.9	100.7	100.2	100.7	100.7
8 January 2019			99.9	100.4	100.4
9 January 2019			98.7	99.2	99.2
10 January 2019			99.0	99.5	99.5
13 January 2019					99.9
14 January 2019					100.1

We'd continue this process until we had adjusted the oldest contract in our data history.

Keeping the price series up to date

A useful property of back-adjustment is that the current back-adjusted price is equal to the price of the dated product we're currently trading. So ordinarily we can just add new rows as follows:

	C	Back-adjusted price
2 January 2019		100.8
3 January 2019		101.0
6 January 2019		101.1
7 January 2019		100.7
8 January 2019		100.4
9 January 2019	99.1	99.2
10 January 2019	99.5	99.5
13 January 2019	99.9	99.9
14 January 2019	100.1	100.1
15 January 2019	**101.6**	**101.6**

This would continue until we were ready to roll on to a new contract (D). On the roll date (16 January) we get a price for both contracts:

	C	D	Back-adjusted price
2 January 2019			100.8
3 January 2019			101.0
6 January 2019			101.1
7 January 2019			100.7
8 January 2019			100.4
9 January 2019	99.1		99.2
10 January 2019	99.5		99.5
13 January 2019	99.9		99.9
14 January 2019	100.1		100.1
15 January 2019	101.6		101.6
16 January 2019	101.0	101.5	101.0

We take the difference in price between the new contract D and the existing contract C on the expiry date: 101.5 − 101.0 = 0.5. We now add this difference **to the entire back-adjusted price series:**

	C	D	Old back-adjusted price	New back-adjusted price
2 January 2019			100.8	100.8 + 0.5 = **101.3**
3 January 2019			101.0	101 + 0.5 = **101.5**
6 January 2019			101.1	100.1 + 0.5 = **101.6**
7 January 2019			100.7	100.7 + 0.5 = **101.2**
8 January 2019			100.4	100.4 + 0.5 = **100.9**
9 January 2019	99.1		99.2	99.2 + 0.5 = **99.7**
10 January 2019	99.5		99.5	99.5 + 0.5 = **100.0**
13 January 2019	99.9		99.9	99.9 + 0.5 = **100.4**
14 January 2019	100.1		100.1	100.1 + 0.5 = **100.5**
15 January 2019	101.6		101.6	101.6 + 0.5 = **102.1**
16 January 2019	101.0	101.5	101.0	101 + 0.5 = **101.5**

We can now discard the original back-adjusted price series, and on subsequent days add additional prices for contract D to the new back-adjusted price series.

Instrument risk calculation

I recommend that you calculate standard deviation using the last 25 trading days of returns. To do this in a spreadsheet package assuming that column A contains daily prices (excluding weekends and market holidays), then we populate column C with percentage returns:

C2 = (A2 − A1) / A1, C3 = (A3 − A2) / A2, ...

If you are using back-adjusted prices then the above calculation will give weird results for long series of prices. This is because back-adjusted prices can become very small and even go negative. For back-adjusted prices, we populate column A with the back-adjusted prices, and column B with the current price of the contract we're actually trading. Then column C should read:

$$C2 = (A2 - A1) / B1, C3 = (A3 - A2) / B2, ...$$

We then calculate the standard deviation from row 26 onwards:

$$D26 = STDEV(C2:C26), D27 = STDEV(C3:C27), ...$$

This is a daily measure, so we annualise it by multiplying it by 16 (standard deviation scales with the square root of time, and there are about 256 trading days in a year):

$$D26=D26*16, E27=D27*16, ...$$

Moving average calculations

Assuming column A contains daily prices (ideally prices which are back-adjusted), then the 16-day moving average would be:

$$B16 = AVERAGE(A1:A16), B17 = AVERAGE(A2:A17), B18 = AVERAGE(A3:A18), ...$$

Then a 64-day moving average is calculated as follows:

$$C64 = AVERAGE(A1:A64), C65 = AVERAGE(A2:A65), C66 = AVERAGE(A3:A66),...$$

Finally, the 16,64 crossover is the difference between columns B and C:

$$D64 = B64 - C64, D65 = B65 - C65, C66 = B66 - C66, ...$$

It's straightforward to adapt this for other crossover lengths.

Breakout calculations

Assuming column A contains daily prices, then for a 10-day rolling window the rolling maximum will be:

$$B10 = MAX(A1:A10), B11 = MAX(A2:A11), B12 = MAX(A3:A12)$$

The rolling minimum will be:

C10 = MIN(A1:A10), C11 = MIN(A2:A11), C12 = MIN(A3:A12)

The rolling average is:

D10 = AVERAGE(B10, C10)/2, D11 = AVERAGE(B11,C11)/2, ...

Finally, the scaled price is:

E10 = (A10 – D10)/(B10 – C10)

Performance ratio

Assuming column A contains a list of trade returns, as a percentage of capital, e.g.: if the first three trades had returns of +3.1%, –1.2% and +5.4%:

A1 = 0.031, A2 = –0.012, A3 = 0.054, ...

Then the average return will be:

B1 = AVERAGE(A:A)

The standard deviation will be:

C1 = STDEV(A:A)

The performance ratio will be:

E1 = B1/C1

It is also useful to know the number of trades:

D1 = COUNT(A:A)

Acknowledgements

I resigned from AHL in 2013 and left the financial industry without a particularly clear idea of what was going to happen next. I hoped that something would come up, a sentiment shared by my wife who was not overjoyed about the prospect of spending all day in a house with an aimless middle-aged man. Fortunately, something did come up. My crazy idea for a book about trading with systems was commissioned by Stephen Eckett at Harriman House. After many months of writing by myself, and a few more months of editing by Craig Pearce to turn it into a readable book, it was published.

No longer did I have to answer the question "So what do you do?", with "Well I used to be...": now I could confidently state "I write books", before adding "Well... I've written one book...". My second book followed a couple of years later, so I could now answer with an unqualified "I write books". Much to my wife's relief, I have successfully avoided becoming aimless.

One of the best things about the last few years has been meeting some great people, who I might otherwise never have known. Three of these great people generously agreed to help me with this latest book.

Tomasz Mylnowski is currently my teaching assistant at Queen Mary, University of London. As well as being very knowledgeable about both the theory and practice of finance, he has an excellent eye for detail. This complements my own skill set very well; I'm more of a 'big picture' guy (i.e., lazy, bored by the granular stuff, and prone to making silly mistakes). Tomasz found time to wade through both my lecture notes and the manuscript for this book, correcting numerous errors in both.

I originally met James Udall after he emailed me, asking if I thought it made sense to implement my trading system (a) with spread bets and (b) entirely on a spreadsheet. I was sceptical but agreed to help, and James proved me wrong by successfully managing both. Although I have traded plenty of futures contracts, I am a relative novice when it comes to spread betting and CFDs. Fortunately, James was happy to fill in the gaps in my knowledge from his own extensive experience.

I was very lucky indeed to meet Riccardo Ronco, who was an early reader of my blog. Riccardo has been very generous in connecting me with his wide network of industry contacts (frequently I've tried to introduce him to someone at a trading conference, only to discover that he has known them for many years). He deserves special mention as he also helped with my second book and should have known better this time round. Like me, Riccardo has a young family. Unlike me, he works ridiculously long hours and I didn't really expect that he would have time to read through my drafts. But he did, and his feedback was invaluable in pointing out where I had made my usual error of assuming that the reader already knew everything I did.

It seems fitting that both Stephen and Craig from Harriman have also had a role in this book. This time they exchanged roles; Craig was an excellent commissioning editor, patiently exchanging emails with me for weeks while I went through at least a dozen ideas before finally settling on the proposal for this book. Then Stephen stepped in as editor extraordinaire to read the completed draft, helpfully suggesting improvements to both content and structure, whilst also solving numerous assorted crimes against grammar.

I'd also like to thank the rest of the team at Harriman. Through speaking at conferences, I have now met several other authors of trading books. Having listened to them complaining about their publishers, I appreciate mine even more.

Finally, I would like to thank my family. Living with a middle-aged writer probably isn't quite as bad as living with an aimless middle-aged man, but it is not always easy. Without your love and support I wouldn't be able to do this.

Index

401Ks 29, 44

AHL 32, 46, 166, 317
arbitrage trade 16, 32
asset classes 35, 172–87, 211–13, 220, 271, 281–4, 287
auto-liquidation 12–13, 19, 27, 30, 33, 281, 285
Average True Range (ATR) 129–30, 281

back-adjustment 124–9, 160, 281, 307–8, 310–14
back-testing 48, 52, 74–7, 87–92, 98, 110–11, 121, 125, 166, 169–70, 173, 182–6, 208–9, 218, 238, 242, 247–50, 252, 267–8, 270, 276, 281, 286
backwardation 125
bankruptcy 41, 44, 120
Barclays 55
bids 18–19, 145, 281, 287, 301–4, 306
binary trading 241–3, 281, see also non-binary trading
bitcoin 4, 37, 94, 177–8, 281, 283
Bollinger bands 55
Bonaparte, Napoleon 20
bond indices 22, 37, 180
bonds 4, 10, 22, 34, 36–7, 46, 63, 69–70, 74, 77, 81–2, 92, 109, 125, 137, 166–9, 171–8, 180–2, 187, 189–91, 207, 253, 255, 281, 301
box and whiskers plot 76–7, 89–90, 169, 193, 226, 243, 282
breakout 196–201, 209–10, 214–17, 242,

245, 249, 251, 282, 314
broker
  alert service 161
  choosing 42–5, 142
  versus exchange 41
Buffett, Warren 165
Bund 81–2, 168–9
buying on margin 16, 21, 35, 282

calculations 307–15
candles 55
capital, definition 282
capital gains tax 29, 31, 85
carry, cost of 10, 14, 32, 69, 282
carry rule 201, 208–10, 214, 217, 227, 242, 250–1
carry trade 10, 14, 245
cash price 125, 282, 287, see also spot price
cash settled futures 143
Chicago Mercantile Exchange 32–3
Citigroup 18–19, 22, 25, 37
clearing house 41–2, 282
closing rule 56, 107, 110, 120, 124, 131, 145, 217–18, 220, 228, 259, 282, 288
commission 3, 10, 15, 18–20, 22, 24, 26, 30–1, 33–4, 45, 51, 66, 69, 121, 140, 144, 148, 150–1, 153, 155–9, 230–2, 235–8, 254, 279, 282, 288, 293–6, 300–2
commodities 22, 27, 36–7, 125, 137–8, 143, 173–80, 282
confidence interval see box and whiskers plot
contango 125
continuous trading 225–7, 241, 268, 282, 299

contracts for difference (CFD),
   definition 25–35, 283
copy trading 52
correlation 173, 175–9, 182, 281, 283
cost of carry 10, 14, 32, 69, 282
costs 67–71, 293–306, *see also* holding costs;
   spread cost; total costs
crude oil 31, 37, 59, 82, 84, 137, 165, 174–
   5, 177, 180, 196–9, 250
cryptocurrency 3–4, 27, 35, 37, 63, 94,
   173–4, 178, 281, 283, *see also* Bitcoin
current exposure 254–7, 259, 263–4, 266
curve fitting 50–1, 283, *see also* over fitting
cynicism 169

daily closing prices 108, 111–12, 114, 117,
   124, 130, 140–1
daily funded bet 30, 35, 56, 69, 83, 283,
   288, 298
data feed 38–9
dated product 15–17, 31, 33–4, 36, 40, 55–
   6, 69, 83, 124–5, 136, 138, 141–2, 281,
   283–4, 286, 311, *see also* undated product
day trading 1, 28, 44, 80, 83, 112–13, 116–
   18, 140, 160, 192, 283, 306
derivatives 15–17, 27, 29, 31, 33–4
discretionary traders 269–70, 272, 283
diversification 48, 161, 165–86, 188–9,
   193–5, 213–14, 220, 251–2, 270–2, 275
diversification
   advantages and disadvantages of 165–72
   of trading rules 193–6
   theory of 172–87
dividends 10, 18, 21–2, 25–7, 29–31, 34,
   37, 201–3, 214, 225, 228, 283, 297

equities 10, 12–13, 15, 31, 37, 44, 57, 74,
   81–2, 84, 88, 93, 96, 104, 121, 137, 166,
   172–8, 180, 182, 201, 203, 208, 228, 240,
   253, 281, 283, 301
EURIBOR 37, 287
Euro Stoxx 50 81–2, 92–3, 104, 116, 121–
   3, 126, 128, 130, 132, 134–5, 139–40,
   142–5, 147, 149, 157, 160, 166, 207, 233,
   235, 238, 250, 260, 262–4, 266, 296, 299
Eurodollar rate 37, 82, 106, 137, 177–8,

204, 287
European Union 13
exchange, definition 283
exchange, versus broker 41
exchange traded fund (ETF) 17, 22–3, 27,
   29, 34–6, 42, 60, 82, 94, 99, 103, 105,
   121–2, 128, 133, 136, 138, 140, 150–1,
   159–60, 178, 202, 228, 237–8, 262, 265,
   295–9, 302
ex-dividend date 27
expiry date 31, 33

fake stop loss triggers 43
FCA 44
Fibonacci 55
financial crisis 2007--2008 20, 89, 192, 253
financing cost 26, 29, 31, 34, 151, 283–4,
   286
financing spread 14, 16, 32, 69, 201
fitting 283, *see also* curve fitting; over fitting
fixed stop loss 107
forecasts 48, 50, 98, 107, 225, 227, 241,
   244–57, 259–60, 262–3, 265, 268, 271,
   275–6, 284–6
foreign exchange (FX), definition 23–5, 284
forward FX 176, 283–4
FTSE 100 37, 44, 81, 84, 283
full hedging 42
funding spread 18, 24, 34, 69, 80, 121, 201,
   283–4, 298, 302
futures, definition 284

gambling 28
Gaussian normal distribution 57
gearing 9, *see also* leverage
government bonds 4, 37, 46, 63, 74, 137,
   207
guaranteed stop loss 13, 43, 115, 225, 227,
   284, 306

hardware 38–9
hedge funds 2–3, 5, 20, 32, 41, 44, 46, 55,
   99, 166, 192, 284
high watermark 55, 108, 111–12, 141, 145,
   284, 287
holding costs 34, 69–70, 80, 83, 90–2, 142,

148, 155, 158, 200–1, 208, 232, 275–7, 283–4, 288, 293, 297, 299, 301–2
home currency 56, 58, 60, 92–3, 101–3, 135–6, 149, 151, 154, 254, 258, 261–2, 264–5, 284
human biases 47–8

Ichimoku 55
income tax 29, 85
incremental trade size see minimum trade size
insider trading 46
instrument, definition 284
instrument currency 56, 101–2, 123, 284, 293–4
instrument diversification multiplier 166–8, 179, 181–6, 188–9, 213, 220, 252, 270, 272, 275
instrument risk 63, 69–70, 80, 93–6, 103–5, 109, 111–13, 117, 120–1, 124–5, 129–30, 134, 138–41, 148–9, 151–4, 161, 187, 189–90, 217, 244, 246–50, 253–7, 259–60, 262, 270, 284–7, 290–300, 313
interest rate spread 18, 34, 284
interest rates 14, 18, 36–7, 46, 173, 214, 242, 245, 282, 287, see also STIR
IRAs 29, 44
ISAs 29, 44

Kelly criterion 66, 98, 185, 284

Lefevre, Edwin 279
Lehman Brothers 41, 44
leverage, definition 9–11, 285
leverage factor 11–13, 15, 18–19, 22, 24–6, 30, 32–3, 40, 61–6, 69, 93–5, 104, 113, 134, 237, 285, 297–8
leverage ratio 11–13, 18, 23, 285
leveraged product 9, 15, 17–18, 23, 35–6, 40, 73, 77–9, 83, 85, 119, 179, 201, 242, 255, 283, 285, 287
London Interbank Offered Rate (LIBOR) 18, 24, 37
London Stock Exchange 20, 283
long, definition 285
losing traders 1–4

margin account 18, 20–1, 41, 44, 56, 66–7, 94, 103, 215–16, 219, 262, 265, 285
margin call 12–13, 21, 27, 30, 33, 40, 120, 281, 285
margin percentage 11
margin trading 9, 11, 21, 23, 35, 44, 69, 78–9, 119, 121–3, 128, 130, 134, 136, 151, 159, 237, 282, 285–6, 295–9
mark to market 12–13, 19, 285
mean reversion trading 285, 305–6
MF Global 41, 44
minimum capital 66–7, 78–82, 84–5, 103–6, 116, 118, 121–2, 137, 166, 168, 171–2, 174–9, 181, 186–90, 196, 214, 252, 270, 285, 300–1
minimum trade size 66–7, 117, 171, 258, 284–5, 293–4, 300
momentum 48, 50, 87–8, 110, 285, see also trend following
mortgages 9–12, 14–15, 18–19
moving average crossover 87–91, 107, 109–10, 116, 120, 130, 145, 160, 193–4, 196, 201, 208–10, 214–17, 226, 245–6, 248, 285–6, 288

Nasdaq 81, 84, 116–17, 174, 176–8, 192, 301
negative carry trade 10, 14
net liquidation value 141
new markets, adding 165–91
New York Stock Exchange 20, 283
non-binary trading 240–3, 251–2, 259, 267, 281
notional exposure 58–60, 92–3, 100–1, 103, 105, 113, 120, 134, 148, 151, 153, 189, 244, 253–60, 262–3, 285, 300

offers 18–19, 286–7, 301
one-third of costs rule 78
opening rule 86–7, 98, 107, 109–11, 115, 120, 130, 133, 145–6, 149–50, 152, 161, 169, 174, 190–2, 194, 196, 209, 214, 217–20, 224–8, 231–2, 236, 240–2, 259, 268–71, 274, 282, 284, 286, 288, 299
optimism 4, 6, 52, 117, 211
over betting 2–4

over fitting 50–2, 87, 100, 107, 193, 209, 268, 283, 286

over the counter (OTC) 1, 15, 17–18, 25, 27, 31, 33–5, 41–2, 114, 283, 286

overconfidence 2–4, 51

overtrading 2–4

Panama adjustment 125

partial hedging 42

Pattern Day Trader rule 44

payment date 27

performance monitoring 272–4

performance ratio 272–5, 277, 286, 315

physical product 15–16, 23, 25

physically settled futures 143

pips 24, 33, 286, 294

point, definition 286

poker 47, 223, 239

Pope, Alexander 279

position, definition 286

position adjustment 239–66

position management 138, 259–60, 262, 267

position size 40, 49, 56, 67, 92, 100–1, 109, 113, 117–18, 123–4, 138, 148, 158, 161, 236, 239–40, 242, 253–4, 297, 300

positive carry trade 10, 14

price unit volatility 111, 286–7

product, choosing 40–1

product, definition 55, 286

profitability 1–2, 5, 20, 49, 56, 73, 94, 98–100, 104, 160, 171, 199, 267, 272

quarterly spread bet 34–6, 56, 69, 79, 83, 91, 200, 208, 216, 219, 283, 286, 297, 302

reference rate 18, 24, 283, 286

rent 9–10, 14–15, 18, 21

risk, definition and measurement 56–66, 129–30

risk control 223–5, 267

risk targeting, definition 62

risk-adjusted costs 68

risk-adjusted returns 60–2, 68, 168, 243–4, 246

rolling 17, 33–4, 69, 125, 142–3, 161, 197–9, 286, 314–15

Royal Mail Group 225, 228

S&P 500 22, 31, 37, 55, 57–60, 67, 81–2, 84, 88, 91, 93–4, 96, 99, 101–3, 105, 109, 121–3, 128, 130, 133–4, 136, 138–40, 142–3, 145, 149–52, 159–60, 166, 172, 181, 192, 200, 202, 208–9, 215–16, 219, 236–8, 250, 260, 262–6, 283, 296, 299, 302

scaled forecasts 247–50, 259

scaling factor 244, 247–50, 268, 286

SEC 44

semi-automatic traders 267, 269–72, 274

settlement date 31

share indices 36–7, see also FTSE 100; S&P 500

Sharpe ratio 5, 56, 61–2, 66, 68, 71, 74–8, 80, 83, 89–92, 96, 98–100, 104, 116–17, 167–70, 174, 182–6, 193–5, 200, 208, 211–14, 216, 226, 243, 252, 267, 272–5, 277, 282, 284, 286–7, 299

short, definition 287

short selling 14–17, 20–2, 35, 40, 285, 287, 297

Short Sterling 137, 287

SIPPs 29, 44

social media 5

software 38–9

speed limit 78, 80, 82–4, 90–2, 98, 117, 174–5, 178–80, 200, 216, 270, 272, 275, 287

spot CFDs 30, 35

spot FX 29, 32, 35–6, 56, 67, 69, 73, 78–83, 85, 91, 116–17, 119, 121–3, 128, 130, 134, 136, 138, 140, 143–4, 148, 158, 160, 174, 178–9, 182, 200–1, 203, 208, 214–16, 219, 238, 254, 261, 263, 284, 286–8, 298–9, 302

spot price 16, 32, 125, 201, 205–7, 214, 282, 287, see also cash price

spread betting 264, 282–3, 285–8, 294–9, 302

spread cost 140, 144, 148, 150, 153, 155–9, 230–2, 235–7, 287–8, 301, 303, 306

spread order 142–3
spreadsheets 39, 52, 87, 119, 124–5, 130,
   139, 160, 171, 201, 209, 214, 227, 238,
   268, 292–3, 307, 313
SPY ETF 60, 82, 94, 103, 105, 121–2, 128,
   202, 262, 265, 295–6
standard deviation 56–8, 60–3, 66, 68–9,
   75, 77, 93–4, 96, 100, 105, 109, 111, 120,
   129–30, 138–9, 149, 152, 154, 167–8,
   183, 225, 247, 251, 259, 272–4, 281, 284,
   286–8, 296, 299–300, 313–15
Starter System
   adapted for multiple instruments 188–91
   funds needed 45, 52
   improvements to 267–8
   overview of 72–118
   position adjustment 239–66
   trading the 119–61, 188–91
   without stop loss 219–38
statistical uncertainty 74–6, 243, 287
STIR 137, 173, 177–8, 180, 287
stop loss
   definition 56, 287
   fraction 110–13, 218, 224, 270, 272, 274,
      276–7, 287
   gap 108–9, 111–12, 120, 138–9, 141–2,
      145, 149, 152, 154, 161, 270, 287
   guaranteed 13, 43, 115, 225, 227, 284,
      306
   trading without 219–38, 268, 271
   trailing 108, 120, 138, 288
stop profit 107

target risk 62–3, 68–70, 93–4, 103–5, 113,
   120, 134, 167, 181, 187, 189, 241, 254–7,
   259–60, 262, 288
tax 29
third party trading systems 52
time-based exit 107
top-down allocation method 215
total costs 71, 80, 91, 200, 208, 275, 288,

299, 302, 305
trade logs 139–40, 143–4, 147, 150, 152–3,
   155–9, 229–32, 234–5, 237
trade plans 119–20, 189, 220, 259, 288
trading hardware 38–9
trading rules
   adding new 192–220
   definition 56
   diversification of 193–6
   removing 219
trading software 38–9
trading spreads 17–18, 20, 22, 24, 29, 31–2,
   34, 45, 51, 60, 69, 121, 179, 288, 293–4
trading systems
   arguments against 49–50
   characteristics of 51–2
   reasons for using 47–9
   third party 52
trailing stop loss 108, 120, 138, 288
transaction costs 31, 69–71, 74, 83, 90–1,
   116, 200, 208, 275–7, 287–8, 293, 296,
   299–300, 304–5
trend following 48, 87, 107–8, 125, 215–17,
   224, 227, 242, 245, 285, 288, 304–5, see
   also momentum
Turtle Traders 209

undated product 15–17, 23, 25, 27, 29, 31,
   34, 36, 56, 69, 83, 116, 125–6, 128, 138,
   282–3, 287–8, see also dated product

volatility 36–7, 56–7, 62, 82, 94, 109–11,
   117, 129–30, 137, 173, 175–8, 180, 217–
   20, 225, 231, 247, 249–50, 270, 275–7,
   286–8, 304
volatility fraction 110, 217–20, 225, 270,
   275, 277

weighted average 110, 169, 210, 217, 219–
   20, 226, 251

www.ingramcontent.com/pod-product-compliance
Ingram Content Group UK Ltd.
Pitfield, Milton Keynes, MK11 3LW, UK
UKHW011451130325
455887UK00013B/134